Ben Jonson:
Public Poet and Private Man

Ben Jonson:
Public Poet and
Private Man

George Parfitt
Department of English Studies
University of Nottingham

LONDON
J. M. DENT & SONS LTD

© George Parfitt, 1976
All rights reserved
Made in Great Britain
at the
Aldine Press, Letchworth, Herts
for
J. M. DENT & SONS LTD
Aldine House, Albemarle Street, London
First published 1976

This book is set in 10 on 11 point Baskerville 169

Hardback ISBN 0 460 10429 2

Contents

For my mother, wife, children
and the memory of my father

Preface

Ben Jonson has never been ignored, although the attention he has commanded takes many forms, some of which help to make up this book. Even when his personality and literary achievement have been used primarily as a foil to illuminate Shakespeare's radiance, or— more generally—as an 'awful example' of what happens when study sullies creative talent, Jonson has been taken account of, has refused to lie down and die—and this is true even though the masque is a dead form, his plays are refused any real place in our (partly mythical) national repertory, and his poems have been resolutely unfashionable.

Committed critics are apt to see dawns where only false dawns exist, but there do seem to have been signs in recent years of a more sympathetic, fruitfully inquisitive response to Jonson (particularly in North America); a willingness to listen to his voice rather than to abuse it for not being like someone else's, and to investigate neglected areas of his achievement—the masques, the poems, the late plays. But this response has been mainly academic. At its best it has been a genuinely perceptive and stimulating response, not a pedantic one in the pejorative sense, but the stir of interest has none the less been largely confined to universities and colleges. Perhaps something about Jonson's work makes this inevitable—that is a question which I hope this book concerns itself with, both directly and obliquely— but my aim is to help re-establish Jonson as an active ingredient of our culture; to indicate why and how his achievement is important as an individual element of our consciousness of ourselves and our living. Doing this necessitates the claim that Jonson's achievement can only begin to be seen adequately if an effort is made to consider individual works in the context of the total output, a view which has helped determine the book's structure. Each chapter is, in a sense, an essay on a particular aspect of Jonson which I think can profitably be reconsidered; I cannot claim to have dealt fully with all aspects of Jonson's output or equally fully with each of the aspects that I do touch on, but this seems a good time at which to ask a number of questions about Jonson and his reputation in the hope that this will help the re-examination which should define and establish Jonson's importance.

In one way the book is arrogant, in that many things are omitted and complex issues are often tersely dealt with; in another it is humble, in that it seeks to raise issues rather than necessarily to settle them. Jonson means a lot to me, his art teases and stimulates, and proceeding by asking questions is one way of suggesting that this art has the vitality which should make criticism a process of seeking to ask those questions which lead to more searching questions, which in turn lead back to the art itself and also reach into the critic's heart and mind.

I am grateful to the editors of *Studies in English Literature, Studies in the Literary Imagination* and *English Studies* for permission to make use of material which has appeared, in somewhat different form, in their periodicals. I am also genuinely grateful to many other writers and have not deliberately neglected to acknowledge any work which has helped shape my thinking on Jonson; but it would not suit the purposes of this book if it were weighted by small print and academic in-fighting, so I have kept notes to a minimum and most of the acknowledgments are general rather than specific. I should, however, like to thank my friend Tom Paulin for his help with the proof-reading.

Chapter 1

Personality and Early Life

No one doubts that Ben Jonson was one of the great characters of English literature. The force of his personality emerges in almost everything he wrote—in, for example, the confident gratitude expressed to William Camden in the Folio Dedication to *Every Man in his Humour* ('. . . I am none of those, that can suffer the benefits confer'd upon my youth, to perish with my age . . ' [1]) or in the splendidly maintained mixture of humorous appeal, a sense of anxious poverty, and retention of dignity in that fine minor poem 'To Master John Burges'.[2] Moreover, the strong impact of his own writings is paralleled by the reactions of other men to him, both during his lifetime and in the centuries since his death. So we have the cheap scorn of Alexander Gill:

> Butt to advise thee, Ben, in this strict Age,
> A Brickehill's fitter for thee then A stage;
> Thou better knowes a groundsell how to Laye
> Then lay the plott or groundeworke of A play . . .[3]

Or there is the reaction of Charles Macklin, the actor, for whom Jonson is a malignant traducer of Shakespeare:

Ben was by nature splenetic and sour; with a share of envy . . . This raised him many enemies, who towards the close of his life endeavoured to dethrone this tyrant . . . And what greatly contributed to their design, was the slights and malignances which the rigid Ben too frequently threw out against the lowly Shakespeare . . .[4]

Macklin, writing in 1748, is making no effort to be fair, but the vehemence of tone marks the impact Jonson had made on him. The impact on Edmund Wilson, in his famous eassay 'Morose Ben Jonson',[5] is rather similar, for Wilson allows prejudice, an easy acquiescence in a stock view of Jonson, and misuse of Freud to lead him to a position of almost wholly blinkered high intelligence.

But, as these few references may have suggested, it does not follow from the impact of Jonson that typical responses to his life and work create an accurate, consistent, or—more important—coherent figure, and this is true of more favourable reactions as well as of wholeheartedly hostile ones. It is interesting that a positive and warm response to Jonson is relatively rare after the middle of the seventeenth century: men who knew him often showed real warmth towards him, but this note dies as these men die. When the reaction is not hostile (and even Hazlitt felt Jonson's power to be 'of a repulsive and unamiable kind' [6]) its quality is usually that of Dryden, who admired Jonson and loved Shakespeare,[7] and is famously summed up by T. S. Eliot:

> To be universally accepted; to be damned by the praise that quenches all desire to read the books; to be afflicted by the imputation of the virtues which excite the least pleasure; and to be read only by historians and antiquaries—this is the most perfect conspiracy of approval.[8]

The nature of Jonson's art partly accounts for this 'conspiracy of approval', which shades—as we have seen—into hostility in some cases. More specifically, the fact that Jonson is usually thought of in terms of a few of his plays, a handful of the poems, some scattered remarks in *Conversations* and *Discoveries* and a smattering of violent incidents in his life, has meant that the warmer, more humane and generous side of his personality (most evident in the poems) has not usually modified admiration to include love or even real liking. William Gifford is a notable exception, but I suspect that the entertaining pugnacity of Gifford's edition comes mainly from Gifford's sympathy with the tough and obdurate side of Jonson. Yet with Gifford there is a real sense of contact having been made: Gifford cares about Jonson, and one feels that he also cares for him. But what emerges from even a perfunctory survey like this is that there is no single 'Ben Jonson': there are a number of them (historical, anachronistic) and some are grossly misleading, so that one of my purposes is to try and find Jonson, as man and artist, in the belief that a proper understanding of his art can only come through a serious and sympathetic attempt to appreciate the complexity of that art and of the personality responsible for it. To an unusual extent the distortions of history and legend (themselves an oblique tribute to Jonson's power) have been allowed to inhibit sympathetic approaches to his work—and we shall not get far with Jonson unless we try to listen to him without the buzzings of the tribe of Macklin and Wilson in our ears.

It may, at first, seem odd that very little is known with any certainty about the early life of a man who was to make so strong an impact upon his own period and upon posterity, but the apparent oddness vanishes when we remember how sparse and accidental Elizabethan records of ordinary families are, that Jonson's eminence dates only from 1598 (when he was about twenty-six years old) and that modern attitudes to biography and autobiography are very unlike those of Jonson's period. England was a country to which the Renaissance came late and so, although biography is a Renaissance development, Fulke Greville's *Life* of Sidney is unusual in English Renaissance writing by its very existence, and it is more a prose eulogy-cum-character-sketch than what we would now call biography. Again, Lord Edward Herbert was doing something unusual by English standards in writing his own life, and—at least ostensibly —his purpose is partly to provide moral guidance for his family: 'I have thought fit to relate to my posterity those passages of my life, which . . . may . . . be most useful to them.' [9] Even in the eighteenth century Cibber's *Apology* and Davies's *Life of Garrick* are as much concerned with anecdote and general reflection as with biography proper. Much of what we 'know' of Jonson's early life comes from seventeenth-century writers like Fuller and Aubrey, who, while they were extending the growing interest in history towards what we would consider biography, are still much influenced by the tradition of the formal 'character', and who enjoy recording striking anecdote rather than mundane detail, often allowing tradition or the seductiveness of a good story to dominate probability and hard evidence (or its lack). The nature of the material these men provide is such that we can only hope to produce a plausible outline, giving it flesh by what we hope are reasonable hypotheses, and drawing some tentative conclusions about what aspects of Jonson's early life may have significantly affected his adult personality.

Of course a man is not born from or into a vacuum: the background to his birth and ancestry is an important factor in his shaping, and needs to be recognized as such, although preferably without leading the writer to produce another *Tristram Shandy* or to emulate the modern trace-him-back-to-Adam school of biography. But although no man is born into a vacuum one may still have difficulty in finding out what sort of air he was born into, and this is the case with Jonson, at least as soon as we try to go beyond generalizations about Elizabethan life.

What we know about Jonson's ancestry depends almost entirely upon the few scraps recorded by William Drummond in his *Conversations*, written after Jonson had visited the Scottish poet at Hawthornden in 1618. We shall see that Drummond's notes cannot be safely regarded as tape-recordings of facts and sayings, nor do I think that the remarks in question constitute a straightforward or complete account of what Jonson knew, or thought he knew, about his ancestry and early life. Leonard Woolf has sensibly remarked that, 'Some of the things which one seems to remember from far, far back in infancy are not, I think, really remembered; they are family tales told so often about one that eventually one has the illusion of remembering them.' [10] In addition, the particular circumstances of Jonson's visit to Hawthornden (discussed more fully in the next chapter) and the fact that he is looking back across several decades suggest an account which is shaped to fit a specific occasion. But there is no alternative to taking Drummond's record as the basis for an account of Jonson's early life.

His grandfather, Jonson told Drummond, 'came from Carlisle, and he thought from Annandale to it, he served Henry VIII, and was a gentleman'.[11] He went on to say a little about his father, who 'lost all his estate under Queen Mary, having been cast in prison and forfeited, at last turned minister'.[12] Slightly later in the text there is the famous anecdote which is almost all we know of Jonson's mother. After the poet's release from prison for allegedly having slandered the Scots in *Eastward Ho* he gave a banquet for his friends, and, 'At the midst of the feast his old mother drank to him, and shew him a paper which she had (if the sentence had taken execution) to have mixed in the prison among his drink, which was full of lusty strong poison, and that she was no churl, she told, she minded first to have drunk of it herself.' [13] The only other piece of information which is important at this point is Jonson's claim that he was 'posthumous born, a month after his father's decease' [14]—it is now generally accepted that the birth was probably on 11 June 1572, and in London.

There is no reason to doubt the basic accuracy of what Drummond records: nothing is intrinsically improbable and there is no evidence of weight to discredit any of it. But this does not mean that Jonson told all he knew, nor that he spoke without shaping or embellishment. In fact it seems to me that the remarks are presented by Jonson in a way which reflects important aspects of his life and outlook up to the time of the meeting with Drummond. It is interesting, for example, that Jonson claims descent from a gentle family. This is not at all unusual in itself at this time but fits in well with his concern, as public artist, with status. This concern emerges at the personal level with Jonson seeking to increase the prestige of the professional literary artist (as with the 1616 folio) and to maintain his own hard-won position against the growing power of Inigo Jones and of younger playwrights. At the level of Jonson's thinking about social organization there is the same interest in position, with Jonson

4

seeing a vital relationship between hierarchy and a stable common-wealth, something which underpins the satire of Mammon (*The Alchemist*) and Overdo (*Bartholomew Fair*), as well, perhaps, as defining his attitude to Lovewit (*The Alchemist*) and Clement (*Every Man in his Humour*); which is presented directly as a positive force in 'To Penshurst'; and which leads to the disturbed anger towards the feckless young noblemen of 'A speach according to Horace'.[15] It is also perhaps significant that, in talking of his father, Jonson stresses the fact that he turned minister after persecution under Mary, for Jonson himself showed a continuing interest in religion and was notably stubborn about acceding to politico-religious pressures to conform to state Anglicanism.[16] Again, the anecdote about his mother suggests not only that she shared her son's largeness of gesture and concern with integrity, but reads as if Jonson is seeing her in an heroic role, reminiscent of someone like the Roman lady-Stoic, Brutus' Portia.

In 1574 or 1575 Jonson's mother remarried, her new husband being a master bricklayer from Westminster, a man of whom we know nothing. Jonson himself touches only obliquely upon this marriage, while Walton simply tells us that 'his mother married a brickelayer, who made him (much against his will) to help him in his trade'[17] and Fuller, still more laconic, that 'his mother married a bricklayer for her second husband'.[18] Jonson's own silence on this marriage does not necessarily mean that he resented the match or disliked his stepfather, although the gibes in later life about his connection with bricklaying hint that this was a sore point with him (which, bearing in mind Jonson's concern with status, is scarcely surprising).[19] Certainly it seems that Jonson felt no love for his step-father's trade and it is possible that part of his dislike of it was con-nected with a sense that his mother's remarriage had lowered the standing of the family.

This combination of factors—the death of his father before his birth, the remarriage of his mother, growing up without his natural father and with a stepfather who wanted him to work at an uncon-genial trade—may have helped to produce that seeming paradox in the adult Jonson, of a man who values good relationships greatly but who also sees them as hard to attain. The poems supply the best examples of Jonson's celebration of friendship, in the civilized warmth of 'Inviting a friend to supper', in the epigrams to Sir Thomas Roe, and in the fine 'Epistle answering to one that asked to be sealed of the Tribe of Ben',[20] which provides a good summary of Jonson's attitude:

. . . if I have any friendships sent
Such as are square, wel-tagde, and permanent . . .
These I will honour, love, embrace, and serve . . . (ll. 63–4, 71)

But the warmth of Jonson's friendships, as seen in the poems, is to be balanced against the difficulties which characters in his plays have in forming and maintaining satisfactory relationships. Of course both comedy and tragedy are usually concerned to a considerable degree with human relationships, but it is striking that in Jonson's drama characters seldom find their difficulties resolved. In *Julius Caesar* Brutus and Cassius achieve comradeship despite major differences of personality; in Middleton and Rowley's *The Changeling* Isabella and De Flores come to have a genuine (if perverse) union even in death; in *Sejanus* there is no equivalent—friendship is either ineffectual or merely an expedient partnership in evil. Comedy is often built around the efforts of some characters to establish valuable relationships against the plot and other characters, and traditionally in comedy some success is ultimately achieved. But in Jonson's greatest comedies this final harmony is either denied or made peripheral, even ambiguous—as with Celia and Grace Welborn. Even in as early a play as the 'Italian' version of *Every Man in his Humour* the formal harmony of the ending is an imposition upon the natural energies of Thorello and Lorenzo senior.

The long interval between 1574 and 1597 (when Jonson's name begins to appear in Henslowe's *Diary*) is one of which we know little, except that Jonson spent a period at Westminster school, that he seems to have worked for some time at what Drummond enigmatically calls 'another craft',[21] and that he fought for a period in the wars in the Netherlands. The hard evidence is sparse, some information is unreliable, hypothesis becomes inevitable.

Fuller alleges that Jonson's formal education began 'in a private school in Saint Martin's church'.[22] There is nothing particularly unlikely about this (although there is no contemporary evidence to support Fuller's claim) but the matter is of little importance since it is clear that the major educational impact came from the much more famous school at Westminster, where—according to *Conversations*—he was 'put to school by a friend (his master Camden)'.[23] The tradition that the friend was Camden himself rests partly upon one possible reading of Drummond's syntax and partly upon a sentimental extension of Jonson's well-known acknowledgment of his debt to Camden, 'to whom I owe / All that I am in arts, all that I know'.[24] But there is no good reason to believe that the friend was Camden: we have no evidence of any connection at this date between the teacher and Jonson's family or the school in Saint Martin's church, and Drummond's remark may mean no more than that Camden was, at some stage, Jonson's master at Westminster.[25]

There is no need to labour the point that Jonson was lucky to be taught by Camden. We can know little about their relationship while Jonson was a pupil, but Camden was clearly an outstanding teacher—at least of receptive children—and a remarkable scholar, and Jonson obviously felt that the older man had taught him much. There is no need to conclude from Jonson's later expressions of gratitude that he had had special attention—he may simply have been more concerned to absorb, and better able to value, the education which all the boys at Westminster were being offered, and he could have had few better examples of diligence, of a feeling for the past, and of the importance of accuracy in thought and reference than that which Camden could provide. Much has been written about the decline of pure humanist educational ideals in the late sixteenth century, but Jonson's career was to show that he, at any rate, was able to see beyond the letter of his texts and to feel the life behind the letter, an aptitude which contact with Camden can only have developed.[26]

Fuller states that Jonson went from Westminster to be 'statuably admitted into Saint John's College in Cambridge . . . where he continued but few weeks for want of further maintenance', and Gildon claims that his education was finished at 'St John's-Colleg of Cambridge, and Christ-Church of Oxon . . . where he took his Master of Arts Degree'.[27] These claims lack corroboration: Jonson himself never said that he had been to either university, although his pride in later contacts with Oxford and Cambridge, with the Inns of Court, and with learned men in general suggests that he would have wanted to claim community if he could reasonably have done so. In fact Jonson's remark to Drummond that both Oxford and Cambridge made him M.A. 'by their favour, not his study'[28] seems clear evidence that he had little if any formal connection with either university. It looks as if Fuller and Gildon are trying to rationalize Jonson's learning—rather as do those who attribute Shakespeare's plays to other men, finding it impossible to believe that his education could have been adequate for the authorship of these plays.

It seems altogether more probable that Jonson left school in 1587 or 1588 to work for his stepfather. He had not managed to become a Queen's scholar of the school[29] and the evidence is that he did not make the usual Westminster transfer to university. If Jonson did leave as I have suggested there can be little doubt that having, by his own account, learnt so much from Camden, he must have finished school bitterly disappointed, and resentful about the prospect of laying bricks for his living. And at this point we come across two versions of what is essentially the same story. John Aubrey provides another slant on the idea of Jonson at Cambridge with his anecdote that when Jonson was laying bricks one day 'on the

Garden-wall of Lincoln's Inne . . . a Bencher, walking thro', and hearing him repeat some Greeke verses out of Homer, discoursing with him and finding him to have a Witt extraordinary, gave him some Exhibition to maintaine him at Trinity College in Cambridge . . .' [30] This is pretty unconvincing, particularly since it is very unlikely that someone of Jonson's temperament would have forgotten to express public gratitude to a man who had done him such an extreme favour. But Aubrey's story has echoes of Fuller:

> He helped in the new structure of Lincoln's Inn, when, having a trowel in his hand, he had a book in his pocket.
> Some gentlemen, pitying that his parts should be buried under the rubbish of so mean a calling, did by their bounty manumit him freely to follow his own ingenious inclinations. [31]

It is very difficult to decide whether or not these stories have any basis in fact. Both look suspiciously like further *post facto* rationalizations, but the detail about Lincoln's Inn is plausible enough and there may be a substratum of truth in the claims that Jonson received some help from one or more of the Inn's students. Certainly, in later life, Jonson had quite a close relationship with the Inns of Court, but this proves nothing, since someone like Jonson would naturally cultivate relationships with Inns' men, who themselves tended to seek connections in the literary and theatrical worlds. What is, however, more important—and symbolically if not literally true—is the indication that Jonson was not resigned to the role in which he had been cast: like Hardy's Jude (though with more success) he was determined to get education somehow.

The chronology of these years is a nightmare. According to Drummond Jonson 'could not endure' his 'craft': 'then went he to the Low Countries, but returning soon he betook himself to his wonted studies'. [32] But how long did Jonson 'endure' bricklaying? How long was he in the Netherlands? What were these 'wonted studies'? There is a period of about a decade to fill, and—to make matters more complicated—it seems that somewhere between 1592 and 1595 Jonson married.

There is reason to believe that Jonson completed his apprenticeship in the building trade, [33] and if this is so it is likely that most of the missing decade was taken up with work for his stepfather. Yet Drummond's phrasing suggests that the decision to join the troops in the Netherlands was taken quite soon after Jonson left school, and so I am inclined to guess that he worked at bricklaying for about two years on leaving Westminster and spent a similar period in the Netherlands, before returning to his original job. [34]

This leaves us with that phrase about 'his wonted studies'. This can hardly be regarded as a facetious reference to laying bricks and Herford and Simpson take it to mean that Jonson occupied himself on his return by 'play-making and poetry'.[35] But this is only plausible if we assume that Jonson had had some previous experience in these fields (*wonted* studies) or that his formal education is somehow to be seen as having continued in 'play-making and poetry'. The first assumption lacks any corroborative evidence (although Jonson may well have been writing poetry before he went to the Low Countries) and the latter ignores the fact that when Jonson published his 1616 Folio he rejected all his early playmaking (even *Every Man in his Humour* is only admitted in a revised version). He would scarcely have regarded cobbling scripts for Henslowe or anyone else as 'studies' and it is more likely, if the Lincoln's Inn story has any truth in it, that Jonson was able, after his return from the wars, to mix bricklaying with study of the classics. It would be natural for him, looking back, to stress to Drummond what would have seemed to him the important element—the continuation of his reading of the classics—even if that study was part-time and intermittent.

Unsatisfactory though this kind of guesswork is, not much more can be said, and further guesses would lead to conscious fiction. It is particularly annoying that we know so little about Jonson's activities with the English forces in the Netherlands and as little about his marriage. Jonson's later career shows a continuing interest in physical courage, while his marriage may have considerably affected his general view of human relationships, but we lack the sort of information on these two matters to make more than tentative speculations.

As Drummond hints, it is probable that Jonson's service in the Netherlands came about less from any strong desire to be a soldier than from his wish to escape working with his trowel. That said, it is likely that serving with the army abroad had some appeal to Jonson: he was never to be satisfied merely with using words and his life was one of action—sometimes of violent action. Also, he was no coward, as his later clashes with authority were to prove. We know little of what actually happened to Jonson while he was with the English forces, but *Conversations* does yield one anecdote. Jonson told Drummond that, 'In his service in the Low Countries, he had, in the face of both the camps, killed an enemy and taken *opima spolia* from him . . .'[36] Once more it is necessary to remember that Jonson was talking many years after the event and that often during the visit to Hawthornden he was trying to impress his host. Yet the story is psychologically true, with Jonson standing alone and proving himself in single combat: the figure is that of the man who duelled with Gabriel Spencer, defended himself against charges of failing to comply with regulations concerning religious observance, aggressively asserted the importance and novelty of his art. Also, Jonson often uses the figure of the soldier as an example of the relationships between seeming and actuality and between true valour and the semblance of courage. Characters like Bobadilla (*Every Man in his Humour*) and Captain Hungry (*Epigrammes* CVII) arouse his contempt not because of their profession but because they degrade that profession: they are social parasites who use their real or supposed military service to gain attention and eke out a living. They are soldiers of a sort, but what interests Jonson particularly is their hypocrisy. These points are underlined by the fact that when Jonson published *Epigrammes* he followed his attack on Hungry with the epigram 'To true Souldiers', and his admiration for such soldiers is explicitly linked with a degree of pride that he had been a soldier himself:

> I sweare by your true friend, my Muse, I love
> Your great profession; which I once, did prove:
> And did not shame it with my actions, then . . .

Jonson's marriage is bound to seem rather casual to us, granted how little is known of his movements during this period of his life; and what we do know of the marriage suggests that Jonson was neither particularly faithful nor much of a family man. His wife is laconically described to Drummond as 'a shrew yet honest' [37]—the only description we have of her, and a remark which, while clearly not notably affectionate, indicates some respect for the woman. We also know that Jonson lived apart from her at times; [38] that there were several children of their marriage; and that when Jonson and his wife were in trouble over their religious observances he was willing to defend her from charges which he accepted in relation to himself. [39] But the wife remains shadowy, like so much else in Jonson's personal life, very much in the background, so much so that we cannot even identify her with certainty. All we can say is that there is neither any reason to believe that the couple were ever seriously alienated nor that the relationship was particularly satisfying to either party. It is interesting that although Jonson wrote great epitaphs for a son and a daughter, [40] his wife (like his parents and stepfather) is ignored in his poetry. There is nothing to suggest that this marriage was ever for Jonson comparable, say, to John Donne's marriage with Anne More, and it is possible, without being too facile, to speculate that the apparent limitations of Jonson's marriage may have encouraged not only that painful sense of schism which marks his treatment of relationships, but also the notable split in his literary attitudes to women.[41] Both difficulties of relationship and a dual view of women are literary commonplaces, but the degree to which Jonson dwells on them suggests more than purely artistic interest in the *motifs*. At the least we have no reason to believe that Jonson's marriage did much to heal any stresses caused by his earlier background. The tension in that phrase 'a shrew yet honest' sums up well the duality of attitude which marks much of Jonson's writing about how people are and how they relate, his belief in virtue and awareness of vice, his feeling for the value of friendship and his sense of how difficult it is to sustain any relationship.

Jonson begins to emerge as some sort of public figure connected with the theatre with the first entry in Henslowe's *Diary* that mentions him by name:

(Received of Benjamin Jonson's
    Share as follows, 1597)
Received the 28th of July, 1597 . . . 3 shillings, 9 pence.[42]

The entry tells us little and we shall probably never know exactly how Jonson came to Henslowe's notice, but it is generally accepted that he must have had contact with the theatre—probably as an actor with a touring company—before entering Henslowe's employ. Solid contemporary evidence for this is lacking but the idea is consistent with Jonson's career-long interest in travel and experiment, and—more important—there are allegations in later years which only make sense if they contain some truth. The most important material here comes from Thomas Dekker, and when Dekker wrote *Satiromastix* (1601–2) he was clearly not interested in providing an unbiased account, but his satire of Jonson is simply inane unless it has some basis in fact. In Dekker's play Tucca tells Horace, 'I ha seene thy shoulders lapt in a Plaiers old cast Cloake, like a Slie knave as thou art . . . and when thou ranst mad for the death of Horatio : thou borrowedst a gowne of Roscius the Stager', and later, 'thou hast forgot how thou amblest . . . by a play-wagon, in the high way, and took'st mad Ieronimoes part, to get service among the Mimickes'.[43] Dekker's lines only have point if they refer to an episode in Jonson's actual life and if we accept that they would annoy Jonson, as seems certain when we remember the latter's determination to lift himself and his drama out of the common rut of playmaking and above the common status of playwrights. Kyd's *Spanish Tragedy*, to which Dekker's remarks allude, was a play which lived with Jonson for some while : Henslowe was to pay him for 'additions' to the text and Jonson himself uses Kyd's script as a butt for humour with a frequency which suggests that that text was more to him than simply an obvious target for the satire of outmoded styles. If Dekker is right in claiming that Jonson had acted in the play with a strolling company, and if, as the evidence indicates, Jonson's early work for Henslowe was in patching and part-writing pot-boilers, then Dekker's gibes have meaning—he is reminding Jonson of just those parts of his earlier career which he would most like to forget.

Plausibly enough, Herford and Simpson also use *Satiromastix* to provide the link between Jonson's time as strolling player and his emergence as part of Henslowe's writing-circle.[44] Tucca asks Horace, 'Thou hast been at Parris garden hast not?' and the reply is, 'Yes Captaine, I ha plaide Zulziman there.'[45] This may indicate two things—Jonson's first theatrical encounter with London and his first contact with Henslowe, who had owned Paris Garden (basically a bear-baiting pit, and hence a fairly humble point of entry into the London theatrical world) since 1595. Here Aubrey comes into the picture again and his remarks seem to have a general if not a particular truth: Jonson 'went into the Lowe-countreys . . . Then he came over into England, and acted and wrote, but both ill, at the Green Curtaine, a kind of Nursery or obscure Play-house, somewhere in the Suburbes (I think towards Shoreditch or Clarkenwell)'. And in his notes on Shakespeare Aubrey adds that 'B. Johnson was never a good Actor, but an excellent Instructor'.[46] It has been widely accepted that Jonson was not an actor of any great ability, but there is no real evidence about his competence, although the fact that he seems to have stopped acting as soon as he could afford to do so does suggest that he found the business either uncongenial or incompatible with the role he wished to play in English letters.

Jonson's documented entry into the writing side of the Elizabethan theatre coincides—prophetically enough—with his first known brush with the government. At some time before 28 July 1597 (when the theatres were closed because of an outbreak of the plague in London) a play called *The Isle of Dogs* was performed. Thomas Nashe was basically responsible for it but claims, in *Lenten Stuffe*, that he did not write it all.[47] Acting 'on information received' the Privy Council took the view that the play contained 'very seditious and sclanderous matter',[48] and had some of the actors imprisoned for their participation in the production (Nashe had prudently retired to Great Yarmouth—and thus out of reach of the authorities —some while earlier). According to the Acts of the Privy Council [49] one of the actors committed to the Marshalsea was also 'a maker of parte of the said Plaie'. When, on 8 October, Gabriel Spencer and Robert Shaa were released so was 'Beniamin Iohnson', and since neither Spencer nor Shaa is known to have done any playwriting or patching it seems almost certain that Jonson was 'the maker of parte' referred to. Annoyingly the play is lost, but it was almost certainly topical and satirical and, as Herford and Simpson comment,[50] it is appropriate that Jonson should come to our attention as playwright in this context of satirical writing and governmental disapproval.

The remaining links between this turbulent start and Jonson's emergence as a major dramatist, with the first version of *Every Man in his Humour*, can be filled in quite briefly through Henslowe. Two entries refer to the payment of £1 on 3 December 1597 'upon a Bocke which [Jonson] was to writte for us befor crysmas next',[51] and there are other glimpses, in 1598, of Jonson working as one of Henslowe's group:

lent unto the company the 18th of August, 1598, to buy a book called *Hot Anger Soon Cold* of Mr Porter, Mr Chettle and Benjamin Jonson, in full payment the sum of . . . 6 pounds

and again:

Lent unto Robert Shaa and Jewbey the 23rd of October, 1598, to lend unto Mr Chapman one of his play-books and two acts of a tragedy of Benjamin's plot, the sum of . . .[52] 7 pounds

Jonson does not yet rate a title and the entries give no indication that he was to become England's second greatest dramatist, while he himself felt that nothing he wrote for the stage before *Every Man in his Humour* was worth preserving,[53] but the tension between popular and coterie writer which was to run through Jonson's career is prefigured here, where one entry links him with the hack-writers Chettle and Porter, while the other mentions him in the company of George Chapman; like Jonson a scholarly writer and, again like Jonson, a man who saw the public theatre as an expedient rather than an ideal way of earning a living.

Chapter 2

Two Ben Jonsons

I said in the opening chapter that there were, in a sense, many Jonsons: now, however, I want to establish that so far as the man's relationship to his work is concerned there are two main figures, and that although they are inevitably ultimately less distinct than I may make them sound, they do nevertheless provide a helpful way of approaching his writing.

The idea of two main Jonsons is not new. Some critics, usually those suffering from a Romantic hangover, have sensed a split between the classicist and the innate romantic (who they see struggling for life in some of the lyrics and in the unfinished *Sad Shepherd*).[1] Some have been—and this is more useful—concerned with what they see as a gap between the classicist and the realist, the close observer and recorder of London and regional customs and speech habits (it is presumably partly this realism which Dickens found sympathetic in Jonson). But there is still a tendency to see Jonson monolithically, as truculent, arrogant, uncertain of temper, narrow-minded, dogmatic, ungenerous. One of the main sources for this picture is the 'Ode to Himselfe'[2] with which Jonson struck back at the public for rejecting his comedy *The New Inn* in 1629. The vigour of the rhythms and precision of the language work to refute the idea that Jonson was by this time a spent force artistically, but the unweakened technique sharpens the bitterness of the attack:

> ... give them graines their fill,
> Huskes, draffe to drinke, and swill.
> If they love lees, and leave the lusty wine,
> Envy them not, their palate's with the swine.

For failing to appreciate *The New Inn* the audience is reduced to pigs and there can be no common ground between the poet and his detractors: 'They were not made for thee, less thou for them.' It is not even a matter of equal disaffection—Jonson's allegation of superiority is stressed by the word 'less' and is part of that tone which seems (and probably was) designed to infuriate. Jonson aims at lofty indifference:

> Leave things so prostitute . . .
> Strike that disdaine-full heate . . .

but the fury keeps denying the claim that his withdrawal from the stage will punish only 'such as have no taste'. Nowhere does Jonson contemplate the possibility that he could be wrong and the play simply a failure, while the furious certainty seeks peace in turning away to the 'Alcaick Lute / Or thine owne Horaces, or Anacreons Lyre'. Two other things need mentioning—the seeming confidence of the closing stanza, with its determination for revenge, and the sad moment when Jonson turns on Richard Brome, perhaps his most faithful and successful disciple in stage comedy:

> Brome's sweeping do as well
> There, as his master's meal . . .[3]

The bitter pun on Brome's name leaves Jonson so exposed in his rage that one almost feels pity as it is followed by the arrogant contrast between Brome's sweepings—'the almes-basket of wit'—and his own full 'meal'.

Certainly, then, although this is only a partial reading of Jonson's poem, there is evidence here to help create the picture of an angry, ill-tempered, unforgiving man who sees himself as a giant, but who emerges, perhaps, more like the Samson of the early part of Milton's *Samson Agonistes*. Yet the impression made by this 'Ode to Himselfe' is bound to seem incomplete to anyone really familiar with Jonson's writing. Elsewhere in the poems, for example, a capacity to see himself humorously rather than complacently emerges, as it does in the *Charis* sequence, where the *motif* of the poet as helpless lover is given a comic, self-mocking twist:

> But she threw
> Such a Lightning (as I drew)
> At my face, that tooke my sight,
> And my motion from me quite;
> So that, there, I stood a stone,
> Mock'd of all: and call'd of one
> (Which with griefe and wrath I heard)
> Cupids Statue with a Beard,
> Or else one that plaid his Ape,
> In a Hercules-his shape.[4]

There is the same wry self-awareness in his reply to the lines sent to him by Burlase [5] and in 'My Picture Left in Scotland':

> Oh, but my conscious feares,
>   That flie my thoughts betweene,
> Tell me that she hath seene
> My hundred of grey haires,
> Told seven and fortie years,
> Read so much wast, as she cannot imbrace
> My mountaine belly, and my rockie face . . .[6]

This last lyric is more personal than is usual with Jonson, who is seldom as self-concerned a poet as, say, Donne. Self-examination of Donne's type is not Jonson's main interest (which is not, of course, to say that his poems do not reveal anything about him: that is quite a different matter). We are accustomed, in modern critical writing, to the idea of personae which can stand in a variety of relationships to the poet himself, but the concept is not one which has been applied very much to Jonson, perhaps because the sense of a real, sweaty, highly emotional individual has become so strong a part of the Jonson myth as to obscure what actually goes on in his work. But without wishing to suggest that Jonson creates personae which are wholly divorced from himself as poet (which would be absurd) I do think that it is important to recognize that, even in poems like 'To Heaven',[7] with its unusual humility, and 'On his first son',[8] the poetic drive is to fashion a public poet-figure rather than to reveal the quiddities of self. I have drawn on *The New Inn* ode to point to aspects of Jonson which come *through* the poem, but even in this extreme case the emotions generated are aimed at others and self-exposure is accidental. And when one notices that the poems where Jonson presents himself as a comic figure dwell entirely upon physical appearance, on features like obesity and a blemished skin, something interesting begins to emerge, something which becomes clearer in a fine—though largely neglected—late poem, 'An Epistle Mendicant'.[9] Jonson's fury in the 'Ode to Himselfe' is fundamentally anger at the rejection of his art, although it would be ridiculous to deny the sense of personal rage which informs that poem. 'An Epistle Mendicant' was written some two years later, out of illness and poverty, and its mood is quite unlike that of the earlier poem, except for a moment when he wonders if

> . . . some saving-Honour of the Crowne,
> Dare thinke it, to relieve, no lesse renowne,
> A Bed-rid Wit, then a besieged Towne.

This may at first look like arrogance—although audacity might be the better word—but what is important is the value comparison, and what removes any impression of personal arrogance is the way in which Jonson presents himself as vehicle. In other words the comparison is not between 'a besieged Towne' and the poet as person but between town and muse. Jonson is specific about this: it is 'The muse' which 'not peepes out, one of hundred dayes'.

An important result of this stress on the muse is that the poem is wholly free from self-pity or servility (an effect aided by the firm control of rhythm and by the predominance of a single image, that of siege). But what really matters for my present purpose is that Jonson here makes a clear distinction between 'self' and 'muse': it is the art that counts rather than the artist as individual. In the 'Ode to Himselfe' this distinction is blurred by rage but now it is specific, and I want to suggest, by looking at *Conversations* and *Discoveries*, that this man/muse distinction is one version of a dichotomy between 'natural' Jonson and 'ideal' Jonson. One way of seeing his career (and I think it is a rewarding way) is as an unremitting effort to make himself and his art into something defined by his deepest beliefs and ideals, an effort thwarted time and again by the personality of the man, but also an effort which gives his art its individuality and greatness.

By 1618 Jonson was clearly the dominant figure on the London (and therefore British) literary scene. At the age of forty he had written all his major plays, was firmly established as the chief masque-writer for the court, and had supervised, in 1616, the publication of his Folio *Works*, a typically Jonsonian assertion of the importance of the status of the artist in society. We shall probably never know exactly why he decided, at this point in his career, to walk to Scotland and back. There was a vogue around this time for peregrinations of various kinds—some straightforward, some bizarre—but it is scarcely likely that this was Jonson's chief motivation. Possibly he felt a wish to see the country from which he believed his ancestors came and it is in character that he made such a journey, in the sense that his life was a restless one and his mind endlessly inquisitive, marked not only by the desire for book-learning but for that accuracy of observed detail which is so strong in *The Alchemist, Bartholomew Fair* and the late masques. But the reasons for this walk are less important than the fact that while in Scotland he met and stayed with William Drummond of Hawthornden, a meeting which led to Drummond's *Conversations*.

Conversations is far too often seen as in essence a straightforward account of what sort of man Jonson was, whereas it is manifestly too biased and too patchy to be anything of the kind. It is simply a record of what Drummond remembered (or chose to remember) of a meeting with a stranger whose temperament was quite unlike his own. Moreover, it is a record of a brief encounter and thus totally unlike works such as Boswell's life of Samuel Johnson or Lockhart's of Scott. Even by the standards of the reminiscences of Trelawney and De Quincey it is a limited document, an account of a man whom Drummond would not meet again. But *Conversations* remains an enjoyable and valuable piece of work—and its value is much increased if we take into account the context of the visit which produced it.

Drummond was a poet himself, and not a bad one. His talent was slight and derivative but not despicable. He still makes pleasant reading but his verses are old-fashioned when we remember what was being written—at least by the forward-looking poets—in the London of the early decades of the seventeenth century. Drummond was no innovator, but worked contentedly to old models. Yet this does not mean that he was unaware of what was going on in London nor that he lacked interest in it. Indeed, *Conversations* takes the form it does partly because Drummond knew that Jonson was the great man up from town and was very anxious to learn from him what was going on and who were the personalities of note. Still, there was a great difference of character: Drummond seems to have been a gentle, sensitive individual—even a rather isolated one—and thus hardly the sort of figure to respond easily to Jonson or to bring out the best in him.

This curiosity in Drummond and his sense of being flattered by a visit from the great man, as well as Drummond's own personality, must be taken into account as we read *Conversations*, because these things clearly affected the way in which Jonson responded to his host. Also, we need to take account of an element of something like *post facto* vengeance: Jonson seems to have irritated Drummond and when the Scot came to write up his notes he took the opportunity to get in some sharp digs at his ex-guest, with the result that there is an element of distortion in the record. As far as Jonson at Hawthornden is concerned two other things have to be remembered. First, he was never averse to being treated as a great man: one thinks of the imperiousness with which, in his later years, he sought his 'rights' from the City of London and, more immediately, of the pleasure he took at the public reception given to him at Edinburgh before he went on to visit Drummond. Secondly, drink. There is no reason to think of Jonson as an alcoholic, but he was clearly a confirmed and outstanding drinker and made no secret of the fact. Drummond himself, in the summing up which ends his report, speaks, in one of his finest phrases, of drink as 'one of the elements in which he [Jonson] lives'.[10] Jonson's consumption of his host's liquor and Drummond's reaction to Jonson's great reputation are both relevant when we try to assess accurately what *Conversations* can tell us.[11] Far away from London, living in his 'element', flattered by Drummond's interest in his news and views, it is scarcely surprising that Jonson let himself go, that he took this fine chance to pay off old scores verbally, boasted, condescended, and generally indulged himself, sometimes teasing his quieter host, sometimes using him as a sounding board.

What emerges from *Conversations* is, I think, more caricature than character: important facets of Jonson's personality are revealed but the proportions are distorted. Yet this version of the 'real' Jonson has, like all good caricature, enough verisimilitude to reward close examination, and although it is caricature the picture which emerges when we read *Conversations* as a whole is more complex than when only a few of the more famous and/or outrageous remarks are considered, usually out of context. It is also important to remember that the text is indeed, as its sub-title says, 'Certain informations and manners of Ben Jonson's to W. Drummond':[12] it is not an essay or formal 'character' and the point is worth stressing because the rough groupings of *Conversations* tend to give particular emphasis to famous remarks where they occur in a context of similar comments. Thus, although we may not care enough now about Abram Frauncis to be distressed that, according to Drummond, Jonson said that 'in his English hexameters [he] was a fool',[13] the crushing, blunt-headed impact of the remark is obviously increased by its coming after a number of similar denunciations.

Two comments early in the text I am using [14] have a particularly authentic feel and suggest that at least something of the 'real' Ben Jonson will be revealed. The remark that he had written against Campion and Daniel, proving couplets 'to be the bravest sort of verses',[15] joints neatly with his own preference for couplets in his poetry, while the indication that he had taken part in controversy on the subject introduces a typical whiff of gunsmoke, and the assertion that he had 'proved' couplets to be best has the Jonsonian note of confidence. There is no proper critical modesty here: not 'seeks to prove', just—flatly—'proves'. Almost at once this is followed by the advice to Drummond to read Quintilian, Horace, the younger Pliny, Tacitus, Martial, Juvenal. The classics are to be the teachers and it is true to Jonson that the authors named are ones whose emphases are upon satire, moral advice and—Juvenal excepted—clarity of expression.

When Drummond moves to Jonson's 'censure of the English Poets' and 'judgement of stranger poets' [16] the mixture richens and, at times, confuses. On occasions Drummond seems only to half understand what Jonson is saying, while the latter appears to be teasing and releasing spleen far away from London. Some remarks echo with common sense and a directness which stops well short of unfair comment: there is nothing unintelligent or particularly sour in the criticism of Sidney and Guarini for their failures of decorum (by Jonson's artistic standards the objection makes perfect sense) nor in the distinction made between Lucan 'taken in parts' and Lucan as a whole. We also find a distinction drawn between man and poet: to Jonson Daniel is 'good' and 'honest' but not a poet. There is, too, a moment of pleasing frankness when Jonson, scorning Sylvester's version of Du Bartas, admits that his earlier verses in Sylvester's praise [17] were written before he could compare the French adequately with the English. There is self-praise, as if to balance this flash of modesty, in the anecdotes about Harington and Du Perron, but there is also discriminating willingness to praise others: Ronsard, Bonnefons, Chapman, John Fletcher all get the nod (in passing, T. J. B. Spencer's remark that 'Jonson was not much given to praising his literary contemporaries' is oddly misguided [18]). But two particular comments in this early section of *Conversations* are often quoted, and not usually to Jonson's credit: '. . . Donne, for not keeping of accent, deserved hanging', and '. . . Shakespeare wanted art'.

Much commentary on these remarks assumes that they represent Jonson's definitive, considered opinion; but it is simply ridiculous to make much of either in isolation. Jonson was fond of epigrammatic statements and his writing is full of terse dicta, but it is necessary to remember that Drummond is recording those pieces of Jonson's conversation which struck him most forcefully, and so almost every brief remark is a fragment isolated from its conversational context. In any case the remark about Donne is perfectly fair from an orthodox view of prosody and there is nothing surprising about it, except that Jonson, hyperbolically, would have Donne hang for the sin. It is clear from other evidence that Donne intrigued and sometimes irritated Jonson: elsewhere in *Conversations* he is 'the first poet in the world, for some things' and Jonson shows that he knew some of Donne's verse by heart, yet he also says that Donne's work will perish 'for not being understood'.[19] In fact the references to Donne in *Conversations* are more numerous than those to anyone else and, in sum, represent a rather baffled but genuinely involved response: Jonson clearly felt that Donne was a man worth giving thought to, and one needs only to consider how different the two poets are to realize that Jonson is not responding arrogantly or gracelessly: how many men in Jonson's lifetime even bothered to think seriously about Donne?

So far as Shakespeare is concerned there is little defence needed. Jonson never pretended that his literary views and Shakespeare's coincided, and from Jonson's position Shakespeare clearly did lack art. In passing, it is worth noticing that Jonson's remark does not have to mean that Shakespeare was incapable of working artistically: it need mean no more than that in Jonson's opinion the other dramatist was not *sufficiently* artistic. But this is detail—anyone who takes these three words to Drummond more seriously than the considered remarks in *Discoveries* [20] or the superbly generous elegy [21] is beyond reasoning with.

These early notes give a fair idea of the range of response in *Conversations*. The section on Jonson's views on foreign authors ends with one of Drummond's flashes of irritation which remind us that this is no impartial record—'All this was to no purpose for he neither doth understand French nor Italian'—and then the flow of remarks continues, with the sense of self-satisfaction as Jonson is said to have admired his own translation of Horace's 'Beatus Ille', something echoed in the poet's recitation of other pieces of his own work, yet mitigated by Jonson's expression of admiration of his host's 'Forth Feasting' and his recitation of lines by Donne, Wotton, Chapman and Spenser. Praise and abuse continue to be mixed and we continue to feel that judgments made on others are largely and powerfully subjective. But the overall impression of Jonson which emerges is not one-dimensional or single-toned—it is of him relaxed and dominant, yet revealing signs of instability ('volatility' may be a better word). Daniel, earlier 'good' and 'honest', is now 'at jealousies with him', while the earlier moderate condemnation of Drayton is replaced by 'Drayton feared him, and he esteemed not him', and the suggestion of Beaumont's self-pride conflicts oddly with the evidence elsewhere of their friendship,[22] although this inconsistency is only discreditable if we insist on seeing Jonson as other than a human being. Few of us have friendships lacking any spark of irritation, and few of us resist the impulse to give vent to this irritation occasionally. There is also the typical flicker of Jonson's violence: 'He beat Marston and took his pistol from him.' But there is consistency too, in the love expressed for Sir John Roe, for Chapman and Fletcher, and there is the admirable generosity of the response to Robert Southwell's poetry, which collides with the scorn for the epigrammatist Owen, 'a poor pedantic schoolmaster'. And the tone changes again as Jonson speaks of his own background, the matter-of-fact voice cutting away any strong sense of boastfulness as he speaks of his exploit in the Netherlands and of the duel with Gabriel Spencer.

As *Conversations* continues the 'sense' of Jonson dilates and this opening up reveals surprising areas of the man. If the famous remark about his wife has the shock, epigrammatic quality of earlier comments it also reflects simultaneously a kind of open criticism of her nature and a willingness to give her her due, but it scarcely prepares us for the revelation of Jonson as a man of imagination—superstitious imagination in the account of his premonition of his son's death; humorous imagination in the anecdote of how he 'cozened a lady' by dressing up as an astrologer (almost a real life equivalent to moments in *Volpone* and *The Alchemist*) and in the glorious story of his 'consuming . . . a whole night lying looking to his great toe'. We also now come across the pride in his mother; the flash of humour aimed at himself as he talks of his humiliation in Paris at the hands of Raleigh's son; pride again when he speaks of an incident at Salisbury's table and in the iteration of, 'He never esteemed of a man for the name of a lord.' Jonson could gossip too: what *Conversations* refers to as his 'jests and apothegms' surprises us with the almost childish sense of humour. The rest is largely repetition and reinforcement: pieces of information, moments of pride, comments on literary matters, a reminder of Jonson as grammarian, odd scabrous scraps. Then Drummond, epitomizing his own rather haphazard manner, briefly describes Jonson's departure, inserts a note about Cecelia Bulstrode, copies two poems sent to him by Jonson, and concludes with a summing-up in which he vividly relieves himself of the strain the visit had clearly imposed—before tagging on a passing comment about *Epicoene*.

Drummond's attempt at a 'character' of Jonson is an odd affair. It seems ignorant or inept to talk of Jonson as being 'oppressed with fantasy, which hath over-mastered his reason', or to say that he 'above all . . . excelleth in a translation', but the first comment may be Drummond's reaction to the heavy-drinking Jonson-on-holiday and the second probably reflects Drummond's willingness to follow Jonson's own hints. Drummond is splenetic in his summary—'He is a great lover and praiser of himself, a contemner and scorner of others'—but he says little which is wholly untrue, and one finishes a reading of *Conversations* feeling that one has gained a partial but real insight into Jonson's personality. Even the jerkiness of the text as we have it helps to convey a sense of the contradictions, fluctuations and variety of the man: if there is spite there is also generosity; if there is blindness to merit in some men there is openness to others; there are various shades of pride but also the ability to see himself as an object of fun; there is imagination and boastfulness. And it is finally to Drummond's credit that he records, even if half-unwillingly, Jonson's volatile but not vicious nature:

. . . he is passionately kind and angry, careless either to gain or keep, vindictive, but—if he be well answered—at himself.

The last words contain a vital clue to Jonson's character. He set high standards, for himself and for others, and failure to match those standards accounts for much of the apparent arrogance and violence in his words and actions. He is impatient when others fail to live up to the ideals he himself believed in, but this impatience could also turn inwards. Drummond's record stresses certain elements in Jonson at the expense of others: reference to other sources of information would serve partly to underline the dogmatism, the lack of tact, the liking for a quarrel, but such evidence would also draw out more strongly the better side of Jonson—a side which is understandably understressed by Drummond—by putting more weight on his integrity, his courage, his generosity, and on those moments when he is revealed as desperately trying to make himself into his ideal of the good man and creative artist. This ideal is most conveniently studied in *Discoveries*.

Timber: or Discoveries ('made upon men and manners: as they have flow'd out of his daily Readings; or had their refluxe to his peculiar Notion of the Times' [23]) is a more formal document than *Conversations* but it is not a work which Jonson saw into print. We don't know if he planned it for publication and it is apparently not in a finished form. It was first printed in the Digby folio of 1640 and Jonson's own prefatory remarks indicate that it is primarily a commonplace book. As we read we become aware that it is a mixture of aphorisms, notes, observations, and more or less complete essays, but—regardless of whether or not we feel that Jonson had his eye on publication—we also become aware that *Discoveries* consists largely of considered, pondered statements: the whole is not finished, but most of its units are. This sense of considered comment cannot safely be accounted for by a picture of Jonson, in his last years, writing down his final comments on human experience. This is partly because we have no reason to believe that the material belongs solely to his late years (indeed the full title suggests that the manuscript, in some form, covers a considerable period) and partly because Jonson's creative work suggests strongly that his views about human experience were never fixed in the ways and patterns indicated by the cool, controlled prose of *Discoveries*. It is far more likely that the sense of considered comment originates in the fact that so much of *Discoveries* is derivative, that it 'flow'd out of his daily Readings'. Jonson is here very often translating and adapting, an exercise which encourages polish and the creation of a sense of conviction. The same impression is helped by Jonson's tendency in all his work to seek clarity and precision in his handling of language.[24]

There is no doubt at all that Jonson borrowed extensively in

Discoveries—just how extensively the Herford and Simpson notes (and they are not exhaustive) show at a glance—but this makes the book neither a work of plagiarism nor a document which has little to tell us of Jonson. The range of borrowing and the selectiveness, together with Jonson's additions and the quality of the writing, make *Discoveries* an original synthesis. More important for my present purpose is that Jonson is clearly selecting material or wording congenial to him. The process is that of the borrowings in the more directly creative work : other men may say just what Jonson believes, and if they do he is willing to let them say it for him. This kind of selection is intensely subjective and hence potentially very revealing. But if we come to *Discoveries* by way of *Conversations*, and if we accept what has just been said of the former, we cannot fail to be struck by considerable differences between the two works, differences which cannot be accounted for purely by dissimilarities of circumstance and composition.

Conversations, though partial, is directly personal; concerned with the impact of Jonson on Drummond and with the latter's memories of what interested him most in the former's statements. This, not surprisingly, proves to be mainly personal opinion about individuals and current literary controversy. *Discoveries*, on the other hand, is much more theoretical and deals with Jonson's reflections on how life should be lived, how it is lived, and on the nature and function of art. This is scarcely surprising : we expect artists to comment from time to time on their art, and if we know something of Jonson we should expect him to comment also upon the bases of human nature. So *Discoveries* is much concerned with ideals and statements of belief —and this may lead us to see the book as the epitome of Jonson's position on a variety of issues. Indeed, more famous Jonson dicta come from *Discoveries* than from any other single work, and they tend to be used by critics as touchstones for Jonson's more directly creative writing : they are the texts upon which we preach our sermons. Granted the high quality of these texts this is perhaps not surprising, but it does encourage a distorted reading of *Discoveries* as a whole. Bearing in mind its formal status as polished commonplace book *Discoveries* is remarkably homogeneous and presents something close to a consistent philosophy, and therefore the distorting effect of isolated texts is less than it would otherwise be. But such texts give an impression of confidence, and we shall see that the philosophy of *Discoveries* is less serene than it may at first look. In fact, the work is much more accurately seen as an attempt towards a philosophy, as the effort of a man to establish in himself belief in what he wants to believe. In other words the book has the tension of creative thought running through it, and if this makes it less easy to handle than a collection of aphorisms it also makes it a more valuable reflection of Jonson as a living, thinking and feeling person.

It is appropriate in relation to Jonson's lifelong concerns and artistic aims that *Discoveries* opens with general emphasis upon the good man: 'Heaven,' he says in his first note, 'prepares good men with crosses; but no ill can happen to a good man' ('Fortuna').[25] That is a version of Christian stoicism, but Jonson puts a similar point more aggressively later: 'A good man will avoide the spot of any sinne' ('De Bonis et malis'),[26] and elsewhere he celebrates the glory of his good men:

> Good men are the Stars, the Planets of the Ages wherein they live, and illustrate the times . . . they, plac'd high on the top of all vertue, look'd downe on the Stage of the world, and contemned the Play of Fortune. For though the most be Players, some must be Spectators.
>
> ('De piis et probis') [27]

Already something of Jonson's consistency can be seen, for all three remarks suggest that the good man must develop, or be given, a kind of inviolability. With this there goes a degree of detachment, summed up well in the image of the good man as star or planet. But the same image conveys the fact that this inviolability and detachment do not relieve the good man of function and responsibility—his role is to 'illustrate' (here 'illuminate') the times, a role which is more complex than may at first appear. In one sense Jonson seems to mean that the good man epitomizes what is possible to mankind, and is thus a model or inspiration to others, while in another the implication is that he may illuminate both what is good and what is bad in others. And this second function is very close to what Jonson sees as the role of the artist: at once we have a potentially intimate connection between Jonson's views on life and those on art.

Naturally we cannot get very far just by looking at moments where Jonson uses phrases like 'the good man': we must go on to ask what these phrases mean to him, and the first step is to see what qualities Jonson emphasizes when speaking primarily of man as individual.

Even in the remarks already quoted one key stress has emerged— the need for the good man to be 'round within himselfe',[28] to achieve the symbolic perfection of the circle. To Jonson this inviolability calls for such qualities as awareness, self-knowledge and fortitude. The first of these is the subject of the very first sentence of *Discoveries*: 'Ill Fortune never crush't that man, whom good Fortune deceived not'.[29] Jonson develops the point, but its essence is present at once—the man who cannot be crushed is the man who is aware that good fortune may prove deceit, the man who therefore cultivates indifference (in the philosophical sense) to whatever fortune may bring. This indifference allows the man 'to make his Base such, as no Tempest shall shake him: to be secure of all opinion' ('De sibi molestis') [30] and it is perhaps best exemplified by fortitude during adversity. The most moving example of this in *Discoveries* comes when Jonson is writing about Francis Bacon—moving because it has a ring of authentic human concern and respect, communicating a sense of Jonson at his best:

... I have, and doe reverence him for the greatnesse that was onely proper to himselfe, in that hee seem'd to me ever, by his worke, one of the greatest men, and most worthy of admiration, that had been in many Ages. In his adversity I ever prayed that God would give him strength: for Greatnesse hee could not want. Neither could I condole in a word, or syllable for him; as knowing no Accident could doe harms to vertue; but rather helpe to make it manifest. ('Horat: de art: Poetica') [31]

Here, in relation to a specific man, Jonson is describing theory in action, allowing Bacon to prove the truth of the assertion that the man of virtue will not be harmed by 'accident' and seeing also that to intervene would be to intrude upon the exercise of fortitude and integrity, the latter being that wholesomeness or circularity in which strength lies.[32]

But this awareness and fortitude can only be achieved through the attainment of self-knowledge. *Nosce teipsum* is, of course, a famous Renaissance tag. It has classical *loci* and the work of historians like Haller [33] has given it another dimension as one of the corner-stones of puritanism at its best. But the concept must be reanimated if we are to understand Jonson. He would have hated the association, but the best way of indicating the importance of self-knowledge to him may be by linking it with the puritan discipline of self-scrutiny. Anyone who reads Haller with a willingness to see beyond the encrustations of prejudice which have surrounded puritanism cannot fail to become aware of how vital self-knowledge was to the puritan's life, for it was the only way in which he could find out if he was one of the elect, and in all the best puritan minds there is an integrity which makes this searching tense and constant. So it was with Jonson, with the obvious difference that he is less concerned with religious salvation than with how self-understanding can enable a man to live honestly and morally in the secular world which presses in upon him.

One sign, I think, of how active this concern was for Jonson is that several of his comments on the issue of self-knowledge go well beyond simply stating its importance and into the area of how it is to be achieved. Thus:

> No man is so foolish, but may give an other good counsell sometimes; and no man is so wise, but may easily erre, if he will take no others counsell, but his owne. But very few men are wise by their own counsell; or learned by their owne teaching. For hee that was onely taught by himselfe, had a foole to his Master. ('Consilia') [34]

Wisdom is a matter of an interrelationship between what we can teach ourselves and what we can learn from others. By implication the man who knows himself knows that there must be this continuing interaction and a process of cross-checking as the wisdom emerges. And Jonson knows that this is difficult:

> Many men beleeve not themselves, what they would perswade others; and lesse doe the things, which they would impose on others: but least of all, know what they themselves most conveniently boast. ('Impostura') [35]

In another note Jonson goes superbly to the core, and the tone is one of real weight and confidence: 'I know no disease of the Soule, but Ignorance; not of the Arts, and Sciences, but of it selfe'.[36] That, for Jonson, is where you start, and without knowledge of your own soul you are diseased. Being diseased you are, by definition, incapacitated in your self, but the incapacity goes beyond this. Although Jonson does not explicitly make the point, it seems clear from the organiza-tion of this note ('Ignorantia animae') that benefiting from 'the Arts and Sciences' depends upon the soul achieving knowledge of itself. If it cannot then ignorance of arts and sciences will take its sombre toll, for such ignorance is 'a pernicious evill: the darkner of mans life: the disturber of his Reason, and common Confounder of Truth . . .' Yet beyond even this lies something else:

> In being able to counsell others, a Man must be furnish'd with an universall store in himselfe, to the knowledge of all Nature . . . But especially, you must be cunning in the nature of Man . . . ('Cognit universi') [37]

The man who does not know himself cannot benefit from what learning (the distillation of human experience) can teach, but he is also unable to 'counsell others' and thus unable to act in society.

The key to self-knowledge is reason; reason which is disturbed by ignorance but which is the means whereby a man can 'account' what fortune gives and make something from this ('Fortuna').[38] From the exercise of reason comes knowledge but, so Jonson suggests, the reason he is thinking of is not purely intellectual in its operations, and so from proper use of it spring the other manifestations of the good man—qualities like truth, honesty, wisdom, dignity.

Truth is full centre in the moral world which Jonson so strongly wants to see made real: 'Truth is mans proper good; and the only immortal thing was given to our mortality to use . . . without truth all the actions of mankind are craft, malice, or what you will, rather than wisdom' ('Veritas proprium hominis').[39] Take away truth and there are no foundations for humane intercourse: the choice is as stark as that between the medieval heaven and hell and, for Jonson, as urgent—'For a lying mouth is a stinking pit, and murders with the contagion it venteth'. Without truth there cannot be wisdom and without wisdom there cannot be, in any real sense, life.

So Jonson is again drawing together things which may at first seem unrelated, and we see again that he is indeed trying to achieve a world-picture, a philosophy. For wisdom brings us back, in part, to the 'Arts, and Sciences'. Just how far Jonson's aesthetic views are bound up with his moral ones will become clear later and for the moment it will be enough simply to notice one example. It comes in the note 'Controvers scriptores' where Jonson is complaining about theological disputation of the worst rhetorical sort—such 'Controverters in Divinity' are, he says, 'like Swaggerers in a Taverne, that catch that which stands next them, the candlesticke, or pots . . .' [40] But the complaint is not primarily about the style of such discourse: it is 'odious' because 'most times the truth is lost in the midst; or left untouched'.

Jonson's good man is hardly a startling figure: his virtues of self-awareness, reason, truth, wisdom, fortitude, honesty and dignity (the last best felt in the note 'Beneficia' [41]) are all commonplaces and they make up a figure closely related to the good man of the poems.[42] But the value, or lack of value, of a commonplace does not depend upon its category as commonplace. Instead it depends upon the truth (or otherwise) of the concept and upon the conviction with which that concept is held. I cannot see how the importance of Jonson's commonplaces can be denied, nor can I see how any reader of *Discoveries* can doubt Jonson's conviction of their importance.

But in treating Jonson's good man mainly as an individual I have been forcing an artificial division upon his book, because much of Jonson's concern with individual goodness arises directly from his continuing involvement with man in society. The good man, as we saw earlier, may have the detachment of a star or planet, but even then he has a social role, and there are passages in *Discoveries* which make it clear that the role includes involvement as well as detachment.

Not everything which Jonson has to say in *Discoveries* about public life and its actual or desirable organization needs concern us here, although it is another sign of the homogeneity of the book that discussion of any particular feature tends to merge with consideration of a number of others. But my chief concern at this point is with how the good man (so often coterminous in Jonson with the good artist or scholar) functions, or should function, in society.

Jonson's view of what society should be was conservative, in the sense that he wanted to maintain or restore values which he believed had operated in the past and should operate in the present, and so his consideration of society centres upon the figure of the ruler. At a time when many men were scrutinizing again the issue of a possible conflict of loyalties between God and king Jonson speaks clearly and unequivocally:

> After God, nothing is to be lov'd of man like the Prince: he violates nature, that doth it not with his whole heart. For I am a wretch, and put of man, if I doe not reverence, and honour him: in whose charge all things divine and humane are plac'd. ('Princeps') [43]

Some were asking what happens when the king seems to forget the common safety and the public good, but Jonson does not here contemplate that possibility,[44] which is not, however, to say that he sees kingship with dewy-eyed sentimental royalism. For him the job of the ruler is strenuous and, more important, needs the active support of those equipped to help, since the king is surrounded by a variety of dangers. The mass of people are not only not useful, they are often a positive danger:

> The vulgar are commonly ill-natur'd; and always grudging against their Governours: which makes, that a Prince has more busines, and trouble with them, then ever Hercules had with the Bull . . . ('Vulgi mores') [45]

It follows naturally enough that Jonson is no great believer in parliaments, for 'Suffrages in Parliament are numbred, not weighd: nor can it bee otherwise in those publike Councels, where nothing is so unequall, as the equality: for there, how odde soever mens braines, or wisdomes are, their power is always even, and the same' ('Comit. Suffragia').[46]

Yet Jonson does not turn from this position to adopt a blind élitist view, since he is fully aware of the existence and potential danger of 'parasites' ('Imo serviles') [47] whose advice to the ruler is self-centred rather than state-focused. He turns instead to the idea of a partnership between the monarch and the good counsellor, who is seen as virtually indistinguishable from the *properly* learned man:

Learning needs rest: Soveraignty gives it.
Soverainty needs counsell: Learning affords it.
There is such a Consociation of offices, between the Prince, and whom his

favour breeds, that they may helpe him to sustaine his power, as he their knowledge . . . ('Mutua auxilia') [48]

The same idea of interrelationship, with a stronger stress upon the function of learning in providing good counsel, appears in 'De Augmentis scientiarum'.[49] The 'wise Patriot' will 'take care of the Common-wealth of Learning' because 'Schooles are the Seminaries of State', a point which is expanded later when Jonson tersely remarks that, 'A Prince without Letters, is a Pilot without eyes'. The prince needs good counsel, 'And how can he be counsell'd that cannot see to read the best Counsellors (which are bookes) for they neither flatter us, nor hide from us?' The solution to the prince's need lies with good counsellors: they are 'the best instruments of a good Age' ('Illiteratus princeps').[50]

Jonson is not putting faith in learning pure and simple: the long discussion of Machiavelli on cruelty not only indicates that Jonson had grasped more of what the Italian was about than most of his contemporaries,[51] but also that he was aware of the possibility of the learned man providing evil advice. So we have again the combination of learning and moral goodness (indeed for Jonson true learning cannot finally be distinguished from moral goodness): 'The two chiefe things that give a man reputation in counsell, are the opinion of his Honesty; and the opinion of his Wisdome' ('Consiliarii')[52]—thus we come to the famous 'A good life is a maine argument' ('Vita recta')[53] and see again how tightly knit Jonson's world is. Almost literally, the world only makes sense if the efficacy of virtue is admitted: without its operation we live by mob-mindlessness or by the selfishness of parasites or by the counsel of cynical empiricists. The moral world is the only alternative to chaos. Thus the good man has not just the need to learn in order to become truly virtuous but also the obligation to serve the state through counselling the prince. This counsel will be good because it will spring from the achieved moral goodness of the adviser and because the king (in this ideal world) will know the value of such a man's advice, advice which is to be offered 'modestly, and with respect. Yet free from Flattery, or Empire' ('Modestia').[54]

Discoveries is full of 'precept' and the fine epigrammatic ring of many of its statements conveys the impression of reasoned and mature confidence in the rightness of the prescriptions. These go to build up a picture of the good man operating virtuously (both in relation to himself and to society) in a right-minded state where the prince appreciates his need for counsel and the necessity for that counsel to come from the good man. And although direct personal intrusion into the discussion is relatively rare there can be little doubt that Jonson sees himself as having the role of the good man in this society. But this does not mean that he thought the society in which he actually lived was such an institution: in fact his creative life is a sustained effort to bring it into existence. It follows from this that while the picture of the good man of *Discoveries* is of one whom Jonson would wish to see himself as exemplifying, it is not one which should be seen as a simple self-portrait. One reason for this is that the formal impersonality of most of *Discoveries* indicates a certain objectivity or distancing, while another—which I now wish to illustrate—is that the terse confidence of the book's style masks considerable tension.

By 'tension' I mean that *Discoveries* is less a record of things discovered during Jonson's long life than of the process of discovering and of Jonson's refusal, or perhaps inability, to conceal elements in experience which hold him back from presenting the world he so strongly wants realized as if it had been realized or was likely to be so. The introduction into his thoughts on the good counsellor of awareness that the actual world contains powerful dangers for the prince is an obvious example of this, and the same realism recurs, in a variety of forms, throughout the book. Jonson knows about our imperfections and he does not exclude himself from them. 'Opinion,' for example, 'is a light, vaine, crude, and imperfect thing' but, 'Wee labour with it more then Truth', and although he knows that 'An ill fact is one thing, an ill fortune is another' he also knows that 'both often-times sway us alike, by the error of our thinking' ('Opinio').[55] Similar knowledge of how difficult it is to attain and sustain virtue appears here, in a more personal form:

I am beholden to Calumny, that shee hath so endeavour'd, and taken paynes to belye mee. It shall make mee set a surer Guard on my selfe, and keepe a better watch upon my Actions. ('Calumniae fructus')[56]

The tone of this is far from arrogant. It is scarcely even confident; more in fact the voice of a man who, knowing his frailty, will try to mitigate it. It could almost be a note by a self-searching puritan.

What keeps *Discoveries* alive and makes it finally non-utopian is the persistent sense of Jonson's awareness of the resistance of human nature to even obvious moral truths. So when he is writing of envy ('Non nova res livor')[57] he is aware of its ubiquity—'Envy is no new thing, nor was it borne onely in our times. The Ages past have brought it forth, and the comming Ages will'—and he is clear about its 'barbarity'. The personal application of this (if it is personal, for the 'I' need not be here) emerges as patient and shrewd, but there is also the impression that Jonson realizes how persistent is the vice which so clearly is a vice:

> Is it a crime in me that I know that, which others had not yet knowne, but from me? or that I am the Author of many things which would never have come in thy thought, but that I taught them? [58]

This sense of a world which should be able to grasp right reason but which will not is central to Jonson's effort as artist. It links up with his attempts to define the good man, to present him in art, to use his satirist's vision to pin down vice and folly, and to keep his awareness of the struggle between seeming and being, appearance and reality, true to the world around him. It seems to me that behind the calmness and assurance of notes like 'Vulgi expectatio' [59] there is an emotional pain coming from a feeling that the calm statement of truth matters—but will probably make little difference in the end:

> Expectation of the Vulgar is more drawne, and held in with newnesse, then goodnesse; we see it in Fencers, in Players, in Poets, in Preachers, in all, where Fame promiseth any thing; so it be new, though never so naught, and depraved, they run to it, and are taken. Which shewes, that the only decay, or hurt of the best mens reputation with the people, is, their wits have out-liv'd the peoples palats . . .

This is not far from the Jonson whose greatest work questions with real insight and painful thoroughness the very premises he most wished to believe could operate in society.

There is no need to spell out the numerous occasions when *Discoveries* takes on substance because of the direct or oblique questioning of its own positives. The evidence is at times obvious, as in notes like 'De mollibus', [60] which bring us close to Jonson's satirical vision, and at times it is a matter of quiet awareness of the complexity and intractability of human nature:

> What a deale of cold business doth a man mis-spend the better part of life in! in scattering compliments, tendring visits, gathering and venting newes, following Feasts and Playes, making a little winter-love in a dark corner. ('Iactura vitae') [61]

With that wonderful final phrase Jonson has gone beyond satire and into the sad resignation of a man who has seen just how absurd life can be.

I do not, therefore, believe that the Jonson who emerges from *Discoveries* is the assured, magisterial figure that can be assembled from the most famous phrases or the finest periods. This, for example, is magnificently thought and expressed :

Natures that are hardned to evill, you shall sooner breake then make straight; they arc like poles that are crooked, and dry: there is no attempting them. ('Ingenia') [62]

But the confident judgment of this is neither arrogant nor abstract. On the contrary it has the feeling of a deal of experience behind it and also a sense of something close to defeat. It is the voice of one who knows that Man can reject the good man. Exactly this tension between prescription and realism spreads out in *Discoveries* to make the whole much more than the parts, and not so much more as other, for the whole is wise whereas even the finest moments are only parts of wisdom.

The Jonson of *Discoveries* both qualifies and complements that of *Conversations*. Much more of what is finest—most humane—in Jonson appears in the former and so serves to counter the Drummond caricature which has had so much influence. But *Conversations* itself is, as we have seen, more complex than is often thought and it is this relative complexity which provides a connection with *Discoveries*. We can compose two Jonsons from these two works—the seemingly calm philosopher, the good man of *Discoveries*; the involved, impatient, arrogant being of *Conversations*—and it will be useful at times to remember this duality in later chapters. Certainly we need to take from *Discoveries* the idea that Jonson was, among other things, creating an idealized portrait of the good man, a picture of what he himself would like to be. But we need also to understand that Jonson seems aware that he was not in practice always that man, an insight which will leave us free to consider the possibility that he could, in his plays, masques and poems, look critically at the validity and value of his presentations of figures of virtue—not excluding alleged portraits of himself. But the real justification for using this dual Jonson in this way is, paradoxically, that the duality is a distortion. The degree of complexity in *Conversations* merges with the tensions of *Discoveries* to create awareness in us that Jonson was a rich character, but not primarily in the usual sense of that phrase. Jonson was clearly a character in the sense of a forceful personality with strongly marked traits which encouraged caricature, but the evidence of *Conversations* and *Discoveries*—taken fully and together—is that he was also a varied, many-faceted man, capable of surprising us by his variety, capable (like all great men) of defeating our conventional expectations. Only by seeing Jonson as character rather than caricature can we hope to read him properly, and it is because the dual Jonson spoken of above is a simplification from a richer truth that it may be a useful tool for analysis.

Much of *Discoveries*, however, is taken up with Jonson commenting on aesthetics and I want to end this chapter by showing that this area of commentary is not separate from the moral concerns which have been emphasized up to now, thus (I hope) enabling us to turn to the directly creative writing with the awareness that Jonson sees no final division between life and art.

We have already seen how, in talking about religious discourse, Jonson objects to a certain style of disputation because it obscures the truth which in theory is being looked for. That position is a typical one, closely linked with Jonson's place in the famous literary debate about form and content. For Jonson there is no debate, in fact, 'For what is so furious, and Bethl'em-like, as a vaine sound of chosen and excellent words, without any subject of sentence, or science mix'd?' ('Lingua sapientis . . .').[63] To Jonson (and his position is not in itself unusual) words and ideas can be distinguished and the former are finally justified by the quality of the latter. It is the literary creed of the man who believes 'things' to be more important than words. As a view of the relationship of idea and language it is undeniably over-simple, apparently showing little appreciation of the complex interrelationship of the two. But in practice Jonson, like other literary artists of his time, was quite capable of grasping the complexity of the situation, and while his basic prescription indicates a tendency to put 'matter' above 'form' it does not imply a lack of concern for the latter. 'Form' is finally the bodying forth of 'matter': that is its limitation but also its importance, because unless the embodiment is appropriate and wholly adequate the matter will not be apprehensible without distortion and will thus be vitiated. Jonson, in fact, postulates a very close relationship between what (in 'De corruptela morum') he calls 'mind' and 'wit':

> There cannot be one colour of the mind; an other of the wit. If the mind be staid, grave, and compos'd, the wit is so; that vitiated, the other is blowne, and deflower'd.[64]

This is close to the neo-platonic theory about the relationship between the beauty (or otherwise) of appearance and the virtue (or otherwise) of the inner being. And although Jonson's claim has similar limitations to such theory it does lead him to a firm statement of the importance of the interrelationship between language and society: 'Wheresoever, manners and fashions are corrupted, Language is' (*ibid.*).[65]

The task of the poet now begins to become clearer. It is the poet who 'can faine a Commonwealth . . . can governe it with Counsels, strengthen it with Lawes, correct it with Judgments, informe it with Religion, and Morals', and so that he can fulfil this task, 'Wee do not require in him meere Elocution; or an excellent faculty in verse; but the exact knowledge of all vertues, and their contraries; with ability to render the one lov'd, the other hated, by his proper embattaling them' ('De malign : studentium').[66] The poet operates in society as, in effect, the epitome of Jonson's good man and his task is a moral one, his prime concern thus being with 'matter'. But Jonson does not say that we do not require 'elocution' in the poet or 'an excellent faculty in verse'—he says we do not *only* require these things and he thus leaves plenty of room for showing awareness of their importance as embodiments of 'matter'. So when Jonson spends considerable time discussing varieties of style and matters of aesthetic definition he is not departing from his expressed opinion as to the balance of importance between manner and matter but is investigating the ways in which the latter can fulfil its function in relation to the former. This gives a completely unified view of life and art. Aesthetics is finally at the service of ethics; the poet's task, as good man, is to make himself virtuous by self-examination and by learning from others, and to place this virtue and wisdom at the service of society. His art will be of little importance unless it serves this end, but—conversely—the end can only be served through the art. There are other views of the nature and function of art, and Jonson's may seem unwarrantably optimistic, but it is neither a despicable nor an unworthy view of the artist's role, and we shall see that it is not one which Jonson clung to with blinkered faith. In fact, the tension between this view—which meant much to Jonson—and the difficulties of applying it in the face of the variety and stubbornness of experience—which Jonson also greatly respected—goes far to indicate the nature of his achievement and to define its greatness.

Chapter 3

Self-Projections and Teacher Figures

The emphasis in the opening chapters has been upon Jonson's complexity, but I have also hinted that it may be useful to think further about the relationship in his work between 'poet' and 'persona'. The force of Jonson's personality, together with the interest of the quarrel with Marston and Dekker, has tended to encourage identification of 'poet' with 'persona' and an inclination to believe that Jonson—one of our greatest dramatists—has little or no idea of how to dramatize himself in his art; could, in fact, only dramatize poet figures where these were the objects of satire.[1] The evidence is that this is simply untrue, although we shall see that the relationship between personality and character is not always the same and not always handled with the same success. It seems to me that *Conversations* and *Discoveries* provide evidence that Jonson was aware of tension between himself and the role of the artist as teacher,[2] and I now want to look at this tension in some examples of the art itself.

Jonson's non-dramatic poetry is, like most of his work, highly marked by his personality; it is notable for its assertiveness, for the sense of urgency in the satirical and moral drives, and for the effort to reduce experience to sharp-edged categories of behaviour.[3] But this is not to say that Jonson's poetry provides the soul-searching of Donne or Hopkins: it doesn't, and the difference lies mainly in a different attitude to the relationship between man and muse. Donne is a great self-dramatizer but has little sense of any real division between man and muse: he clearly does use personae (and so attempts to read his verse as literal autobiography are usually disastrous) but there is small doubt that his poems are the dramatization of aspects of self, the emphasis being upon the individuality of the poet-figure and there being little sense of the muse as something ultimately independent of the individual. Much later, poets like Coleridge and Wordsworth quite clearly did have a sense of something like a muse which existed apart from themselves, and both were certainly concerned with personae, but they were very much interested in the relationship between muse and individuality. Wordsworth writes of how

> . . . poetic numbers came
> Spontaneously, and clothed in priestly robe
> My spirit, thus singled out, as it might seem,
> For holy services . . .[4]

—and the spirit which has thus been singled out is something which interests him greatly.

Jonson's muse is pretty robust and has something of the nature of the good and bad angels of *Doctor Faustus*, being neither a purely psychological phenomenon nor a wholly independent being. Jonson sees the poet as vehicle for the muse and clearly believes that the poet can train himself to be a better vehicle than he would be purely by his natural gifts (the training being along the lines indicated in *Discoveries* for the good counsellor). Thus the poet is not passive in the relationship with the muse, is not merely 'possessed' by it, and can also be a worth-while object for scrutiny, but in the final analysis the muse retains its separate identity or personality. This is very clear in 'Epistle. To Lady Covell',[5] in which Jonson tells Lady Covell that she has won 'a Servant, and a Muse', going on to develop a contrast between the servant—

> a tardie, cold,
> Unprofitable Chattell, fat and old

—and the muse, which

> . . . can tread the Aire,
> And stroke the water, nimble, chast, and faire,
> Sleepe in a Virgins bosome without feare,
> Run all the Rounds in a soft Ladyes eare . . .

The poem's tone is light but Jonson has caught something of the pathos of 'An Epistle Mendicant'[6] and is making much the same point—that the muse has value and may be worth fostering, even if the vehicle is breaking up under decay through time.

Here, as in the *Charis* poems and 'My Picture left in Scotland',[7] it is clear that Jonson can present himself dramatically. But he concentrates on outward appearance, and in place of the projection of inner states of consciousness such as we find in poems as different as Marvell's 'The Garden' and Coleridge's 'Frost at Midnight', he sets against the picture of poet-as-body that of the muse-as-soul. But more usually Jonson's poems are not directly concerned with either self or muse and then we encounter a third figure, one which

37

draws on both of these but yet is focused elsewhere. This figure varies from poem to poem, sometimes growing close to the self-projections already mentioned, sometimes becoming virtually disembodied, but it is a figure which should be seen less in terms of the powerful individuality of Jonson the man than in relation to the idea of the poet as the type of good man defined in *Discoveries*. Essentially, what Jonson tries to achieve is analysis of experience in moral terms, through a poet-figure which is presented as being equipped to make such an analysis with conviction and authority. There is no space here to show how Jonson achieves this sense of authority, but it is largely a matter of the humanity and consistency of his moral position, of the energy with which he communicates this position, and of the manner in which he gives it density and a background in traditional native and classical commonplaces.[8] Here I shall concentrate upon only one feature of this achievement, chosen because it relates closely to what Jonson does in the plays and masques. This is the way in which Jonson projects the poet figure as essentially an *impersonal* guide and commentator.

In 'An Epistle to a Friend, to perswade him to the Warres',[9] for example, the poet-figure is shadowy. It directs and urges the friend, pointing to things in society which should amaze and disgust him, seeking to define the proper attitude to these features of experience. The figure is not itself an object of much interest, either for the reader or, apparently, for Jonson himself, and there is no sense in which the poem can be said to be about the poet, as the subject of Donne's first satire can be said to be the persona. Elsewhere, as in the satirical epistles to the Countess of Bedford and to Lady Aubigny,[10] the genre (with its traditional stress upon decorous intimacy) brings the persona more fully into the poem, but the figure remains a device for establishing a moral viewpoint and making that viewpoint convincing: it is neither a centre of dramatic interest nor the subject of analysis. In so far as the figure is dramatized it is as moral guide, the figure presented in *Discoveries*, and has little individual personality.

We might expect to find a more individualized persona in the lyrics, and Jonson is quite capable of conveying such individuality, as he does with great assurance in 'My Picture left in Scotland'. But even here the lyric is organized to a conclusion which refers outside its occasion to a moral distinction—between appearance and reality —which is central to Jonson's views about public ethics:

> . . . my conscious feares,
> That flie my thoughts betweene,
> Tell me that she hath seene
> My hundreds of gray haires,

> Told seven and fortie yeares,
>   Read so much wast, as she cannot imbrace
>   My mountaine belly, and my rockie face,
> And all these through her eyes, have stopt her eares.

This is obviously a self-portrait but it is not analytic and the portrait is designed to illustrate a general ethical distinction. More often in the lyrics, however, the poet-lover is not individualized at all, a point best demonstrated, perhaps, by comparing Jonson's 'Song. That Women are but Mens shaddowes' [11] with Donne's 'Woman's Constancy'. Both are of a common seventeenth-century type in that they are based on general propositions about the nature of women, but the resemblance scarcely goes beyond this. Jonson's poem has no first person in it: the 'you' of the opening lines—

> Follow a shaddowe, it still flies you;
> Seeme to flie it, it will pursue:
> So court a mistris, she denyes you;
> Let her alone, shee will court you . . .

—could be the self regarded impersonally, but is more probably impersonal, as is suggested by the general categories of the lines which follow ('us men . . . men . . . us men'). The proposition is discussed formally, almost abstractly ('a shaddowe . . . a mistris') and reaches a general conclusion. Nothing in the poem operates against this generalized effect: no attempt is made to test the validity of the proposition against individual experience. Technically, too, this generalizing is present, in the neatness of the organization of the stanzas, in the tendency towards a medial caesura, and in the easy linear structure of the ideas. In an obvious sense this is, as the title claims, a song: nothing is done to disturb the direct presentation of a general proposition and the poet-figure exists only behind the scenes, as director.

In 'Woman's Constancy', on the other hand, the title itself is almost the only generalization. Jonson's 'you' and 'a mistris' are replaced by the familiar 'thou', by 'I' and 'We', while his concern with a neat statement of a general case gives way to the typical Donne urgency of the opening 'Now'. Similarly, the simple structure of ideas in Jonson's poem (all that his exposition requires) contrasts with the repeated 'or' in Donne, with the urgency of his poem, with the feeling that ideas are being rapidly developed under pressure, and with an overall structure which involves variations in line lengths and caesural pattern. The difference is well summed up by Donne's use of the 'oaths made in reverential fear of love' and of the 'lovers contracts'. In that these refer to categories of behaviour beyond the particular lovers of the poem they are generalizations,

39

but here they are not used as general truths. Instead they seem rather paltry excuses. But what matters is that they are examined in a particular context and it is this which brings them into the poem. Jonson, by contrast, uses generalization without such a context and is interested in it for its own sake.

The poems, then, provide support for the claim that Jonson was well aware of man/muse distinctions and capable of presenting personae in a number of different ways, although the tendency is usually to focus our interest upon something other than the poet-figure itself (this, incidentally, is perhaps what we should expect from a dramatist). His personae often serve the function of teachers or moral guides, but usually unobtrusively and never with the kind of ostentation common in Elizabethan formal satire.

This use of personae is clearly a way of trying to control the response of reader/addressee to the poem's material, and this concern to control response is an obvious feature of most of the plays as well, so much so that one way of looking at his drama is as a series of experiments in audience control and manipulation.[12]

We know almost nothing about Jonson's plays for Henslowe: titles like *Hot Anger Soon Cold*, *Robert II*, *The Page of Plymouth* and *Richard Crookback* are tantalizing but do nothing more than suggest types of drama: we can scarcely even guess how they were structured, although Meres's reference to Jonson [13] suggests that he soon developed a high level of competence and the titles are worth remembering as evidence of Jonson's professional range. *The Case is Altered* is extant, but although it is almost certainly a refurbished early play Jonson seems not to have wished to have it counted as part of his *œuvre* and did not concern himself with its publication. The play has a conventional moral pattern which is unobtrusive without being subtle and which lacks almost totally the questionings which mark such comedies as *As You Like It* and *The Merchant of Venice*. It seems a play written to order or else one which Jonson wrote as an experiment in a conventional comic mode. It is only with the quarto version of *Every Man in his Humour* (1598) that we begin to see Jonson's characteristic use of teacher figures who act as controls within the play. Granted Jonson's reputation as a rigid moralist we might expect these controls to be extremely tight in an early play, but they are not, although I think the lack of rigidity comes less from any sense that moral teaching may not be efficacious than from some confusion in Jonson's handling of Lorenzo senior and Doctor Clement, confusion which suggests that Jonson is not yet sure what sort of play he wants to write.

Lorenzo is often seen as merely a comic figure; Jonson's adaptation of the old father who cannot cope with the witty, 'modern', ultimately victorious son of Roman comedy. Such a view makes the play tidier and allows us the pleasure of neat theories of influence, but Jonson seldom forgot his own formula that the classics were to be seen as 'guides' rather than 'commanders',[14] and his play is wrongly simplified if we see the elder Lorenzo as no more than a version of the stock figure of Roman comedy. For if we listen to the text, rather than impose our preconceptions upon it, it is hard not to feel that Lorenzo in Act I is in some ways an admirable man. He is concerned about his son's education and general development and, while his contempt for 'idle poetrie' suggests that in Jonson's eyes his awareness of what good education involves is limited, he comes across as fundamentally sane and moderate in his attitude to the younger Lorenzo. So he is more than a stock comic figure in his final speech of the act:

> I am resolv'd I will not crosse this journey.
> Nor will I practise any violent meane,
> To stay the hot and lustie course of youth.
> For youth restrained straight growes impatient,
> And (in condition) like an eager dogge . . .
> Therefore ile studie (by some milder drift)
> To call my sonne unto a happier shrift.[15]

This may not be very individualized but it is responsible and sensible; and this attractive side of Lorenzo senior is strengthened when we remember how quickly he sees through the pretentious fool Stephano. His dismissal of the latter as 'a prodigal, and self-wild foole'[16] is abrasive but no more than Stephano has been seen to deserve. Nor is Lorenzo just a talker, for his treatment of the servant who has been so boorishly insulted by Stephano shows him enacting the kind of gentility he preaches to the appearance-besotted fool.

On this evidence Lorenzo senior could be intended not as the old-fashioned father but rather as a model of the moderate, morally upright man, a figure by whom others might be measured and who could be relied upon to point out to the audience how the words and deeds of others are to be judged—a function he has already performed in relation to Stephano. But even in Act I Lorenzo is more complicated than this. A letter is brought from Prospero for his friend, the younger Lorenzo, but is handed by mistake to the father, who decides to open it even though he knows it is not for him:

> Now (without doubt) this letter's to my sonne.
> Well: all is one; ile be so bold as reade it,
> Be it but for the styles sake and the phrase;
> Both which (I doe presume) are excellent . . .[17]

The excuse is feeble: does Jonson want us to see the action as culpable, or is he allowing plot to dictate characterization? The latter is improbable (since it would have been easy enough to have had Lorenzo open the letter by mistake) and the revisions in the Folio version suggest the former, in that they point up both the curiosity and casuistry of Lorenzo/Edward Knowell's behaviour here ('Yet I am Edward Knowell too . . . (Old men are curious . . .)).[18] This sense that Lorenzo is not to be wholly admired is increased when we realize how he fails to understand that Prospero's letter is not really insulting to him at all—he allows the style to blind him to the respect indicated by Prospero's, 'how if thy Father should see this now? what would he thinke of me? Well (how ever I write to thee) I reverence him in my soule, for the general good all Florence delivers of him'.[19] Jonson may be trying to fuse two type-figures (those of teacher and old fool) and may be getting confused, but by the end of Act I the older Lorenzo is a figure of some complexity and potential interest.

It gradually becomes clear, however, that Lorenzo senior is not able to be an adequate teacher. By Act II. ii, while still showing real concern to find out how best to help his son, he has come to seem a seeker rather than a teacher. When he encounters his disguised servant Musco he appears as a responsible orthodox moralist, but again questions arise about the desired response to him: are we to see Musco's gulling of him as Jonsonian criticism of the limitations of Lorenzo's insight, or are we to see him as vulnerable innocence?

The answer has to be given partly by reference to Roman comedy, which defines, at least in part, Lorenzo's position in the play in relation to his son and to Musco. The plot requires Lorenzo to be gulled and he therefore has to have limited insight. As a result he is drawn into the group of figures who require comic 'absolution' at the play's end. But Lorenzo is not a simple buffoon and the nearest we can get to making the figure consistent is to see him as basically good but rather old-fashioned, a man who needs to learn that his wisdom is inadequate for the world he lives in. To his credit he proves willing to learn, but in so far as my description is accurate Lorenzo senior is less a standard by which to judge others than an illustration of the common comic allegation that man must and can learn through experience.

Even if we feel that Lorenzo senior is a somewhat confused creation it remains true that he is not a rigidly controlled character, and *Every Man in his Humour* as a whole is more complex in its moral awareness than we might expect from a moral dramatist at this stage in his career. Characters like Cob, Matheo and Bobadilla are all firmly placed early in the play by their attitudes to art,[20] and Bobadilla is partly a parody of what a teacher should be, but neither Giuliano nor Thorello is as simple as this. The former is antithetical to Bobadilla, for he is willing to back up his words with forceful actions, and might thus seem an example of the real man set against Bobadilla's hypocrisy. But such a positive view is undercut by the emergence of his rightness as self-righteousness, and his conciliatory attitude at the end suggests that Jonson wanted us to see this limitation. Thorello is something else again, for even in the quarto version he is a study in obsession, having the type-role of the jealous husband but extending it by trying to understand himself and control his jealousy.[21] Again, any expectation we might have that *Every Man in his Humour* is a play of simple moral patterns is disturbed if we look (again trusting the tale, inconvenient though this may be; attractive as prejudice undoubtedly is) at Prospero and Lorenzo junior, who clearly regard themselves as superior to Bobadilla and the others of that group. In terms of wit they *are* superior, and neither is vicious. Bryant suggests that Lorenzo junior is the play's hero,[22] but that is true only within terms of play-as-plot. I would not deny that *Every Man in his Humour* is a play in which the aesthetics of plot are important and enjoyable, but I would suggest that neither Lorenzo junior nor his friend can qualify as 'hero' in anything more than a lightweight sense, for neither has the maturity and wisdom (as distinct from 'wit') to qualify as adequate moral guide or standard by which to judge others.

It is, however, Doctor Clement who is the most interesting character in relation to Jonson's future development. Clement is the earliest of Jonson's teacher-moralists but his role is not that of straight moral censor. His use of the law is eccentric since he treats it basically as a means of entertaining himself, an arbitrary way of behaving which must weaken the ethical strength of his judgments, even though his role in the play requires him to be the benevolent agent for organizing final harmony. Clement is the proper mixture of teacher and comic figure for the demands of this play: Jonson, I think, saw that it would be heavy-handed and indecorous to present Clement as a straight moral judge when the follies which need correction are relatively slight. When Jonson came to revise *Every Man in his Humour*, however, he deepened the portrait of Thorello/Kitely in a way which made for pressure on Clement which that character was unable to bear. In the revised version Clement seems a minor Falstaff run into a minor Lord Chief Justice, and his genial eccentricity is inadequate for the agent of Kitely's reform. But the world of the quarto is one of folly—folly amusing and treated with toleration, but folly none the less, and there is no character who stands outside this folly, exempt from it and thus able to comment on it with detached authority. Clement is adequate here because Jonson has organized the play-world so that there is no judgment needed beyond what the amiable eccentric can provide, but yet there is in Clement the basis for the avocatori of *Volpone* and for Overdo in *Bartholomew Fair*. Because of the structure of *Every Man in his Humour*, where—despite the relative simplicity of the play—the moral distinctions are not black and white, it is possible to argue that Jonson has produced a sketch of the far more disturbing patterns of his finest work, where there is no guarantee that moral authority will be efficacious or free from corruption.

But Jonson's development towards these patterns—patterns which involve him in questioning his most deeply felt beliefs and make him a great artist—was by no means direct: it can, in fact, be seen as having come about almost against his artistic (as well as his ethical) wishes, for the plays which immediately follow *Every Man in his Humour* show him concerned less with extending that play's moral flexibility than with didactic statement articulated by way of more rigid audience control: a development which has been largely condemned.

The success of *Every Man in his Humour* presumably pleased Jonson: it established him as a dramatist of importance and individuality, and it seems that he had another success soon afterwards with the Children of the Chapel's production of *The Case is Altered*.[23] But the success of this latter play may well have encouraged Jonson to move away from the manner of that harmless and undemanding comedy and from the more interesting but still entertainment-biased *Every Man in his Humour*. The movement to new efforts was to mark his whole career: Jonson was an experimenter right up to the end and his attitude to public success was far from simple. It must have pleased him, but he seems to suspect such success, either feeling that it means he is deserting his ideals or that it indicates that the public is ready for something more demanding. Certainly *Every Man out of his Humour*, *Cynthia's Revels* and *Poetaster* show Jonson becoming tougher, demanding more from his audiences, seeing himself more and more as an isolated voice fighting for standards against philistinism. This sense of isolation may well have been encouraged by the imprisonment over the killing of Gabriel Spencer (although Jonson seems, on what limited evidence we have, to have been acting in self-defence) and by his conversion to Roman Catholicism, which seems to have taken place while he was in prison as a result of the Spencer affair of September 1598. The Jonson who turned away from the successful manner of *Every Man in his Humour* is recognizable as the man who went over to Rome with such bad timing that it would be blasphemous to deny the integrity of the conversion.

The results of the change of manner which begins with *Every Man out of his Humour* have, as I have already commented, usually been condemned, and in so far as the plays have interested writers on Jonson and Elizabethan theatre it is because of the so-called 'War of the Theatres'. Kay has argued that the plays in question were not, as has been glibly assumed for so long, failures, and we are beginning to understand more about the Children's Companies and their methods, so that we may be able to see that the methods of *Cynthia's Revels* and *Poetaster* are not necessarily undramatic. Some of these matters will need more discussion later, but for the moment it is enough to point out that there is nothing necessarily undramatic in long speeches or in choric or framing material (Greek drama has plenty of very long speeches; while *The Taming of the Shrew*, *The Knight of the Burning Pestle* and a more modern play such as *Under Milk Wood* are obvious examples of framing material being thoroughly effective). Once again we need to look at what Jonson is doing rather than to parrot clichés about what he should have done.

There is no doubt that Jonson uses the induction of *Every Man out of his Humour*, for example, both to pre-empt possible criticism of what he plans to do and to put his defence of what he is planning aggressively. But this induction is not static. On the contrary it is both verbally and theatrically interesting, while it also performs its task of emphasizing the formality of the stage [24] to prepare the audience for a play which is demonstration rather than exploration. One aspect of the induction is the presentation of Asper and Cordatus. From the start Asper is the moral analyst, but his analytic methods are the railings of Elizabethan formal satire. He sees himself as fearless, free from control by those who fear the truth:

> (with an armed, and resolved hand)
> Ile strip the ragged follies of the time,
> Naked, as at their birth . . .
> . . . and with a whip of steele,
> Print wounding lashes in their yron ribs.[25]

This fits well enough with the prose 'character' of Asper:

He is of an ingenious and free spirit, eager and constant in reproofe, without feare controuling the worlds abuses. One whom no servile hope of gaine, or frosty apprehension of danger, can make a Parasite, either to time, place, or opinion.[26]

We don't have to be too bothered at this point about Jonson's intentions, but Asper is certainly not an anaemic figure. As the induction proceeds his function as analyst-cum-author becomes clearer and we begin to feel that his vision has Jonson's approval, but it does not follow that Asper gains this position easily or undramatically. His 'furor poeticus' sounds excessive and that is how Cordatus sees it. There is at least the possibility that Jonson knows what he is doing here, for the use of Elizabethan versions of Juvenalian satiric rage suggests that Asper's reaction to folly may be meant to seem excessive (Jonson had a personal dislike for Marston and contempt for formal Elizabethan satire) while the attempts of Mitis and Cordatus ('The Authors friend . . . of a discreet, and understanding judgement . . . a Moderator'[27]) to restrain him produce some early tension. There *is* drama in our uncertainty: will Asper's rage prove appropriate to the experience of the play? Will the moderation of Cordatus prove more relevant? It is also worth noting that the interventions of the Prologue, Carlo and the boy, together with the quietly comic portrait of the poet himself, break up the theoretical element in this exposition; help to give variety and to remind us that the theatre and plays are artifice and not actuality—which is important, granted the sort of play this is.

I am not concerned to give a full account of *Every Man out of his Humour* here, but the stock idea that the play's 'choric' figures are rigid and obtrusive is worth questioning. Thus in Act I Jonson uses a very formal, almost pageant-like technique which extends commentary on folly beyond Asper and Cordatus: Sogliardo's stupidity is obvious and is seen by Carlo, but Carlo himself (already 'placed' by Cordatus) is in turn 'penetrated' by Macilente, who is more self-aware than Carlo and more philosophical, but who (as we are told on his first appearance) is 'your envious man'. Macilente's role has connections both with the figure of the malcontent and with that of the formal Marstonian satirist—which places him not all that far from Asper. When Asper leaves the stage before the end of the induction it is to 'turne an actor, and a Humorist',[28] and at the end of the play Macilente tells us that he 'was Asper at the first'.[29] Macilente has a humour which is purged in the play and, although he is not coterminous with Asper, the fact that he does not change back into Asper at the end produces an interesting paradox. In so far as Asper 'turne(s) . . . a humorist' it is indicated that Macilente's 'envious apoplexie'[30] is not part of Asper's own personality and thus, with the purging of envy, Macilente becomes Asper without the need to discard his costume. On the other hand the resemblance between Macilente's role and Asper's half suggests that the former's humour is not wholly foreign to the latter: if so then Asper is not uncritically viewed. If I am right in thinking that we cannot be wholly certain that even Asper is a straight moralist we are in a position where none of the figures mentioned can be completely trusted, and where if we insist on identifying Asper with Jonson it can be argued that Jonson is not presenting 'himself' arrogantly. Such a view of Asper makes the roles of Cordatus and Mitis more meaningful for they become the figures who are meant to guide our response. But they are not over-obtrusive or heavily didactic: they do not force upon events in the play didactic interpretations which it will not bear. On the contrary, folly exposes itself so clearly in the body of the play that the main charge against the characters of Cordatus and Mitis is that they are perhaps redundant, their very presence arising from a lack of confidence in Jonson that he is making the drift of his analysis clear. And we should also remember that the activity of commenting on the follies of others is one which the play views critically—the characters who point the finger are themselves to a greater or lesser extent tainted.

In fact the moral teaching of the play is less overt than is often assumed (which is not to claim that it is particularly arcane) and the choric figures of Cordatus and Mitis are not primarily moral teachers: their main function is to explain and assess the aesthetic quality of the play. For moral teaching we have to look, largely, elsewhere—back into the world of the play proper where, as we have seen, the demarcation lines are less sharp than some critics would have us think. Two examples should be enough. In Act IV the various levels of folly established in Acts II and III remain clear in outline, but there is a striking amount of back-biting going on, of a kind which creates a sense of energetic folly, foreshadowing to some extent the greater dynamic of the finest comedies. Secondly, although Carlo and Macilente are the agents of exposure in the last act, neither can be seen with full approval. Carlo is exposed in the comic drinking scene,[31] while Macilente is at his worst in the poisoning of Puntarvolo's dog.[32] His final major speech indicates a change in him:

> I am as emptie of all envie now,
> As they of merit to be envied at.
> My humour (like a flame) no longer lasts
> Then it hath stuffe to feed it . . .
> I am so farre from malicing their states,
> That I begin to pitty 'hem . . .[33]

—and Jonson makes it clear that the malcontent in Macilente is the product of social malaise, the implication being that the satirist/malcontent is both analyst and victim. Jonson has, in fact, not used teacher figures here in a simple moral way, but has instead operated through self-exposure, confining overt teaching largely to aesthetic commentary. Indeed one could argue that *Every Man out of his*

Humour is a play about the formal satirist as a possible agent for the sort of moral exposition and analysis Jonson wishes to make—and that the play finds the figure wanting.

When we move on to *Cynthia's Revels* and *Poetaster* we have to take account of two contextual factors, the nature of the Children's Theatres and the so-called Stage Quarrel. Herford and Simpson [34] provide a succinct account of the traditional view of the extent of this quarrel between Marston and Dekker on the one hand and Jonson on the other: its relevance to my argument is mainly that it has encouraged critics and scholars to concentrate too much on identifying personalities with characters in the plays which are—or can be twisted to be—connected with the undoubted ill-feeling which existed for a time between the men involved, a concentration which has hampered consideration of what Jonson actually does in his plays. My view of the quarrel should emerge from what follows: so far as my feelings about its extent are concerned my position is close to that of R. W. Berringer's demystifying essay of 1943. [35]

Recent work on the Children's Theatres has been mainly concerned with discussing how far what we know or can reasonably infer about the acting styles and audiences of these theatres can help understanding of John Marston's early plays, notably *Antonio and Mellida* and *Antonio's Revenge*. Professor Foakes has argued that when the Children's Theatres were revived near the end of the sixteenth century the Children of Paul's concentrated mainly on burlesque (Marston being their 'house dramatist') while the Children of the Chapel (at Blackfriars) tended more to what he calls 'humour' plays, such as *Sir Giles Goosecap* and *Cynthia's Revels*. [36] This suggests a situation in which the two companies were not only trying to blear the eyes of the adult companies but were also competing with each other, which may provide a professional reason for the Marston/Jonson quarrel to go alongside the personal animosity which Jonson, at any rate, seems to have felt. But not much attention has been given to how our understanding of *Cynthia's Revels* and *Poetaster* may be increased by thinking of them as plays written specifically for boy actors. For the moment it is enough to note that the fact that the actors of the Children's companies were thoroughly educated in the Elizabethan grammar school tradition (with its emphasis on memory and rhetoric) [37] may well have encouraged Jonson to develop further the formalized type of drama which he had already experimented with in *Every Man out of his Humour*. If we grant as well that the audiences of these theatres were, broadly speaking, similarly well educated [38] it may also be possible to claim that Jonson, although certainly experimenting, was not working with lofty unconcern for commercial issues.

The Induction and Prologue of *Cynthia's Revels* show Jonson's usual concern to be understood, but they also show him well aware of the actors for whom he is writing. The induction is a thoroughly lively piece of work, both in dialogue and in stage business. One of its obvious functions is to present the child actors *as* child actors, and I think Jonson does this not so much defensively (as a way of covering himself in case the production seems inadequate) as to indicate relationships between the performers' youthfulness and the outlook of certain characters in the body of the play. Certainly he conveys a strong impression of childlike behaviour from the very start, with the energetic jealous quarrel as to which boy shall speak the prologue: a gap opens up between the humorous and natural squabbling and high spirits of the actors, and the, presumably, serious business of performing a play. This not only creates some tension as to whether the play will be properly performed but is also a hint that parodic effects may be a part of what we are to see. When the prologue is finally read Jonson defines (having already implied as much in the induction) what the emphasis of the play is to be: his poetry, he says, affords 'Words, above action: matter, above words',[39] which indicates that the play will have a masque-like tendency and that action will be less important than the presentation, through formalized interchanges, of a message about manners and morals. The same tendency is indicated earlier when, in the induction, the third child is allowed to tell most of the plot: Jonson would obviously not have put this in if he had been concerned with plot-suspense.

Crites enters for the first time in the fourth scene of the actual play and Gifford's note neatly establishes the problems he presents:

By Crites here, as well as by Asper ... and Horace ... Jonson undoubtedly meant to shadow forth himself...[40]

Gifford seems not to take account of the possibility, for which there is evidence, that Jonson may not present a self-figure uncritically or always identify an ideal figure with his natural self. There is also the fact that Crites, whom Gifford identifies with Asper, is not an exact parallel with him. If Asper is a self-portrait there is some evidence that Jonson means us to see his initial outburst as excessive, whereas there is little suggestion that Crites needs the controlling which is applied to Asper: it would be perverse to see Amorphus' comments in the opening scene as a valid critique, and Crites' manner is less extreme than Asper's. But there is, in any case, little evidence for the view that Crites was meant as a recognizable portrait of Jonson himself. Obviously he stands, as critical observer, in lieu of the author, but it is the quality and accuracy of his analysis which matter and the emphasis is upon what he says rather than upon building up a character-portrait *through* what he says and does. This is not to claim that Jonson necessarily succeeds with Crites but to argue that his function in the play is part of the allegorical strategy and not an exercise in self-glorification. The point is made clearer in the course of Act II. Crites 'passeth by' and Mercury, in answer to Cupid's question, 'His name, Hermes?', replies

Crites. A creature of a most perfect and divine temper. One, in whom the humours and elements are peaceably met, without emulation of precedencie . . . in all, so composde & order'd, as it is cleare, Nature went about some full worke, she did more then make a man, when she made him . . .[41]

There is more of the same and the total portrait is clearly an idealized one which makes more sense when seen as an attempt at a dramatic version of the good man of *Discoveries* than as a complacent picture of the sort of person Jonson thought himself to be. Only if we accept the most extreme caricature of Jonson as totally and blindly arrogant is it credible that he would say of himself that, 'Nature . . . did more then make a man, when she made him.'

There is nothing, as the play progresses, to require us to change this view. Obviously the presence on stage of a figure who is to be seen as teacher/ideal/moral analyst was likely to encourage enemies of Jonson to claim that he was glorifying himself (thus Dekker's impatient, 'You must be called Asper, and Criticus, and Horace' [42]), and it also becomes clear that the kind of folly to which Crites objects is close to things which Jonson, on other evidence, found objectionable, but it is quite another matter to say that the figure is Jonson's view of himself. There are difficulties with Crites, but they arise because of an imbalance between the objects of attack within the play and the means used to expose and control those objects: the rigidity of *Cynthia's Revels* springs from lack of confidence rather than from arrogance. But there is no reason to believe that with Crites Jonson was doing anything more than trying to dramatize an ideally good and balanced man. If we take the 'straight' view of Prospero in *The Tempest* (that is, the view that he is a benevolent figure) we can argue that Crites stands to Jonson as Prospero does to Shakespeare— as idealized portrait of the artist-teacher.

There is no doubt that when he wrote *Poetaster* for the Children of the Chapel Jonson involved himself in personal satirical warfare with Dekker and Marston: years later he told Drummond that he 'wrote his *Poetaster* on Marston', and we scarcely need this comment to be sure of the fact, but the tendency to discuss the play largely as a contemporary document in a theatrical battle necessarily involves distortion. Unless it can be shown that the play is *in toto* an allegorical attack on one series of writers and an allegorical defence of others, we have to accept that *Poetaster* is essentially a play about art. This is so even if we accept that the impetus behind its creation is Jonson's anger at Dekker and Marston and we should at least consider the possibility that, as with Pope's *Dunciad*, personal animosities are to some extent integrated with a less ego-centred defence of literary and social standards.

The personal element in the play centres upon the figures of Demetrius, Crispinus and Horace, commonly identified with Dekker, Marston and Jonson himself. Yet there are other literary characters in the play—Propertius, Tibullus, Gallus, Ovid and Virgil—and its organization is such as to suggest that Jonson is concerned to do more than to ridicule Dekker and Marston by contrasting the hypocrisy and incompetence of Demetrius and Crispinus with the behaviour of Horace and Virgil. The threat to good art which Demetrius and Crispinus represent is an extreme, but the behaviour of Ovid and—to a lesser extent—Gallus and Tibullus is also dangerous since it involves misuse of talent. Jonson may indeed have written *Poetaster* to settle Marston's hash but it is typical of him that he did so by trying to make a comprehensive analysis of the proper function of poetry and the poet's task. Unfortunately, the effort is not wholly successful (the distinction which Caesar makes between Ovid's offence and that of Gallus and Tibullus, for example, is inadequately dramatized by any standards) and one reason for this is the extraordinary way in which Horace is presented.

Horace does not appear at all until the beginning of the third act, where he is introduced by means of a close adaptation of one of the real Horace's own poems (*Satires* I. ix). Gifford was aware of this and comments 'methinks, Jonson might have found a happier method of introducing himself'.[43] There are two plausible explanations of this remark: that Gifford is taking it for granted that Horace is Jonson glorified, and that he sees a gap between this view and the tone of Horace's satire. In the latter, as in Jonson's scene, the importunate figure who annoys the poet is to be regarded as irritating and feckless, but in the poem the poet-figure itself is viewed with amusement as the object of discomfiture, especially when the long-looked-for rescue by his friend proves a failure. If we look at Jonson's scene without preconceptions about what Jonson may be aiming to do, and forgetting for a while what he may do with Horace in the play as a whole, we notice that something of this discomfiture is carried over from the Latin poem.[44] As Jonson's Horace becomes more fully conscious of what Demetrius is like he grows increasingly anxious to escape from him, and his failure to shake him off builds up into a comic situation in which Horace is partly an object of our laughter. His friend having failed him completely, Jonson's Horace has to take advantage of a diversion and 'exit hastily'—and it is hard not to feel that he has come out of the encounter with his dignity impaired: he leaves the stage routed by the obstinacy and tenacity of Crispinus, and—in isolation—III. i strikes me as an adroit and amusing scene, certainly not one of self-glorification.

If Jonson sees himself in his Horace he has clearly misjudged the effect of this scene or is willing to allow 'himself' to be seen as comically embarrassed. Unfortunately the way in which Horace is presented in the rest of the play suggests that Jonson has not fully realized how III. i operates. The Dialogue which is added at the end of Act III in the Folio, but which seems not to have been acted, does not show any awareness of the comic impact of the first scene of the act. It is essentially a defence of satire and is largely impersonal, neither suggesting the Horace of III. i nor, on the other hand, an individualized portrait of Jonson himself. Taking this dialogue together with III. i and the rest of the play it seems that the figure of Horace has simply not been focused by Jonson, and it is certainly too fissile to be seen as another example of the tentative ambiguity in the presentation of teacher figures found in Lorenzo senior and Clement. When Horace bumps into Crispinus again in Act IV there is another moment when the former seems a comic figure. Crispinus enters:

Horace: Crispinus? Hide mee, good Gallus: Tibullus, shelter mee.
Crispinus: Make your approach, sweet Captaine.
Tibullus: What meanes this, Horace?
Horace: I am surpris'd againe, farewell.
Gallus: Stay, Horace.
Horace: What, and be tir'd on by yond' vulture? No: Phoebus defend me.[45]

But this is just a flicker, and against it must be set the evidence that Jonson sees Horace as a projection of the good man of *Discoveries* and that on this occasion he did expect a connection to be made between this figure and himself. Demetrius' references to Horace's 'arrogancie, and his impudence, in commending his owne things; and for his translation',[46] for example, make little sense unless applied to Jonson, and such remarks add another strand to the confusion which is Jonson's Horace. We have the comic effect which emerges twice and now the satirical references by poetasters to Jonson himself. But, of course, Jonson docs not give to his Horace as a whole idiosyncrasies which parallel those given to Demetrius and Crispinus. Instead Horace is basically the voice of reason, the man who is able to stand above petty intrigue and the incidental difficulties of a poet's life. His role is clear as he deflates the 'dangerous plot' of Lupus and company:

> Hadst thou no other project to encrease
> Thy grace with Caesar, but this wolvish traine;
> To prey upon the life of innocent mirth,
> And harmelesse pleasures, bred of noble wit?

and, speaking of the virtue of true knowledge:

> But knowledge is the nectar, that keepes sweet
> A perfect soule, even in this grave of sinne . . .

Or he acts the part of the good man as counsellor, in the speech which starts 'Caesar speakes after common men in this', which elicits the response:

> Thankes, Horace, for thy free, and holsome sharpnesse:
> Which pleaseth Caesar, more then servile fawnes.[47]

All of this could have come straight from *Discoveries*, and the sentiments are commonplaces of Jonson's view of the functions of the artist.

What has happened, I think, is that Jonson is trying to do too much. He seems to have found adapting Horace's satire for III. i an interesting exercise—but without keeping an eye clearly enough on its impact on the rest of the play. He wanted to put down Dekker and Marston—and his talent for personal satire was such that he makes a good job of this (the emetic scene is cruel, perhaps, but it is also funny) but he could not resist putting into the mouths of Crispinus and Demetrius words which were bound to identify Horace with Jonson himself, and this makes it impossible to see Horace as an impersonal figure of the good poet. Jonson had, it seems, a purpose beyond settling personal scores: he wanted to show how poets should operate and be regarded. But the result of these three elements is partly confusion and partly a blurring of the line between Jonson-as-man and poet-as-ideal which, I have argued, can be drawn with Asper and Crites. The tension can be summed up best by touching on the Apologetical Dialogue in the context of the vomiting scene.[48]

When Crispinus receives his emetic there is no doubt that Marston is the victim and no reason to doubt that Jonson would have enjoyed being seen as the pill-giver. It follows that when, in the Dialogue, the author-figure protests, 'I us'd no name' and claims that the locale was chosen, 'To shew that Virgil, Horace, and the rest / Of those great master-spirits, did not want / Detractors then . . .' he is bound to seem disingenuous. But recognizing that Jonson has misjudged the problem of trying to work personal satire in with a play about poets and their roles is not the same thing as admitting that *Poetaster* is simply the result of spleen and hurt pride. Even the treatment of Crispinus is more than personal: there is at stake the principle of whether or not the incompetent and selfish artist is to be tolerated by society. The real point of *Poetaster* is that it seeks to indicate what the true role of the poet should be. It is fair to claim that the play is over-optimistic about the ease with which abuses can be rectified (Jonson may have been misled here by the sheer pleasure of purging Marston) but that is a comment about insight and perhaps technique, rather than an indication that Jonson here indulged in an orgy of personalities and self-aggrandizement. As on other occasions, it is reasonable to feel that he wanted to be like the real Horace—the difference this time is that he trapped himself into a position where he was bound to look as if he thought he was the Roman reincarnated.

In the plays so far considered three rough groups of teachers can be isolated. Lorenzo senior and Clement are the clearest anticipations of later awareness that efficacious moral teaching may not be a simple matter, while Cordatus represents mainly a teacher of aesthetics who is present to help the audience understand how to 'read' the play, and Crites and Horace stand as figures who are moral guides by what they say and do within the plays themselves. In addition, while it is hard to say how far Jonson meant the seeming immaturity of Prospero and Lorenzo junior to indicate the limitations of wit as a way to education, they do to some extent foreshadow characters like Lovewit and Winwife, while the presence of Giuliano and Bobadilla in *Every Man in his Humour* hints at Jonson's later sense of how 'teaching' may become perverted. Even the odd split in Horace is interesting as a probably accidental reminder that Jonson was to come to look with cold eyes at figures who might have been rigid mouthpieces of his own moral values.

I have spent some time on these plays because they seem to me to have been too often read with unhelpful preconceptions about Jonson's ways of presenting teaching figures. The six plays, written between 1603 and 1614, which represent Jonson's greatest achievement as dramatist have had more and better critical treatment and do not need such full discussion here, but I want to say enough to suggest that part of their greatness is in Jonson's examination of the ways in which moral education can fail, be diverted or ignored. In one sense all Jonson's plays are about how to write didactic drama, how to make an audience see that the image which is the play may be an image of themselves and not of everyone *except* themselves. Behind these great plays lies the positive pressure, most evident in *Discoveries* and in the poems which celebrate moral virtue, to sustain belief in the possibility that art may help man to be better. In these plays this drive collides with Jonson's honesty in the face of experience, and so the examination of teacher figures becomes more complex: Cordatus and Crites have to change now because Jonson's world has become too rich and difficult for their sort of simple response.

For reasons which remain obscure (at least in detail) Jonson seems to have got himself into trouble over *Poetaster* and only to have been saved from prosecution by the intervention of his friend, the lawyer Richard Martin. It seems clear that the trouble had less to do with the quarrel with Dekker and Marston than with satirical comments on soldiers and the law. If this is so then the famous lines in the Apologetical Dialogue where Jonson says,

> Since the Comick Muse,
> Hath prov'd so ominous to me, I will trie
> If Tragedie have a more kind aspect [49]

may indicate weariness and annoyance at what Jonson saw as pigheaded inability to understand his work as much as any feeling that his drama was itself misdirected. It would certainly be strange to present Jonson as suffering a sea-change over method when one remembers that his next play is *Sejanus*, which is not only as demanding as *Poetaster* but which retains quite a lot of that play's formalism, even though there is now scarcely a whiff of the comedy's theoretically efficacious emetic.

Jonson can be accused, in his early comedies, of being facilely optimistic, of seeming to think that if only he can make the folly of folly and the virtue of virtue clear enough man will abandon the one and embrace the other. It is the view of Sidney's *Apology* writ large, and any doubts Jonson may have felt seem to have been about how to present his vision most effectively. After the troubles over *Poetaster*, Herford and Simpson tell us, Jonson, 'For a few months . . . seems to have withdrawn himself literally into a sombre and sullen seclusion, even from his home.' [50] Manningham's diary for February 1602 informs us that 'Ben Jonson the poet now lives upon one Townesend, and scornes the world', and it is in character that Jonson, at this point in his career, felt frustrated and angry. In such a mood the surface response with Jonson is always to hit back, as he did famously after the failure of *The New Inn* and when Inigo Jones began to gain pre-eminence over him in the area of the court masque. It is easy to see *Sejanus*, a tough and uncompromising play, as another aspect of this impulse to strike back, but if we see it mainly in this light we may well miss the fact that although Jonson is making few concessions to popular taste he is working out a new approach to his usual concern with teaching through drama. We may, incidentally, also reasonably be a bit suspicious of Herford and Simpson's alliterative rhetoric, while the point about his withdrawing 'even from his home' looks rather sentimental granted what we know of his marriage and the evidence—which the Oxford editors themselves present [51]—that Jonson seems to have lived largely away from home until about 1607: his success during this period makes it unlikely that being at home or not had much relevance to his moods. *Sejanus* may well be the kind of play it is because Jonson felt angry when he wrote it, but the anger is more than pique—it springs as much, I suspect, from doubts about the possibility of teaching men to be better, doubts which have their origin in fear that man may not, after all, be either reasonable or basically good. Whatever the combination of circumstances which led to the writing of the play, the important fact is that in *Sejanus* the efficacy of the good man is almost wholly destroyed, almost as if Jonson wanted to clear away the earlier optimism completely so that in the comedies to come he could explore possibilities of harmony and rebirth afresh.

The change is not primarily one of technique. Jonson no longer uses a figure like Cordatus to tell us what to look for and admire, but he still makes use of commentators who analyse the corruption of the state. These figures, however, are directly relevant to the action (which links them with Macilente and Horace) but they are frighteningly vulnerable and there is a sense in which the good men of *Sejanus* are commentators for a new reason: the force of corruption has driven them towards the periphery of the action upon which they comment, and comment is all they can do. The same force renders them weak, something symbolized by the fact that virtue in this play is much more widely scattered than in the comedies which precede it, involving Silius, Sabinus, Cordus, Arruntius, Lepidus and Agrippina. This disintegration of virtue is indicated in the first scene, in which Silius and Sabinus present themselves as men out of step:

> ... wee are no good inginers;
> We want the fine arts, & their thriving use,
> Should make us grac'd, or favor'd of the times:
> We have no shift of faces, no cleft tongues,
> No soft, and glutinous bodies, that can sticke,
> Like snailes, on painted walls ... [52]

They say true and the image of snails is a perfect summary of this

Rome, but although their voice could almost be that of a Horace or a
Crites Jonson does not allow us to believe for long that there is much
chance that these men can save the state. They are part of a group
which resists the glutinous corruption of the power party, but their
resistance is fatally weakened by their involvement in a degenerate
society. Sabinus speaks of the 'flatteries, that corrupt the times' and
Silius remarks

> . . . all is worthy of us, were it more,
> Who with our ryots, pride, and civill hate,
> Have so provok'd the justice of the gods.[53]

It is significant that Silius says 'us'—not 'them'—and the present he
describes is contrasted (by Arruntius) with the past:

> The men are not the same: 'tis we are base,
> Poore, and degenerate from th'exalted streine
> Of our great fathers. Where is now the soule
> Of god-like Cato? [54]

The play's good men are to spend their time looking for the answer
to that question. The decline of which Arruntius speaks has been so
swift that even Germanicus, chronologically almost of the present,
is part of the lost past and of its virtue:

> He was a man most like to vertue; In all,
> And every action, nearer to the gods
> Then men, in nature . . .[55]

Because they are aware of involvement in a degenerate age men
such as Silius and Sabinus, who think of themselves as lesser than
their ancestors, are inhibited—they cannot consider themselves
Catos and so the chance of virtue being active is weakened. Real
opposition to Sejanus and all he represents could only come from
someone who was not intimidated by the sense of decline and defeat
which infects these men. But this is a world of nightmare.

Somewhere near the centre of the power conflict of the play there
is Agrippina. Of the more or less good figures she is the one who is
most closely linked dynastically with traditions of rule and positions
of influence, but because the world of *Sejanus* is a miasma of suspicion
and ambiguity the very fact that Agrippina is linked in this way with
the prevailing ruling powers makes it hard to see her as a source of
hope. Her concern for others in Act IV ('Away, good Gallus, leave
me. / Here to be seene, is danger') appeals to our sympathy, and
she shows awareness of her own situation ('No innocence is safe, /
When power contests' [56]) but she emerges overall as at best inert

and at worst a counter-plotter, concerned with power and dynastic control rather than necessarily with the good of the state. The others are similarly tainted or weak. Silius is clearly framed but not clearly innocent (a more ambiguous case than even Webster's Vittoria). Sabinus preaches obedience to the prince under all circumstances (his views [57] represent good Tudor orthodoxy but effectively nullify him) and Cordus is an historian who refuses to apply his study of history to the present moment—only to be destroyed for allegedly doing just that. Arruntius speaks big but does nothing, while Lepidus is a moderate; helpful and decent but always believing in operating within the system (any system), a kind of liberal Tory or tory Liberal. But it is Lepidus who sums up best the most that the good man can do when corruption is so strong. Arruntius asks him,

> What are thy artes . . .
> That have preserv'd thy haires, to this white die,
> And kept so reverend, and so deare a head,
> Safe, on his comely shoulders

and Lepidus replies:

> Arts, Arruntius?
> None, but the plaine and passive fortitude,
> To suffer, and be silent . . .[58]

This stoicism fits well with Sabinus' doctrine of obedience and it allows a man to live (or die) with integrity, but it is no recipe for reform. Crites has disintegrated and the fragments are compromised, consumed, reduced to impotent analysis. But in so far as Crites was a model of how to live he has also been metamorphosed in Jonson's Roman tragedy, for it is in this play that those who would live parasitically and irresponsibly acquire the insight to be able to do so with some success. Since Jonson is to go on to examine these inverted teachers in the great comedies the point need only be touched on here. Sejanus himself is a study in how far a man may go by using wit and insight to perverted ends, and his 'teaching' is far more efficacious in this Rome than the analyses of Cordus and Arruntius. There is little consolation in recalling Sejanus' downfall either, because behind him (and very much alive still) is another and greater politician—Tiberius. When Jonson wrote *Sejanus* 'Machiavel' seemed more relevant than William Camden.[59]

This sense of perverted teaching working much better than that of the good man is still stronger in *Volpone*, where the savage tone of the comedy draws the play close to the bleakness of the earlier tragedy. Volpone himself stands, on two levels, as a kind of teacher. He has parental responsibility for Nano, Castrone and Androgyno, and we scarcely need the reminder of the closing section of 'To Penshurst' to grasp how twisted that responsibility has become in Volpone's house. But, with Mosca, Volpone also teaches the way in which a vulnerable society can be exploited by perverse application of knowledge of human weakness: his drive is the polar opposite of the reformation-through-exposure organized by such as Clement, Crites and Horace, and the far greater dynamism of Volpone as a character is in itself a comment upon how much more 'natural' his drive is. Further, the perverted teaching of Volpone is echoed at the level of folly by the behaviour of the Politic Would-bees, for whom knowledge is a means to self-advertisement or social prominence. But, of course, Volpone and Mosca are not allowed to teach their morality without opposition and unscathed. They are eventually checked by the avocatori and by the virtue of Celia and Bonario.

The avocatori are not the play's only representatives of the law. The law's function is to ascertain truth and to express society's disapprobation of immoral (here 'antisocial') behaviour.[60] In this sense the law is society's public conscience, voicing what society wishes to be told is acceptable conduct within it. And in *Volpone* the law is indeed a mirror of society as Jonson presents it—corrupt, greedy, morally confused, vicious. There is scarcely a reference to the law in the play which does not prepare us to find that the avocatori will be ironically fitting judges for Volpone, Mosca and their dupes. Voltore, himself a lawyer, is a constant reminder that the law is not necessarily society at its best. We also recall that when Mosca tells Voltore of how his master has always 'admir'd / Men of your large profession' because such men 'coulde speake / To every cause, and things mere contraries, / Till they were hoarse againe, yet all be law',[61] Voltore is pleased rather than in any way insulted. The avocatori, when they seek to unravel the complex web made by Volpone and Mosca, cut sorry figures. Their ability is severely limited: they seem spectators watching a drama rather than investigators of illegal activities and the truth reveals itself with almost no help from them. Their view of how law should work is affected by hierarchical considerations, so that the seemingly ascendant Mosca is seen as 'A proper man . . . A fit match for my daughter.'[62] Their limitations are perhaps best summed up in IV. iii:

Avo. 1	What witnesses have you
	To make good your report?
Bonario	Our consciences.
Celia	And heaven, that never failes the innocent.
Avo. 4	These are no testimonies.
Bonario	Not in your courts,
Where multitude, and clamour overcomes.[63]	

If it is true that, legally, conscience and heaven are scarcely in themselves 'testimonies', it is also true that in this court 'multitude, and clamour' seem almost certain to produce verdict-through-chance. There is no sense in *Volpone* that the law is above the corruption of the play's society—in so far as it teaches anything it is that if you get caught, but have tried to use your wits to avoid getting caught, the law will be vengeful.

So if there are any representatives here of the good man they must be Celia and Bonario, who have firm moral standards and appeal to them continually. But many critics have pointed out, correctly, that their virtue comes over as insipid and enervated—only to draw what I think is a false conclusion, that this points to a failure of Jonson's creativity. In fact their lack of impact is of a piece with the weakness of Sabinus and his fellows in *Sejanus*: they are weak because the forces of perversion are strong, inert because the dynamism of vice binds them. They survive because they are lucky, or—more precisely—because vice tends at a certain point to internecine warfare: they survive by courtesy of their enemies and themselves can do little more than enact the stoic philosophy of Lepidus. They fade out at the end of the play because Jonson sees no reason to regard their paper-victory as validating the orthodox comic celebration of virtue's triumph over vice and folly. In this world the situation Coleridge wanted to see at the end of *Volpone*, whereby Celia could be 'the ward or niece instead of the wife of Corvino, and Bonario her lover',[64] would have been either sentimental or the worst kind of cynicism.

The examination of the value of the good man as teacher or moral guide was not (and there is no reason why it should have been) Jonson's only concern during his greatest period as dramatist, and the line we have been following leads naturally to *The Alchemist* and *Bartholomew Fair* (1610, 1614), so I shall for the moment bypass *Epicoene* and *Catiline* (1609, 1611).

In *The Alchemist* Jonson not only changes locale from Venice to London but anchors his consideration of 'teaching' in a more social context which is provided with more detailed realism, for while the Venice of *Volpone* has strong realistic detail it remains at the same time distinctly exotic, whereas *The Alchemist* moves closer to that merging of play world and real world which is most fully developed in *The Devil is an Ass* and *The Staple of News*, and it is in this artistically heightened London that he produces a strongly jaundiced analysis of figures which are generically related to earlier models of the man of right wit and/or social standing.

On the surface the three main categories of teacher in Jonson's drama—the lawyer, the schoolmaster, the priest—are less fully present here than in *Bartholomew Fair*, and there is only (in Dame Pliant) a very indirect version of the good and innocent Celia. There are representatives of religious orders in the figures of Tribulation and Ananias, but there is no need to labour the point that these are not good men outwitted by rogues: Tribulation is both rogue and hypocrite and Ananias, if not exactly a hypocrite, allows his faith to embrace abuse of the scriptures and permit a blindness whereby the greed of their sect is presented, in a glorious comic moment, when Ananias enters with the momentous—and wholly predictable—announcement, 'Casting of dollars is concluded lawful'.[65]

But, in fact, *The Alchemist* is packed with perverted or failed teachers. Subtle has the sort of mind which could have been directed to society's good and he acquires power which could have been used to this end. He also, like Face, has insight, is a 'knowing' person—and for Jonson knowledge is a necessary part of virtue, but it is twisted here into exploitation. Subtle, in particular, is a variant upon the inverted Volpone, and his career—comically delightful though it is—is one which shows just how far 'politic' wisdom can succeed in the world of the play, one in which the humane virtues, so strongly present in the poems, are almost wholly absent. Even the echo-reminders of that world which survive in Celia and in the fragmented decent men of *Sejanus* have passed into silence, a silence made the more resounding by the existence of Sir Epicure Mammon. Of course, Mammon is a satire upon the mania for wealth and consequent power symbolized in actuality by men like Mompesson and Mitchell, and of course Jonson makes great comic capital out of the Marlovian ring of Mammon's verse. But Mammon has more significance than this might suggest. If we set him in the context of the men whom Jonson praises in *Epigrammes* we see him in a social perspective, and see that he represents the almost total abnegation of all that the classes of lord and knight should, in Jonson's view, stand for. The point cannot be evaded by saying that Mammon should never have been knighted, for if unsuitable candidates are so honoured that is in itself a comment upon the social order and upon the irresponsibility of the ruling classes. Mammon's betrayal of the values which Jonson, in poem and masque, indicated over and over again were for him vital for state health is only pointed up by his fleeting moments of seeming charity:

> I'll undertake, withall, to fright the plague
> Out o' the kingdome, in three months.[66]

One thinks in part of the projects of Sir Pol, and also of the empty 'magnanimity' of Faustus.

Lovewit remains, and the name itself should give pause to those who easily see him as the restorer of harmony. Lovewit is a gentleman and master of the house in which the plots and trickeries have taken place. His return does produce a resolution, but it is sentimental to regard this as a return to supposedly normal decency. *The Alchemist* is not *All's Well that Ends Well* and Lovewit's main concern is partly indicated by his name: provided he does not have to take direct part in the knavery created by Subtle and Face (provided, that is, he does not have to be embarrassed) he is very willing to treat everything as a joke. But Jonson has played the *Volpone* trick again, for Lovewit's indulgence seems both decorous—since we have been made to laugh by the plotting of the knaves—and, on reflection, irresponsible because men have been duped and robbed, and the robbers escape essentially unscathed. Comically this is just enough, but comedy has a human face and that includes recognition that a world in which men can be screwed because another man is cleverer is a world which has abandoned humane morality—and it is insulting to Jonson to imagine that he thought this merely funny. It is to be hoped that we have got beyond the point of thinking that the humour in *Bleak House* and *Dombey and Son* is easily 'genial', and if we have I see no reason to be more condescending to Jonson. There is little cleansing at the end of *The Alchemist*: Dol and Subtle have escaped and are eminently well suited to survive in another environment; what they have lost is not restored to the dupes; Lovewit benefits materially and sexually—this *deus ex machina* has a disturbingly human face. His brand of tolerant exploitation extends the gallery of Jonson's portraits of those who fall far short of the good man of *Discoveries*.

But it is in *Bartholomew Fair* that Jonson provides his most comprehensive account of the failure of moral goodness when confronted with human weakness: there is scarcely any type of model/teacher in earlier plays not found again here, and if the distress and anger which mark Jonson's earlier presentations of vice and folly resisting reformation are less evident this does not mean that the satirist has gone soft. It may suggest some resignation, or—equally well—may reflect the dramatist's greater awareness of how complex are the relationships between seeing what is wrong in society and bringing society to see this, let alone bringing society to do anything about it. It may even suggest something close to despair.

As Jonas Barish has demonstrated so well,[67] the representatives of the 'teaching' world in the play are all failures. Busy is another of Jonson's puritan hypocrites, but too much attention has perhaps been paid to the satire of the precisian as such, for Busy is the play's only representative of a religious vocation and his humiliation by

Puppet Dionysius is the sign that the values of the fair reject those of Christianity. In a sense Busy plays the world at its own game: the world proves better at this game but Jonson gives no sign of thinking that any other type of Christian would survive with greater dignity or seem more relevant.[68] Elsewhere the story is much the same. Wasp is Cokes's tutor, but cuts a wretched figure throughout, never able to control his charge, let alone educate him in any way or even protect him from his own folly. Again Camden seems far away: the figure is reminiscent rather of the story Jonson told Drummond of how he was himself humiliated by Raleigh's son in Paris.[69] Wasp comes to see his own failure but he cannot move from this to a positive statement of future activity: 'I will never speak while I live, again, for ought I know.' [70] Like Wasp, Overdo learns something at the play's end but there is little reason to feel that he has learnt much or that he will remember it for long. It is his catastrophic inability to do his job properly which *we* remember and his corresponding failure throughout the play to be aware of his own blindness. Confusion and humiliation are the lot of these official representatives of religion, teaching and the law, and when we look elsewhere for comfort and secure ground we look in vain, even though it may at first seem that Grace, Winwife and Quarlous provide such ground.

Grace is, on the surface, another Celia, but whereas there is no reason to think that Jonson was questioning Celia's goodness (her efficacy is another matter) it is, I think, wrong to see Grace as a straight virtuous character. Her first line in the play is the aside 'So would I, or any body else, so I might scape you'.[71] She is referring, of course, to her desire to avoid marrying Cokes, and one can sympathize with her, but there is still an impression of wilfulness—almost petulance—which suggests something other than a symbol of virtue. This reservation about Grace is reinforced very soon by her reaction to the plan to go to the fair:

Truly, I have no such fancy to the Fayre; nor ambition to see it; there's none goes thither of any quality or fashion.[72]

The note of snobbery is unmistakable. Grace wants, more than anything, to avoid having to marry Cokes, and does avoid this, but her husband is to be Winwife and could as easily have been Quarlous. This pair have connections with Crites, but also with Lovewit. That is, they see much of the folly around them but are perfectly willing to participate in and exploit it. Jonson's view of Winwife is surely made perfectly clear by his name, while Quarlous accepts his defeat in the marriage lottery with complete equanimity. The superficiality of the duo as moral reformers is summed up in Quarlous's remarks to Overdo:

... remember you are but Adam, flesh and blood! You have your frailty, forget your other name of Overdo, and invite us all to supper.[73]

However one sees Jonson's development this is a long way from the emetic for Crispinus: the advice is sound, but what authority has the adviser and what are the chances of the advice being acted upon?

A full discussion of these questions would involve close examination of all the texts which have been ignored in this chapter, and that is beyond the range of this book. But I want to take the issues further in the next chapter by introducing the complications which arise when we try to see Jonson whole: the playwright-Jonson has the disconcerting habit of reaching positions which are not the same as those of masque-Jonson and/or poet-Jonson, or not the same at the same time.

Chapter 4

Some Periods in Jonson's Art

Few English writers have made substantial and valuable contributions in more than one area of literary activity. Apart from Hardy (and, debatably, George Meredith) none of the major English novelists is also a major poet or dramatist, and apart from Yeats and Eliot no major British poet has much claim to attention as dramatist. A case might be made for Lawrence, but even if his plays and poems are given maximum weight it is hard to see their achievement as matching that of his best novels. Jonson, like his namesake Samuel Johnson, but on a larger scale, demands serious attention on several levels—as playwright, poet, masque-writer, critic and author of *Discoveries*. What I am anxious to show, however, is not so much that Jonson's achievement in each of these areas is considerable as that awareness of his achievement in each is necessary to a full understanding of the total achievement. The tendency of writers on Jonson has been to concentrate upon the plays or the poems or the masques, and the few books which seek to deal with more than one area usually treat each separately. As a result it is difficult for a reader of Jonson to come to terms with the complexity of his work as a whole, something which is made more difficult by Jonson's own tendency (which is tied up with the linguistic attitudes discussed later) to present different facets of his outlook in separate works. This operates to disguise the fact that his mind often covered considerable ranges of manner and attitude within comparatively narrow bands of time, although it is also important to recognize that the fundamental questions remain much the same throughout his career: What is man really like? How far can and does he act morally? How far can he be taught? In this chapter I want to look at Jonson's output in selected time-bands, in an attempt to show how his work in one area relates to, and enriches, our sense of his work in another. One thing which will, I think, emerge is a sense of a mind dwelling upon a variety of aspects of a limited set of problems about human nature and behaviour.

The period 1603–4 is a good place to start, for during this time Jonson had *Sejanus* produced, composed his part of 'King James' Entertainment in Passing to his Coronation' (15 March), wrote his 'Panegyre' 'On the happy entrance of James . . . to his first high session of Parliament . . .' (19 March) and also 'The Satyr' (written for 'the Queen and Prince at Althorpe'). It is also, incidentally, the period of the composite *Eastward Ho*, a fine comedy which landed Jonson and his co-authors in trouble with the authorities. Anyone reading these works is likely to be struck by their range, but it may be felt that this is no more than an indication of Jonson's professionalism. Jonson was certainly a professional and took a professional's pride in doing his work well, whatever the nature of that work. Also, of course, the fact that his living depended upon his continuing to get literary work meant that he would have been a fool (even if a high-principled one) to ignore what his various clients would expect from him and what would please them. This obviously applies particularly to the Entertainment, Panegyre and Satyr, for these mark the beginnings of his career as a writer for public and court occasions. Yet Jonson was not the sort of man simply to do the easiest thing or to tailor his work in sycophantic accord with what his audience might expect, and I do not think that he would have wished to disavow, as elements of his total vision, any of the works of 1603–4.

But if we proceed on the assumption that Jonson worked with integrity we are bound to wonder, when we look at his achievement in different genres, whether his viewpoints can be thought of in terms of any tidy pattern at all. On the surface Jonson wrote *Sejanus* out of anger at public reaction to *Poetaster*, but not (to judge from the tone of the relevant lines in 'To the Reader', appended to the latter play [1]) to satisfy mass taste. *Sejanus* is challenge rather than conciliation, and it failed. But what concerns us is the kind of play this is, and we have seen that it is a very bleak account of how the force of evil can, when mated with intelligence and ruthlessness, splinter the powers of goodness. The play shows considerable awareness of Machiavelli—and not so much the crude distortion of the usual Elizabethan 'Machiavel' as a sense of the cool, seemingly pragmatic thought of Machiavelli himself. In *Sejanus* the expediency which is advocated in *The Prince* is accepted but pushed to totally selfish and evil ends. Authority is brutal, tyrannical, single-minded—but virtue cannot match its organization and 'democracy' is a fickle mob. In *Sejanus* Jonson pushes an aspect of Machiavelli's thought to an extreme and when we consider the play in the light of the discussion of Machiavelli in *Discoveries* [2] we can perhaps see how concerned Jonson was to refute the Italian and also how much he was interested in questions about the nature of power. We may also see a hint in the *Discoveries* discussion of Jonson's usual habit of singling out particular facets of his basic viewpoints for examination in particular works. So *Sejanus* is only one part of Jonson's long-drawn-out examination of the nature and efficacy of moral goodness. We do not know exactly why he decided to write this play in this way at this time, but we do know that he was reacting from a failure in comedy and it is typical of Jonson that instead of turning to some type of drama in which he could be sure of regaining public popularity he chose to challenge the public instead, but now in a different mode. Certainly one of the impulses behind *Sejanus* seems to be anger ('If they won't accept my brand of satirical comedy, they'll have to face my type of cynical tragedy'), but it is I think an anger in which annoyance with the public is mixed with anxiety about the possibility of reform through satire and the presentation of moral positives. It is almost possible to see *Sejanus* as a desperate attempt by Jonson to make his audience see themselves in the roles of those who, in the play, ignore or seek to destroy virtue. Perhaps if the audience could see this and its results it would begin to listen, aware now of the urgency of the issues.

Yet *Sejanus* does not strike me as a play written out of emotional anguish or deep psychological torment. It lacks the personal inwardness of a play like *King Lear*, and I do not mean by this that *Lear* is some sort of allegorical autobiography but that Shakespeare communicates the feeling that the issues of the play are of the gut as much as of the brain, whereas *Sejanus* gains its peculiar effect from the coldness with which its cynical views are put forward. This sense of chill defines the kind of play we are dealing with, one which seems to start from some such proposition as, 'Let us contemplate what happens when evil is intelligent and completely amoral.' Such drama of demonstration need not have the pressure of emotional torment behind it, and this is not to say that the play therefore suffers or that Jonson was not, as an artist dealing with public issues of ethics and authority, disturbed about the ways in which the union of ruler and adviser could go tragically wrong. Since his method is one of demonstration Jonson would naturally (and I think instinctively) be inclined to seek for clarity, to illuminate an area of experience with maximum intensity to make an audience as aware as possible of the consequences of energetic tyranny.

If we grant this there is no need to explain differences between *Sejanus* and 'The Satyr' or 'Panegyre' primarily in terms of professionalism (I have suggested that in this sense of professionalism *Sejanus* was badly judged) or in terms of some fluctuation in the state of Jonson's psyche or alimentary tract. It becomes possible, instead, to look at these works as projecting various possibilities, alternative images of what may be possible for man. Thus in the printed text of 'The Satyr' Jonson preserves a speech which he says was to have been delivered to the royal visitors to Althorpe 'in the person of a youth, and accompanied with divers gentlemens younger sonnes'.[3] It was not delivered, Jonson tells us, 'by reason of the multitudinous presse', but although that may well have irritated Jonson it is immaterial here. The queen and Prince Henry are addressed:

> You are a Goddesse, and your will be done:
> Yet this our last hope is, that as the Sunne
> Cheeres objects farre remov'd, as well as neere;
> So, wheresoe're you shine, you'le sparkle here.
> And you deare Lord . . .
> O shoot up fast in spirit, as in yeares;
> That when upon her head proud Europe weares
> Her stateliest tire, you may appeare thereon
> The richest gem, without a paragon.
> Shine bright and fixed as the Artick starre . . .[4]

The imagery, linking monarchy with celestial bodies, is of course commonplace and the speech is obviously flattering. But it is more than just that, for it is composed so as to remind queen and prince of their roles: it is important, Jonson is saying, that the royal family should remember that part of their sun-like function is to give sustaining warmth to the whole kingdom, and it is important for the kingdom that Henry should grow in quality of personality as well as in age, to the point where he can 'Shine bright and fixed', the latter word pointing to that quality of constancy, firmness of purpose, which Jonson so often presents as part of the essence of the good man.

Decorum requires that complimentary verse such as this should not seem to suggest that the Stuarts might forget their roles. But the advice (which is in a sense a mirror of what *should* be) is still there, and this is typically underlined by the intention that the speech should be presented with the 'accompaniment' of young gentlemen, something which symbolizes the importance of unity between royalty and gentry, a unity which was to be tested to breaking point before very long. Here Jonson is putting foward the alternative picture to that of *Sejanus*: the image is of benign stars, as against the malign ones of the play, but in both cases—and this underlines the essentially secular nature of Jonson's art—the stars are ultimately human beings, and benignity and malignity are human choices. Jonson would be a more orthodox exploratory writer if these alternatives were given full weight in a single work, but his usual method is to break down complexities into their components and to demonstrate particular components in separate works. *Sejanus* is, in terms of what was to happen in England in the next few decades, the more perceptive work, and its greater power makes one feel that there was more conviction here than in 'The Satyr', but it is important to notice that the play and the minor entertainment, taken together, indicate that Jonson was able, within the space of a few months, to articulate visions both of authority totally abused and of effective responsible rule. This dichotomy is made less absolute when we consider 'Panegyre', which is a considerable piece in its own right and which expresses Jonson's belief that princes need to have and heed good advice with an emphasis which suggests that the Roman world of *Sejanus* is not so far removed from the complimentary lines to James as may at first appear.

I don't much like historical generalizations, but it does seem clear that James's journey to England and his coronation were greeted with genuine national enthusiasm. In so far as he was known in England before his accession it was as an able king of Scotland, and his assuming the English throne dissolved anxieties which had grown from Elizabeth's refusal to name her successor; removed fears of a Catholic monarch; and ended the sense of *fin de siècle* associated with Elizabeth's last years of life. James's first visit to Parliament, the context of Jonson's poem, was his first major act of state after the coronation and was of considerable importance, bearing in mind that during Elizabeth's reign it had become increasingly evident that a decent working relationship between monarch and Parliament was vital to the harmonious running of the country. Jonson could easily have been excused if he had written an automatic poet-laureate piece of flattery to James, but 'Panegyre' is more than this, being articulated in a way which gives real weight both to the imagery of compliment and to the advice offered to the monarch. Its opening lines make use of the sun/king motif mentioned above but Jonson conveys a sense of forces genuinely resistant to the power of the sun's rays. He refers to the moral darkness:

> . . . those darke and deepe concealed vaults,
> Where men commit blacke incest with their faults;
> And snore supinely in the stall of sin . . .[5]

These forces are such as would '(if not dispers'd) infect the Crowne, / And in their vapor her bright mettall drowne'. The language of the passage in which Jonson presents this negative is theatrical, even melodramatic, rather than being located in analysis of particular areas of society or particular ways of social thinking. There is no precise indication of where the danger lies, but while this obviously makes the passage fairly useless as social commentary it is nevertheless an effective account of general moral darkness, of Jonson's sense that there is danger and that the king's job is to burn it out. It is also worth mentioning in passing that the theatricality of the language relates the passage to Jonson's world of art—in which *Sejanus* is, chronologically, the most relevant object: the language could almost come from the play.

It is only when this negative has been established that Jonson moves to present his positive. He does this in two ways. First he operates, in the masque tradition, by presenting images or ideals of harmony and unity:

> I saw . . . that rich chaine,
> That fastneth heavenly power to earthly raigne

and

> This was the peoples love, with which did strive
> The Nobles zeale, yet either kept alive
> The others flame, as doth the wike and waxe,
> That, friendly temper'd, one pure taper makes . . .[6]

The idea of a chain-link between God and monarch is scarcely original, and James would have fully agreed with the concept, as would Sir Robert Filmer several decades later,[7] but it was an image which was already being questioned elsewhere.[8] The image of the taper is a beautifully exact summary of the hierarchy-with-responsibility in which Jonson believed and probably caught the prevailing mood of the moment, but elsewhere [9] such images are of brevity and uncertainty, and although here the picture is clearly an idealization of the relationship Jonson wished to believe existed it is interesting that the associations of the image are not conducive to complacency: in terms of the context one cannot help feeling how easily a taper can be extinguished—the mutual fostering of people and nobles is precarious. The second way of rendering the positive is through the view of kingship put forward by Themis, a view which belongs to the tradition of 'advice to princes'; and what is most interesting about this section of 'A Panegyre' is the strong awareness that the monarch may fail to do his duty. Obviously Jonson cannot suggest that this is likely to be the case with James, and obviously James was meant to be flattered by the poem, but if he listened with any care (which is perhaps unlikely—I am haunted by the imaginary picture of a frustrated Jonson, glowering inwardly as his precious words get lost in the general hubbub) he must have been made aware of how difficult at least one of his subjects felt the task of kingship to be.

James is presented within the poem as aware of the difficulties and dangers, and of course 'A Panegyre' does not give any strong direct sense of threat to the new king or to his theories about how the kingdom should be run—it would have been indecorous if it had, and Jonson would have been bold to the point of foolhardiness, but although the world of *Sejanus* may be far away it is not out of sight.

I now want to move forward several years, to the period between 1608 and 1610, one in which Jonson wrote two of his best comedies (*Epicoene* and *The Alchemist*) and also several of his finest masques. The years in question perhaps mark the peak of Jonson's popularity, both as public dramatist and as court poet, and it is therefore a period of great interest—and not least when we look at the overall effect of the products of the period.

The traditional picture of Jonson's development as dramatist has been that after *Volpone* and *Sejanus* his commentary upon society becomes more tolerant, less abrasive: by this account the embattled young Jonson grows more genial, more humane, more able to tolerate man's imperfection, perhaps because he is more 'mature' (though that is a loaded word), perhaps because he becomes more secure in financial and 'place' terms. The return of Jonson to a more aggressive manner in later years is explained by such things as ill-health, the failure of plays like *The New Inn*, and the quarrel with Inigo Jones, accompanied by a more general sense of being displaced by rising, younger men. There is much in this account which I cannot agree with, but for the moment I want to take one aspect of it for further examination.

It is, I think, a mistake to see Jonson as becoming more easy-going in these years, if we mean by this that he was less concerned than previously to persuade men to share his view of how they should live. The change is one of tactics and not due to any abandonment of objectives. But this change of tactics—briefly speaking, the refinement of methods of dramatic subversion towards a complex play/audience relationship which foreshadows the tactics of Swift—does include a change of tone. *Sejanus* and *Volpone* are both sombre plays, and in both the bitterness of near despair informs the tone, dominates the atmosphere. It is reasonable to see both works as aggressive: they are dramatically thoroughly assured and at times subtle, but they attack their audience frontally. At least this is the immediate impression, and although closer inspection reveals complexities these reinforce but do not fundamentally change this first impression. Thus even the ending of *Volpone*, which is a remarkable piece of audience-manipulation, is the logical extension of the mood of that play—in fact it is because the logic is so remorseless that the ending is so disconcerting. *Epicoene* and, more obviously, *The Alchemist* develop techniques which Jonson had worked out fairly fully in *Volpone*, but they do so in a more oblique, more subversive way, one which—it can be argued—makes the views of human nature (views which themselves remain fundamentally unchanged) more difficult to divorce ourselves from, once we have realized how we have been implicated through Jonson's dramatic technique in the worlds of his plays.

Now, while I do not believe that in the period between 1608 and 1610 Jonson became any less concerned about the human condition or any less convinced that his task as artist was to try to convince his audiences that his definition of the good man was essential to man's personal and social welfare, I do sense in the writings of this period something which can be called 'relaxation'. But this is the result of the aesthetic confidence now fully shown, a confidence partly the result of experience (by 1608 Jonson had a substantial body of writing behind him) and partly from the fact of recognition, particularly as the chief writer for the court. Such relaxation need not indicate or include any lapse of purpose, although, of course, it may do so. But here I want to concentrate upon the aesthetic assurance of the main works of this period, assurance which takes in considerable variety of method and material.

So far as *Epicoene* and *The Alchemist* are concerned it is unnecessary to go into detail—Dryden's estimation of the former, Coleridge's of the latter [10] have been developed and confirmed by many modern critics, and there is general acceptance that both plays are structural masterpieces. In addition, only a very imperceptive or bigoted reader can miss the stylistic mastery of these plays: the use of dialogue to create comic confusion at the start of *The Alchemist*, the certainty of touch whereby idiom places and defines character in the same play,[11] the theatrically perfect tormenting of Morose in Act II of *Epicoene*, the splendid merging of language and action in its closing scenes. Rather than simply repeat things said well by others about these two comedies I want to mention some features of the articulation of one or two of the masques of the same period.

'Oberon' is not one of Jonson's more challenging masques (that is, it is not particularly esoteric, nor is it one of the masques which extend our understanding of Jonson as social analyst to any great extent) but it is a beautiful piece of work. Structurally it has a simple design, being little more than the juxtaposition of the wild and rugged satyrs against the grace and harmony of the 'lesser Faies', the adult fays, and Oberon himself with his 'knights'. But this simple basis is given variety and animation by Jonson's writing, as well as by the skilful 'phasing' of the structure so that the 'antique action, and gestures' of the satyrs give way gradually to the concluding 'full song'. Jonson's satyrs are not meant to have the menace of, say, the witches in *Macbeth*, but they are not to be seen as Disney-emasculations either: if they were, the aesthetic balance of the masque would be ruined. They are creatures very much on the edge of civilization, showing a simple desire to see Oberon and hoping that he will give them 'pretty toys', but at the same time fundamentally outside the moral code of society. They are lightly lascivious (Satyre 5: Are there any Nymphes to woo?; Satyre 4: If there bee, let me have two [12]) and their concern to have 'toyes' from Oberon is in part so that they may 'beguile the girles withall' [13] and in part because they want to beautify their deformity. This irresponsible, selfish element is beautifully caught and controlled by Jonson's couplets and moves towards something like menace as the satyrs consider how to wake the sleeping sylvans:

Satyre 3:   Or, that we had a waspe, or two
    For their nostrills.
Satyre 1:   Hayres will doe
    Even as well: Take my tayle.
Satyre 2: What do'you say to'a good nayle
    Through their temples?
Satyre 3:   Or an eele,
    In their guts, to make 'hem feele? [14]

The balance is close to that of *A Midsummer Night's Dream* and the control is of the same quality as in Shakespeare's play. Thus, before the sadism of the lines just quoted can become indecorously disturbing, the satyrs are directed by Silenus into their 'catch', the fine nonsense verse of

    Buz, quoth the blue Flie,
    Hum, quoth the Bee:
    Buz, and hum, they crie,
    And so do wee . . .[15]

Jonson's control need not be spelt out in more detail: it is perfectly summed up by noting how the movement towards the masque proper is achieved through the satyrs' lovely song 'Now, my cunning lady; Moone',[16] which gives way to the reminder of their basic nature in their 'antique dance', a dance which provides the perfect foil to the entry of Oberon and 'the nation of Faies'.[17]

'The Masque of Beauty' also belongs to this period, but here it is only necessary to note that the more elaborate allegorical achievement there adds to our sense of Jonson's range, something extended still further if we recall the witty dialogue between Cupid and the Sphinx in 'Love Freed' and the superb prose of Robin in 'Love Restored'.

What the comedies and masques of this period show is a Jonson who was in almost total control of his material, whether it be the London of *The Alchemist*, with its strong sense of realistic detail, or the fantasy world of 'Oberon'. The control is indicated not by the range as such, so much as by the consistently high quality of the writing in the various styles of these works. The Jonson who wrote the splendidly energetic prose of Subtle and Face was also the Jonson who modified Marlovian blank verse to trap the essence of Epicure Mammon. He was also the Jonson who uses language as torment in *Epicoene*, who can write 'Buz, quoth the blue Flie', produce the controlled menace in the charms of 'The Masque of Queens' and the supple seven-syllable lines for the Graces in 'Hue and Cry'. The range itself should make us pause before constructing simple Ben Jonsons, and the quality should make us very suspicious of those who indulge in this hobby.

But 1608–10 is interesting for other reasons than that it marks a high-water point in Jonson's aesthetic career. When we look at the main works of this period we notice, I think, a decrease of anxiety but a continuing concern to analyse moral and social issues, as well as to create pictures of excellence and its opposite. The Jonson of the comedies after *Every Man in his Humour* is anxious, in the sense that he is seeking ways to convey the moral views he holds, while the dramatist of *Volpone* and *Sejanus* communicates powerfully and confidently his fear that man may slip beyond receiving truth—and part of the power springs from the doubt, which easily shades into anxiety. With the 1608–10 period we come to something of a paradox, for Jonson's artistic assurance allows a remarkable range of stylistic achievement and, at the same time, a deeper examination of moral problems and, more specifically, of the difficulty of communicating them.

The Alchemist is one of the great comedies in the language for a variety of reasons—the quality of the structure, the wonderful sense of comic timing, the fine controlled variety of the writing, the certainty with which Jonson traps and disturbs an attentive audience, and the creation of a large number of memorable comic figures. There is also, playing an important part in the manipulation of audience, the tension between the realism of much of the detail and the extravagance of what is going on behind Lovewit's front door: on one level it is obviously comic inflation working off a realistic base, but on another the comedy is steadily fed back into reality to confuse our responses about the relationship between art and nature and, more importantly, to normal experience and our normal reading of it. The ostensible subject of the play—alchemy—is used as a symbol for greed, gullibility, hypocrisy, deceit and other moral abuses. As Jonson presents the world it is one in which each man is an individual, working to his selfish ends, concerned finally only with himself. There are, of course, harmonies within the play, but they either take the form of agreements in which one partner to the agreement is clearly conning the other (Mammon and Dapper are both victims of this sort of pact) or they are, notably with the 'venter tripartite', agreements among knaves to combine to maximize their chances of gulling others. The opening scene makes it quite clear that there is no genuine harmony between Face, Dol and Subtle; and in so far as their unity operates in the play it is to keep the multi-form impulses to disharmony from wrecking the plot, a plot which is both the comic structure of the play and the indication of how far agile and ruthless minds can go in outwitting and exploiting those of lesser wit and/or less moral depravity. As we have seen, the return of Lovewit involves a double response in the audience: he restores harmony but if this is taken as a return to the normal we should look closely at what this norm consists of. It is worth adding that, in the play's terms, Lovewit is the greatest of the individualists in which this play has specialized.

Critics who argue that we should not get too solemn about works like *The Alchemist* are right to remind us that it is a very funny play, but the emphasis is misleading when it suggests that because the play is funny it is nothing else, and when the insistence upon the humour leads to a sentimental view of the ending. *The Alchemist* has a comic element which is more widely acceptable than that of *Volpone* because not so bitter. In *Volpone* our laughter is closely followed by a distressing sense of what we are laughing at, of how we are indulging aspects of our worst natures; in *The Alchemist* the more relaxed tone means that such realization comes more slowly—but it does eventually come and the slowness makes it the harder to ignore once it has been realized. We have been enjoying ourselves watching greed and ingenuity exploit greed and lack of ingenuity, and play upon weakness and gullibility. The experience of *The Alchemist* is finally that of jungle law, and the laughter is there to draw us into the jungle and to make us aware, on reflection, that in being so drawn we have admitted that Jonson's vision is—at least potentially—true. Having admitted this (so the theory would run) we can then see that coping with this truth requires us to accept the need for the moral positives which Jonson teaches elsewhere. And so, metaphorically, understanding *The Alchemist* might prepare us to understand the purpose of 'The Masque of Queens'.

Jonson's own prefatory note to the masque provides the best summary of how it stands in relation to a stage play like *The Alchemist*:

> I . . . therefore, now, devis'd that twelve Women, in the habite of Haggs, or Witches, sustayning the persons of Ignorance, Suspicion, Credulity &c. the opposites to good Fame, should fill that part; not as a Masque, but a spectacle of strangenesse, producing multiplicity of Gesture, and not unaptly sorting with the current, and whole fall of the Devise.[18]

As this suggests the masque is not tense, it does not seek to create the uncertainties so often the essence of stage drama. The 'opposites to good Fame' are a spectacle: there is no doubt about what they are or how they stand in relation to good fame itself, and the action of the masque is one of displacement rather than struggle. But within this formal framework there are links with the threats to civilized values given life in *The Alchemist*, for the anti-masque is fully presented and with real strength. The threat which the hags embody belongs, of course, more to *Macbeth* in atmosphere than to the London of *The Alchemist* (although we should be careful not to misrepresent the links between alchemy and witchcraft: in *The Alchemist* Jonson satirizes the credulity of foolish and superstitious people, but the strength of the satire is much reduced if we forget that there were plenty of people who not only believed in the chemistry of alchemy but also in its association with the forces of darkness). Yet Jonson's witches are, unlike Shakespeare's, clearly defined in terms of allegorical function, representing 'Ignorance, Suspicion, Credulity &c.'. As such they relate closely to those aspects of human personality which make up the experience of *The Alchemist* and are, in masque terms, a reminder that the world of good fame and virtue (summed up here in Anne of Denmark and extended to James) has to assert itself against the opposing world of infamy and evil. The drive of the witches is to revive 'Old shrunke-up Chaös', to 'let rise, / Once more, his darke, and reeking head, / To strike the World, and Nature dead . . .',[19] and Jonson's presentation of this drive has genuine imaginative force. The fact that it is dispelled by a scene change and the speech of 'Heroique Virtue' is, if we are thinking in terms of orthodox drama, too easy (although it is worth noticing that 'Heroique Virtue' begins his speech, 'So *should*, at Fames loud sound, and Vertues sight / All poore, and envious Witchcraft fly the light'[20]) but, of course, the point is that such terms are inappropriate. Jonson's purpose is to hold up a mirror indicating how Fame and Virtue have the power to banish those forces which would smear or defile them. On one level this is done as a compliment to the king and queen, but the care with which Jonson organizes the masque is indicative of more than just his professional competence: the triumph of genuine Virtue is the assertion of Man's potential against his tendency to drift towards the reefs of ignorance and vice, in fact, the world of *The Alchemist*. 'The Masque of Queens' presents in full a formal picture of that choice between virtuous knowledge and vicious ignorance which so often preoccupies Jonson, and when we look at play and masque together we once again notice Jonson's unusual ability to project different visions of essentially the same issue within a brief space of time. There is something almost Baconian here, a kind of artistic version of scientific process.

'Prince Henry's Barriers' is another of Jonson's mirrors and in it we again see him using a specific celebratory occasion—the creation of Henry as Prince of Wales—to render advice, while blending it carefully into the decorous praise demanded by the occasion. Thus the fiction that Henry revives dormant chivalry is obviously flattery, but it is also a reminder that chivalric values are easily forgotten, and in this section of the 'Barriers' there is something of that concern about the young nobility recognizing their responsibilities which disturbs the poem 'A speach according to Horace'. Similarly the shield which is presented to Henry has historical exempla on it which are patriotic and flattering, but they are also meant to remind the prince that he belongs to a tradition which, according to Jonson, imposes responsibilities upon him. Finally, both the way in which Merlin is presented and the virtues with which James is credited are reminiscent of the views put forward in *Discoveries* about the importance to the monarch of having good counsel and the need for the king to be a good man. It would be silly to argue that 'Prince Henry's Barriers' is a detailed analysis of the particular state of Britain in 1610, or that it shows any precise sensitivity to the stresses which were soon to break through the positive visions which Jonson projects, but the piece does have a firm view of kingship as something more than either simple autocracy or the figurehead role to which monarchy has been reduced today. Jonson's monarch is to be concerned with peace as well as war (Jonson goes out of his way to show two of the Edwards as concerning themselves with 'trades and tillage') [21]—humanity is stressed, and the belief that 'civill arts the martiall must precede' for 'lawes and trade bring honors in and gayne'; [22] while Henry is also reminded of the Black Prince's motto 'I serve'. At times the emphasis is almost prosaic: monarchy has its glamour but it is also hard work and there is awareness that a nation's welfare involves full appreciation of things other than the arts of war, as well as the passing—but not unimportant—reminder that the monarch is finally a servant. Unlike 'The Masque of Queens' this piece does not give direct representation to the forces which challenge the virtues which Jonson so strongly wants nobility to embody and foster, but there are reminders that the world of the court is not finally isolated: it cannot be allowed to forget the world outside, and there, as Jonson's works so often remind us, positive values are tenuously held and often overthrown.

In their different ways, then, the three works I have been discussing all show Jonson's concern with aspects of human nature in relation to a moral world. This concern is given a specific focus in another masque, 'Love Restored', which was presented at Christmas 1610. I have already mentioned Robin's prose as an example of Jonson's artistic confidence and range at this period, and one might add that the familiarity of Masquerado's opening reference to the king [23] is another sign of this. Yet there is something interestingly disturbing beneath the surface of this masque. It is artistically finely controlled and the denials that there is going to be a masque are, especially when extended to Robin, an amusing example of Jonson's ability to play with an audience. But Plutus' strictures on masquing create something which goes beyond this comic situation, though without destroying it. Plutus (disguised as Cupid) says, 'I tell thee, I will have no more masquing; I will not buy a false, and fleeting delight so deare: The merry madnesse of one hower shall not cost me the repentance of an age'.[24] Later he attacks 'prodigalitie' and 'riots' as 'the ruine of states' [25] and goes into some detail about the ways in which this operates by leading people into 'superfluous excesses'. Plutus' disguise is penetrated and he is 'placed' by Robin as 'the god of money'.[26] Robin goes on to make it clear that Plutus represents a view of money which is unacceptable because it elevates wealth above true love (with all that that represents in terms of human values). Several extrinsic factors seem relevant to the shaping of this masque. If John More's letter to Sir Ralph Winwood is to be trusted [27] there had been a cutback in expenditure for the masques of Christmas 1610. It is also likely that Jonson is getting in a blow at Inigo Jones (the expenditure on a masque rested far more heavily upon the mechanics than upon provision of a text) and it is also possible that he was becoming concerned that 'the merry madnesse of one hower' would completely swamp the mirror-lessons which he saw as the true function of the form: instead of the mechanics serving the text they would reduce it to mere decoration. Even beyond this there seems to me to be a concern over display which sees a real danger that the true function of 'munificence' (to symbolize the power and wellbeing of the state) is being displaced by a vicious concentration upon display for its own sake. In this, 'Love Restored' reminds us of 'To Penshurst' (undatable but probably written within a year or two either side of the masque) and of the presentation of Pecunia in *The Staple of News*. If I am correct we thus have a very good example of Jonson's ability to turn particular circumstances to his long-term concerns and to subdue personal feelings to the artistic and moral unity of what he is writing. A virtue is made out of royal economy, in that Jonson stresses that real wealth lies separate from cash, and at the same time the chance is taken to articulate a view of appearance's deceptive potential which reminds us again of the comic worlds of *The Alchemist* and *Epicoene*.

The latter is perhaps Jonson's purest comedy, almost flawlessly organized, with the logic of the best farce backed up by superb writing, a magnificent central comic idea, and deft confidence and fertility in the creation of comic characters. As a play it seems effortless and matches means to ends with the economy of great craftsmanship: it is only when we look at the typically Jonsonian way in which it is built up from hints and allusions (see Chapter 6) that we realize how perfectly it illustrates the formula *ars celare artis*. Yet *Epicoene* is more than just an aesthetic triumph, for the attitudes embodied in its form are complex and its implications about human nature far from flattering. I am not concerned here with the subtlety with which Jonson presents Clerimont and Truewit, subtlety which can be seen by extending the lines drawn in the previous chapter or by contrasting what Jonson does here with the lineal descendants of these characters in Restoration comedy (Congreve's early *The Old Batchelor* is an interesting transitional case). What I want do to is to indicate the disillusionment in the play's view of love and marriage. The minor key is that of the Otter marriage. Captain Otter's marriage is an example of the 'epicoene' element in the play, for he has accepted a reversal of the idea of marriage as an institution in which the male dominates and the female submits. He is capable of bluster but not of effective action: his wife is, in effect, the male and he is precariously allowed his drinking cups, comic-pathetic reminders of his subordinate status, that of child or eunuch. Otter is a victim—although not one we are allowed to pity very much—of a society in which the women (exemplified by the Collegiate Ladies) are seeking to subvert norms by invading male territory, and the Otter marriage is a microcosm of 'the world upside down', one where the established order is being subverted. This, in itself, would scarcely meet with Jonson's approval, but his attitude is less simple than a mere reaction against such subversion, for the facts that Mistress Otter has the control she does over her Captain, and that he lacks the strength to contest her control, involve recognition that subversion is a factor in the play's world: the norm has been inverted and the energy is on the side of the inversion. Lightly though the theme is presented it is basically the same view as that of *Sejanus*, *Volpone* and *The Alchemist*.

But, of course, love and marriage in *Epicoene* are closer to the play's centre than the Otter strand suggests. Dead centre we have Morose, and he certainly intends a marriage which in effect will reflect the relationship he has with his servants. But Jonson never for a moment allows us to imagine that Morose's view of marriage is healthy. It is analogous to the norm mentioned in the previous paragraph but the play both questions the reality of such a norm (in Truewit's tormenting of Morose and in Epicoene's 'discovery' of language after the 'marriage') and makes Morose such an extreme representation of the male-as-master concept that we can no more respect his view than the situation of Otter. Yet the play offers no romantic alternative: the Morose 'courtship' is not only unromantic in itself (to put it mildly!) but is surrounded by the commercial intrigues which centre on Dauphine. The scheming of Truewit and Clerimont is designed to torment and humiliate Morose (reaching the point where we begin to pity him) but it is no part of Jonson's purpose to rescue a woman for a romantic future, for Epicoene proves to be male. Of course Jonson is using the romantic convention of disguise here but his particular version of it rules out the romantic solution, offering instead the comic divorce. Romantic love is only admitted with La Foole, and is there only to be parodied. The wit, speed and comic invention of *Epicoene* do not in the end disguise the fact that in his play Jonson cannot offer a single moment of mutual love— nothing reminds us of, say, the Duchess and Antonio in Webster's *Duchess of Malfi* or of the growth of a relationship such as that of Beatrice and Benedict.

This lack of warmth in sexual relationships is not unusual in Jonson's plays. I mentioned in Chapter 1 that his work is marked both by the high value he puts on relationships and by a simultaneous sense that a good relationship is hard to find and sustain. Sexual relationships seem particularly difficult. Jonson can convey animalism and the selfish itch very powerfully (see, for example, 'An Epistle to a Friend, to perswade him to the Warres') and he is also very sharply aware of the cosmetic cheat and the deceptions of intrigue (as in *Sejanus*), but warm human love between the sexes is something which he seldom conveys. This is not to say that emotional warmth is beyond his scope: he can communicate this impressively, but usually within the context of friendship. When sexuality is not mere lust in Jonson it is either the sort of eroticism found in poems such as the songs 'To Celia' (which is to say the eroticism of Catullus and Propertius, and a perfectly valid and decent emotion to communicate, but one which excludes romantic elements in love) or is generalized and/or idealized. A poem like Donne's 'Good Morrow' is simply not within Jonson's range. What is interesting here is that when he seeks to convey a sense of love as something which enriches human life he either draws deeply on his sensitivity to the value of friendship or works in a formal context, as he does in the masque 'Love Freed from Ignorance and Folly', written close in time to *Epicoene*.

'Love Freed' is short and, like *Epicoene*, seems effortless, with Jonson controlling his couplets with an assured touch which ranges from wit to direct seriousness. There is a minimal plot and the threat to Love is formal rather than theatrically tense. Here, as in other cases, the mirror which Jonson holds up in the masque is complimentary, for the solution of the Sphinx's riddle (upon which, in terms of plot, Love's safety depends) is found where we should most expect it:

> Britayne's the world, the world without.
> The King's the eye, as we do call
> The sunne the eye of this great all . . .[28]

The king/sun imagery is stressed again a moment later, when the priests comment, 'Sphinx must flie, when Phoebus shines'. Here, for a moment, there is a reminder of 'A Panegyre', useful in that the Sphinx stands for ignorance and folly, qualities which Jonson—believer in the social importance of knowledge and reason—must see as the prime threats to the harmony of the commonwealth. But the immediate context is narrower. Love is associated with beauty and both with goodness:

> How neere to good is what is faire!
> Which we no longer see,
> But with the lines, and outward aire
> Our senses taken be.[29]

Several things are important here. Love is helped by Wisdom—as Jonson tells us in a note—'to encounter Ignorance, and Folly: ... ever readie to assist Love in any action of honor, and vertue ...' [30] So, the love Jonson is 'freeing' is served by wisdom for a moral purpose and is associated, when it is real love, with beauty as reflector of goodness: the neo-Platonic view. Several Jonsonian *motifs* are present here: appearance should reflect reality; knowledge should serve virtue; the king should enact these concepts, embody this view of love. Again, we distort the point of the masque if we see it as merely flattering: its didactic element is bound up with its formal pattern and beauty to incite reality to imitate the perfection of Jonson's art, an art which remains resolutely moral.

But the point I really want to make here is that 'Love Freed' celebrates precisely the union of wisdom, beauty and love which

Epicoene cannot envisage. In the play the assumption that when we see that 'faire' and 'good' are close together their reflection in 'lines, and outward aire' convinces our senses, is denied because the play sees neither this association of fair with good nor their reflection in appearances. In *Epicoene* wisdom is merely the wit of Clerimont and Truewit (intelligence used to punish and humiliate, only obliquely to create) or the purely verbal wit of the Collegiate Ladies (used to polish appearance at reality's expense and to disrupt social norms) while beauty and love are pinned to a divorce between what is and what should be: Epicoene is male, the Otter marriage is an inversion, and Morose wants nothing to do with the reality of a mutual relationship. Ignorance and folly dominate *Epicoene* and while wit provides a kind of 'freeing', which is some sort of glide into the masque, it remains far from the wisdom of the latter. Conversely the Sphinx can be seen as a link with the play, but it is formal, whereas ignorance and folly are active in the comedy. Here again we have, closely linked in time, opposing views of similar topics, and the difference in modes is suggestive. The world of the comedy is active and actual—extreme of course but easily referable to actuality—while that of the masque is a beautiful rendering of what should be. Jonson can imagine both worlds, but only in different modes, and these modes, with their different angles on reality, create disturbing reflections when we relate them, for while we are impressed by the ability to enact different viewpoints with artistic conviction we are also drawn to consider that the comedy registers what is, while the more positive view of the masque can only try to mirror what Jonson would like to be the case. Only if the masque could become the comedy could we feel that his ideals were in practice, that Penshursts had multiplied and Mammons had come to their senses.

It might (to return for a moment to an issue raised earlier in this chapter) be objected that the differences of attitude which I have been talking about can be explained purely in terms of differences of genre and audience, but while it would be silly to underestimate the importance of these factors they do not provide a full explanation. Jonson did not have to write *Epicoene* in the way he did—it was not the only formula for commercial success. Also, even if we accept that the view of love in 'Love Freed' was largely predetermined by context it is still true that the detailed exposition of that view need not have taken the form it did. In terms of personal economics Jonson may have had limited control over the genres he worked in, but he had, and exploited, considerable freedom in handling those genres, and hence the differences between *Epicoene* and 'Love Freed' remain instructive even when considerations of genre and audience are taken fully into account. The split between comedy and masque illustrates Jonson's ability to examine and articulate different views of similar issues, but also his sense that these different views cannot be unified in a single response to reality. But I want to finish this chapter by looking at another band; one which, I believe, shows Jonson finding it harder to keep his views of 'is' and 'should be' apart. This band consists of *Bartholomew Fair*, 'The Golden Age Restored' and 'Mercury Vindicated', all products of 1614–15.

There is no need to go into detail about *Bartholomew Fair* here, since most of what is said elsewhere in this book about that play is relevant to the points I now want to make. If we take seriously, as we should, the idea of the Fair as microcosm it is hard to avoid feeling that the play's social view is distressing. Of course the vitality of the characters, action and writing is important (if it weren't we would not be talking about art at all) and it is a vitality which does include more of what 'being human' involves than is admitted by the frenzied dynamism of *Revenger's Tragedy* (or, for that matter, by the terms of reference of Beckett or Ionesco). It is also true that Jonson's comedy is vital in a way which is more generous than the vitality of most Jacobean tragedy, a genre which is dominated by cynical undercutting of traditional moral values. The best of these tragedies have a conviction which makes their cynicism perfectly acceptable as a response, however distressing, to experience, but *Bartholomew Fair* is, I feel, ultimately more distressing precisely because in it moral values are *comically* undercut. The energy of Ursula, Busy, Wasp and Overdo is not vicious as, say, that of Lussurioso in *Revenger's Tragedy* is vicious, but it is still the energy of those who have abandoned moral values or who represent perversions of them; and while Jonson is acutely aware that this matters he seems to have reached the position of believing that this is the social reality, that it will continue to be so, and that it is useless to pretend otherwise or to imagine that change is possible, except the perpetual and meaningless change which is a complicated way of not moving. If that makes *Bartholomew Fair* sound like Jonson's version of *King Lear* I am quite happy. The vitality of Ursula can be 'celebrated', but only because it is at least, paradoxically, honest in its acceptance of the fundamental immorality which is the norm. As such it is preferable to the pretensions of Overdo, Wasp and Busy, but we have to accept that the choice is within very circumscribed limits, and to ask to what use the pretensions of the pretenders are put. Overdo and his colleagues are not created pretentious so that they may come to learn the real nature of responsibility and work to reform others: the time of *Cynthia's Revels* is time past and these characters only learn enough to go into silence or become 'Adam, flesh and blood' (which in this play means Ursula and her like). Thus the proposed feast of the ending *is* an acceptance of the norm, but the norm is the world of the Fair, one of cheating, sweating, pissing, robbing, fucking. These are all parts of life but Jonson is saying that this is all that life amounts to when the pretensions are cut through, and—granted Jonson's own moral commitments—this sounds very close to despair. Where now are the Camdens, the Sidneys, the Wroths, even the Roes? And to evade the issue by restricting the world of the Fair and turning Jonson's play into a misunderstood celebration of the fertility of sweat and blood is to insult Jonson as Breughel and Dickens have both been insulted. More mundanely, it is to ignore those who come to the Fair and the wide social categories they represent. Religion, teaching, the law are all present; they are major aspects of social organization and thus all ultimately the responsibility of the monarch and his advisers. The world of education and wit is there, only to be reduced in Quarlous and Winwife to selfish manœuvrings for pleasure and gain, and that of innocence is remembered also, to be degraded by Grace, burlesqued in Cokes. If the Fair is a microcosm it reflects a society beyond hope, and Jonson's ending may indeed be realistic, but it is the realism of defeat: 'Eat, drink and be merry, for morally we are already dead.' As a comment upon what was beginning to happen in the 1610s this is, when related to Jonson's pattern of values, genuinely prophetic. It is true enough that Overdo speaks, almost at the play's end, of working 'Ad correctionem, non ad destructionem; Ad aedificandum, non ad dirvendum',[31] but (literally and metaphorically) who can understand his Latin? and who can take comfort in these sentiments, expressed in a way which suggests that punctured Overdo is reinflating? Anyway, the final word is with Cokes, that supreme example of impervious stupidity: 'wee'll ha' the rest o'the Play at home'—indeed, Jonson is saying, we will: and that is the measure of the human defeat.

Within *Bartholomew Fair* art is represented by Nightingale's song (typically used as a cover for pocket-picking) and the puppet play. The latter is the agent for 'confuting' Busy and the overthrow of the puritan is a minor triumph of art, but the tone of the ending (and especially Cokes's closing remark) does not allow us to feel that Jonson any longer believed in transformation of the vicious and foolish through art's power—at least not in stage comedy. In 'Mercury Vindicated', however, Jonson again celebrates in masque the defeat of the unnatural by the natural through art. The basic matter of the masque is satire of alchemy and of credulous believers in that distorted art: the bulk of this satire comes in Mercury's two long speeches. In 'Mercury Vindicated' the anti-masque dominates the text, balance being restored by the music and dancing of the masque proper, but before the perverse gives way to the healthy it is given full expression in Jonson's best prose style, and Mercury's speeches extend the scope of the satire beyond the immediate topic to make credulity an active and ubiquitous force in the society depicted, one recognizably continuous with that outside the masque itself. Even the court is not unaffected, and Mercury's appeal to the king is a direct comment on the effrontery and reality of ignorant credulity. The point need not be laboured : all we need to see is that although the masque form allows Jonson to affirm the superiority of real art and monarchy against threats to their power, his own writing here is such as to make the threats real, with an energy which reminds us of *Bartholomew Fair*. Here Mercury is describing how he is abused in the 'laboratory, or Alchymists workehouse' :

. . . It is through mee, they ha'got this corner o'the Court to coozen in, where they sharke for a hungry diet below staires, and cheat upon your under-Officers, promising mountaines for their meat, and all upon Mer-curies security. A poore Page o'the Larder, they have made obstinately beleeve, he shalbe Phisician for the Houshold, next Summer : they will give him a quantity of the quintessence, shall serve him to cure kibes, or the mormall o'the shinne, take away the pustules i'the nose, and Mercury is ingag'd for it . . .[32]

The vigour of such prose is clear enough, but it is also important to note how it creates a world which is dominated by greed, excess and exploitation—a world which is that of the great comedies and which, like them, is a distorting mirror of actuality.

The other masque I am concerned with here—'The Golden Age Restor'd'—could almost be seen as masque to *Bartholomew Fair*'s anti-masque. *Bartholomew Fair* is Jonson's most extreme expression of his sense of man as animal beyond the reach of his moral art, while in the masque he makes use of one of the most potent myths of social and moral perfection, the myth of the golden age. It is easy to see the masque as no more than a well-organized version of a commonplace view of kingship, but I am struck by the emphatic way in which the forces of evil are dispersed. There is literally something rigid in the turning of the Evils into statues, in Pallas' speech of dismissal and in her summoning of Astraea and the Golden Age. The whole thing is done economically (even tersely) and the stress which Jonson then puts upon the restoration of the golden age under the king seems to me to indicate concern rather than confidence. Even at a simple level the question occurs—why talk so much about *restoration* unless the actuality is something very different? The mirror here is a great and beautiful myth and there are echoes of 'To Penshurst', but whereas the latter presents a plausible extension of actuality the former cannot offer the same confident links between ideal and real —it can only hold up the picture of 'should be'. The beautiful unreality of 'Golden Age Restor'd' suggests to me that Jonson could only see hope for society in the court, and could only see it there by invoking an ideal which might perhaps attract and be acted upon. By 1615 the restoration of the golden age was pretty unlikely, and I suspect that Jonson knew as much, even though he could not contemplate the alternative way, the way of conflict, war, redefinition, which was to dominate the rest of the century.

Chapter 5

Language and the Man

Both linguists and philosophers have been much concerned in this century with indicating how tricky language is and, specifically, how complex the relationships are between word and object, referee and referent. Direct or indirect awareness of this kind of problem, however, underlies all creative writing of value: one way of looking at Sterne's *Tristram Shandy*, for example, is as a critique of Locke's arguments that words should be capable of such definition that their relationship to ideas is as precise as mathematical notation. But many writers in the twentieth century have worked out their styles, it would seem, with direct awareness of the theoretical problems raised by the linguists and philosophers—thus, experiments with streams of consciousness, automatic writing, Burroughs' scissors-and-paste method, Sartre's probing of the gaps between the essence of objects and that of words, and the exploration by dramatists like Beckett of the discontinuity and non-communication which go to make up most human discourse.[1] For their part, modern literary critics have investigated the underbelly of poetic writing, concerning themselves with image-strands, myth-patterns, and those probably subconscious groupings and repetitions of language which often indicate the true nature of a writer's concerns and attitudes to them.

There is nothing new in saying that Ben Jonson's use of language does not lend itself particularly well to this sort of critical approach: verbal ambiguity and tentacular linguistic groupings of the subterranean kind are not areas which can be most profitably studied in his work. It does not follow, of course, that Jonson was not interested in the nature of language or unaware of the difficulties of making words do the jobs he wanted of them. On the contrary there are—apart from the large section of *Discoveries* which is directly concerned with language—the *English Grammar* and the passing comments to Drummond about style and decorum; but the job which Jonson usually wants language to do is normally connected with man as

87

social animal and speech as social communication. This, of course, is a logical extension of Jonson's basic artistic concerns: it is not much use having views about the proper moral organization of society if you can't find ways of making words transmit those views.

This attitude to language can be seen very clearly in the way Jonson uses imagery. If, for example, we think of *Volpone* and *The Merchant of Venice* (using the figures of Volpone himself and Shylock as our excuse) one of our first responses is likely to be how much more outward-looking Shakespeare's play is. I mean by this that Shakespeare's imagination responds to Shylock in a way which seems instinctive rather than planned: our fascination with the character is precisely that he is tantalizingly poised between victim and predator, and the play is made both richer and more incoherent by Shylock's challenge to Antonio in the famous 'Signor Antonio, many a time and oft' speech.[2] What Shakespeare may have thought he was doing is now beside the point, but Shylock's words often speak for his race, summing up much of the Jewish experience and asking for acceptance in the human species. In this sense the Rialto speech is an appeal to our subconscious as well as to our intellect and emotional consciousness—and both areas are troubled because both contain prejudices and conflicts. Jonson does not work like this in *Volpone*. Rather than disturbing our subconscious indirectly he seeks to create a picture of appalling clarity, one which—when we have come to see it whole—undermines complacencies and disturbs our hopes for human nature.

To achieve this appalling clarity Jonson needs to make the outlines of his picture as clear as possible: the force of his best work depends to a considerable extent upon tension between pressure of detail and clarity of outline. In *Volpone* the outlines are drawn mainly through a group of words descriptive of wealth, and the most important of these words is 'gold'. It is almost symbolic of Jonson's method that the word occurs in the first line of the play—'Good morning to the day; and, next, my gold'—and that its verbal presence is at once backed up visually as Mosca 'withdraws the curtain, and discovers piles of gold, plate, jewels . . .' There have been several excellent accounts of how Volpone's opening speech sets the tone of the play and of how Jonson establishes Volpone's scale of values, whereby riches, the 'dumbe god', 'art vertue, fame, / Honour, and all things else'. The effect is dual: gold is elevated to the status of deity, and everything seen as valuable by normal moral criteria is correspondingly degraded. The speech is remarkably resonant in one sense, with Jonson playing with the idea of the sun generating gold and setting it against other (more morally valuable) connotations of the sun, and with the complex devaluing of religion by the application of its

vocabulary to wealth. But the speech is resonant in a highly controlled way and at its end we are not meant to be wondering about
the configuration of Volpone's psyche or about how he came to be
the person he is. We are meant instead to have a very clear idea of
what he is and of what his values are, and we are also meant to have
an equally clear sense of how perverted these values are in relation
to a norm which has been fully, if obliquely, stated.

This key image of treasure is kept at the centre of our minds
throughout the play. Visually this is achieved by the obvious device
of having the gulls actually present gold and plate to Volpone, but
it is also done by verbal reminders that gold is the referent for all
values. The most brilliant example of this, perhaps, comes at the end
of Act I, when Mosca is describing Corvino's wife Celia to Volpone.
His speech is organized to a climax in the last line:

> . . . a beautie, ripe, as harvest!
> Whose skin is whiter then a swan, all over!
> Then silver, snow, or lillies! . . .
> . . . flesh, that melteth, in the touch, to bloud!

—and then the climax:

> Bright as your gold! and lovely, as your gold! [3]

Everything is right here. Mosca can only think of beauty in sensual
terms—there is the quietly lascivious touch in 'whiter then a swan,
all over!'; the prefiguring of the last line in 'silver'; the precision of
the idea of flesh melting to blood under the touch; and the final
moment, in which the whole beauty of the picture is guaranteed in
terms of the ultimate standard—gold. It is worth noting that Jonson
is so firmly in control here that he resists any temptation to present
Celia's beauty as all-transcendent: the build-up is close to the
traditional apotheosis of the lover, but in this world the transcendent
element has already been established: gold is 'all things' and Celia
cannot transcend it, although she can be valued to and by its
standard.

I don't want to weary by reiteration. Any reader of the play can
trace how Jonson keeps the central images clear, both as images and
in terms of the value given to them. A count of the references to gold
and associated materials would be impressive, but what is important
is that the impact is massive and its effect centripetal rather than
centrifugal. The effort behind establishing the image of gold is aimed
at valuing it precisely, and so although gold constitutes an image-
strand that strand is metallic rather than fibrous, and this is as it
should be since the point of the play is that everything (Volpone's

values; those of the other characters; our valuing of them, their values and their/our world) ultimately returns to this image, which needs to be firm and hard-edged. This does not mean that the image is without associations or suggestiveness, but it does mean that suggestion and association are limited, wholly comprehensible as part of the play's view of social order and man in society. We are not puzzled by Volpone as we are by Shylock, but we *know* more about aspects of the cost of acquisitiveness at the end of Jonson's play, even though Shakespeare has had moments of insight into complexities of relationship between man and man, man and society, which go beyond anything Jonson saw.

This sort of approach, whereby an image is established as the key to a play's central meaning, has obvious connections with Jonson's interest in formal art. It is not fanciful to see the verbal/visual link at the opening of *Volpone* as belonging to the same mode as the symbolic use of word and visual image in 'The Masque of Blackness', nor would it be fanciful to suggest that both have clear links with the traditions of emblem and imprese. The same emphasis can be seen with another important image, occurring this time early in *Sejanus*. This is the image mentioned earlier, when Sabinus says that he and those of his kind have

> No soft, and glutinous bodies, that can sticke,
> Like snailes, on painted walls . . .

It is one of Jonson's finest images, but its quality lies in the perfect matching of means to ends. Four main points are made: (1) in Rome such walls are painted, disguised, not necessarily what they seem; (2) in Rome there are persons who have the durability and strength of walls; (3) in Rome there are also those who wish to cling to these walls and who have the slimy adhesiveness to do so; (4) the walls, being painted, are smooth—so even for snails clinging on may be difficult.

This image is not used in the same way as that of gold in *Volpone*. It does not have the same kind of visual equivalent and is not reintro-duced as a restated standard of value: but it does have the same quality of controlled resonance. All that I mean by this is that the image is richly significant of the world of the play and is thus a microcosm of it, similarly placed right at the play's beginning. This similarity of placing is important, for it underlines Jonson's concern to get the outlines marked out straight away, and the implications of the image are worked out exactly, without those implications sprouting further suggestions, reverberations and ambiguities. How unlike the Shakespearean method this is can be seen very clearly if the opening of *Sejanus* is compared with that of *Antony and Cleopatra*, where Shakespeare uses the uncertainties of his characters to indicate the ambiguities which make his play. The walls of Jonson's Rome prove to be durable (it matters little in the wide political sense that one wall is destroyed, since others are being built) and they prove to be painted, a point made specifically in the cosmetic scene between Sejanus, Livia and Eudemus [4] and reinforced by the dissimulations of Sejanus, Tiberius and Macro. Adherents to these walls prove to need glutinous personalities and at the same time they have the vulnerability of snails: it is all embryonic in Sabinus' image.

This tendency to put a lot of weight upon a central image and to present that image as clearly as possible works perfectly whenever Jonson achieves, in the play as a whole, a sense that the themes of the play are of massive importance; when, that is, the matter has the weight to balance the weight of the image. This is the case with *Volpone* and *Sejanus*, but an indication that the method is not itself a prescription for success can be seen in *The Devil is an Ass*, a play which should have been a masterpiece but isn't.

Here again we find the establishment of the key image right at the start of the play, and here—as in *Volpone*—the image is conveyed by a visual/verbal union. The basic comic device of the play is simple but potentially very effective—using the idea of a devil sent to earth to show that hell is outclassed and old-fashioned by comparison with the vicious subtlety of mortal man. Part of the point is that Satan knows this sad fact from the start, while Pug wants the chance to find out what the situation really is and to prove himself a worthy devil. Visually Pug's presence on stage for most of the play enacts the starting-truth, that he is pathetically incapable of coping with the diabolic activities of man. Verbally Jonson hammers the point home by constant literal and metaphorical references to devils, hell and possession, this last emerging visually when Fitzdottrell fakes a fit.[5] The reiteration of the basic image is closer to *Volpone* than to *Sejanus*, but what is interesting is that it seems more obvious, not because it is repeated more often but because the image is given emphasis in excess of its import. The hard-edged method works perfectly in *Volpone* because the central image stands for—in a sense *is*—something of massive importance: our sense of dehumanization by greed has to be clear and weighty so that we can appreciate the need to find a force which will escape the confines of the outline and the failure in the play of any force to do so. Hence the pressure and tension of the drama. In *The Devil is an Ass*, however, Jonson does not manage to give to Meercraft and his associates the generalized moral weight of Volpone; the satire remains local in effect and so the key image emerges clearly but—lacking the significance communicated in *Sejanus* and *Volpone*—seems obvious and relatively unimportant.

I have concentrated so far on Jonson's use of imagery, stressing his use of controlling symbols with sharply defined fields of significance and his habit of achieving this definition with the help of verbal/visual unions (other obvious examples being the fountain of self-love in *Cynthia's Revels* and the vomiting scene in *Poetaster*). But this way of working with language is not confined to Jonson's images, and I now want to look at how he deals with more abstract types of language; specifically with moral terms. This can most easily be done by considering examples from the poems.

Although Jonson makes use of a vast vocabulary in the course of his career, he works outwards from a fairly small stock of terms which define his basic moral position, and this stock is largely plain and conventional, not only in that the words themselves are well worn but also because Jonson tends not to decorate or reanimate them in immediately striking ways. The sort of words I am thinking of are words like 'good', 'great', 'virtue', 'honesty', 'honour'. Terms like these run through the non-dramatic verse and are of major importance to Jonson's vision of human life and potential. Oddly, despite the plainness of Jonson's use of such words they do not emerge as vague or weak.

One reason for this is that the terms are given definition by context. These are the opening lines of 'An Epistle to Sir Edward Sackvile';

> If Sackvile, all that had the power to doe
> Great and good turns, as well could time them too,
> And knew their how, and where: we should have, then,
> Lesse list of proud, hard, or ingratefull Men . . .⁶

The strength of this lies partly in the assurance of the voice, the confidence with which Jonson's mind plays sense units across couplet form. There is a feeling of inquiry and also a sense that the poet can control his inquiry, shape it into some illuminating pattern. The abstract moral terms 'great' and 'good' are anchored in context by the presence of quietly concrete language—'power', 'time', 'turns'. Then there is the way in which the potentially too-easy phrase 'good turns' is strengthened by 'great', the two adjectives complementing each other so that the generosity of which Jonson speaks comes to seem a matter of moral range as well as of moral nature, while the scope of the generosity is controlled by the need for it to be 'good'. Again, the words 'good' and 'great' are partly defined by contrast with 'proud, hard . . . ingratefull'.

Such definition by context and by the use of concrete vocabulary alongside abstract terms occurs over and again in the poems. One further example should be enough—the opening of 'Epistle to Elizabeth Countesse of Rutland': [7]

> Madame,
> Whil'st that, for which, all virtue now is sold,
> And almost every vice, almightie gold,
> That which, to boote with hell, is thought worth heaven,
> And, for it, life, conscience, yea, soules are given,
> Toyles, by grave custom, up and downe the court ...

Here Jonson makes use of antithesis to give his terms sharpness—'virtue'/'vice', 'hell'/'heaven'—and again there is characteristic energy in the verbs 'sold' and 'Toyles', as well as the sardonic strength of 'almightie' and 'grave' and the careful precision of 'thought'.

Often Jonson gains precision through juxtaposition, as in the lines to Sackville, or by his habit of using 'good' and 'great' in harness. They are together again, for example, in *Epigrammes*, LXXVI:

> I meant to make her fair, and free, and wise,
> Of greatest bloud, and yet more good then great ...

Here Jonson expresses one of his most consistent beliefs, that great birth is less important than moral goodness (although the goodness is given lustre by great birth and is more likely to be found among those of gentle blood). A more famous example occurs in 'To Penshurst':

> What (great, I will not say, but) sodayne cheare
> Did'st thou, then make 'hem! and what praise was heap'd
> On thy good lady, then!

The value given to the concept of greatness is defined by 'sodayne' (the point being that a state of ready hospitality is more important than ostentation) and this distinction in turn lifts the phrase 'good lady' beyond the commonplace.

Reading Jonson's poetry one gradually becomes aware of how important such words as these are to him; of how consistently he defines them by context; and of how reliable his usage is. Repetition of these words from poem to poem gradually increases a sense of sharp meaning, a sense made stronger as we become aware that Jonson's ethical vocabulary describes a firmly held philosophical pattern.

One other feature of Jonson's use of moral vocabulary needs to be noticed. I have already said that he defines this vocabulary partly by providing a concrete setting, but he goes beyond this at times to use concrete terms for what are basically abstract states. An example of this has already been quoted—the adjective 'hard' in the lines to Sackville, which is a case where Jonson exploits the literal and metaphorical properties of the adjective at the same time. A more extreme case is *Epigrammes* XCVIII:

> He that is round within himselfe, and streight,
> Need seek no other strength, no other height;
> Fortune upon him breakes herselfe, if ill,
> And what would hurt his vertue makes it still.

These lines form a kind of summary of Jonson's way with ethical language. 'Vertue' is given something like concrete status by the verb 'hurt'; 'height' has a similar literal/metaphorical duality to 'hard'; while 'round' and 'streight' are firmly concrete, with Jonson exploiting their moral overtones to the point where the words become moral objects.

There is, in fact, much common ground between the ways in which Jonson uses imagery in the plays and ethical vocabulary in the poems. The basic drive is the same, a drive towards definition, away from ambiguity and towards total clarity. Expressed another way this drive is towards making word and object one: the verbal/visual links spoken of earlier are paralleled in the moral vocabulary by methods which go as far as possible to give the words of that vocabulary the solidity of objects, a process which perhaps reaches its peak in the fine 'A speach according to Horace'.[8] This drive suggests confidence, indicates that the poet has worked out where he stands, what he believes and what he should say. It thus seems to support the common view of Jonson as a didactic artist, certain that he is right. But we should be careful about leaving it at this, because a drive to define, to achieve a hard-edged effect, may as easily indicate fundamental lack of confidence as its opposite: the powerful urge to believe and to know exactly what you believe may well spring from anxiety about the possibility of belief at all. It is almost as though Jonson wants to make words concrete to convince himself that they and the values they represent will not vanish: there are distant reminders of Lawrence's attempts to convince his readers of the psychological validity of an observation by repeating the same words over and over—'If I say it often enough it must be true'. In passing it is worth mentioning that Jonson was a very careful user of punctuation, being particularly fastidious about the use of commas to make clear where he wants emphasis and what the relationship between particular words is. Again the effect is almost as if Jonson is frightened by the thought of ambiguity. If we want to find plausible explanations for this tension between surface certainty and a degree of anxiety there are plenty of possibilities to hand: the death of his natural father, the failure to go on to university from Westminster, and the struggles to become accepted as a serious writer are only three obvious possibilities. With an eye on the final chapter I also want to suggest here that the effort to 'build solid' may be based on a fear of change: you preserve in art what you believe in and want to believe exists, for fear that your beliefs may be swept away by time and flux.

But although the aspects of Jonson's writing which have been spoken about so far suggest tensions in his personality there is no doubt that they also indicate the role of the poet as he sees it, most definitively in *Discoveries*. He once called speech 'the Instrument of Society' [9] and the phrase not only indicates where Jonson's artistic interest lies but also suggests what kind of values he is most likely to concern himself with in language. A man who sees speech primarily as the instrument of verbal intercourse in social relationships will, for example, be concerned with decorum, so that the criticism of Sidney and Guarini for failures of decorum is not merely stylistic, but indicates, in Jonson's view, a breakdown of accurate social communication. Similarly, the famous remark 'Pure and neat Language I love, yet plaine and customary' [10] expresses more than an aesthetic position: the qualities which are celebrated here are those which make communication as easy as possible (which does not mean that Jonson thought that popularization was easy or even desirable, but that he considered that articulation should be as clear as possible, commensurate with maintaining integrity to what was to be expressed). The balance to be struck between the awareness that language is common property and at the same time the writer's special medium and responsibility is brilliantly expressed by the comment that, 'Words are the Peoples; yet there is a choise of them to be made.' [11]

Communication of some sort is fundamental to art, even if it is only a matter of communing with a mirror or a few friends, but for Jonson communication involves wider fields than these. Many critics have pointed to a split in Jonson's sense of audience between the select few who will appreciate his art and the mass, but perhaps not enough attention has been paid to the nature and significance of this split. The appeals to the understanding viewer/reader, the interest in writing for the private theatres, the love of contact with learned men, and the long record of working on court entertainments all suggest some sort of snobbishness—or, at least, may seem to do so.

But Jonson's life shows clearly that he was no sycophant and it seems to me that his interest in writing for, and having contact with, coteries indicates not merely professional common sense but also a desire to communicate to those whom he could reasonably expect to be most receptive to his ideas. But it does not follow from this that the rage of the *New Inn* 'Ode to Himselfe', for instance, sprang from frustration at having had to spend time addressing the mob (although there is reason to believe that economic pressures lie behind the writing of the play [12]). It seems rather to spring from frustration at having tried to communicate with a mass audience and having failed to do so. There seems to me no reason to doubt that Jonson's desire was to communicate his views as widely as possible and that when he speaks of language as the instrument of society he has in mind society as a whole. If we accept that Jonson felt a serenely lofty contempt for the capacity of society to understand him it becomes hard to see why he bothered in his greatest comedies to work so hard to communicate his moral doubts and beliefs in forms both entertaining and instructive. It would have been easier for him just to have ripped off neat, light comedies to bring in the money he needed —and it would be ridiculous to doubt his technical ability to have done just that. Certainly Jonson was proud and impatient, too ready to turn on his critics and assert that they must be wrongheaded, too ready to consign them to the many-headed multitude, something which Thomas Carew saw clearly when he wrote his poem to Jonson during the *New Inn* controversy. But Jonson's record remains one of persistent attempts to educate, and it is possible to see his increasingly subtle manipulation of his audience up to *Bartholomew Fair* as stratagems to increase the number who will see what he is up to. Other features of his drama show the same desire: the explanation of objectives in prologues and epilogues, the careful annotation of the masques, the use of choric figures in several of the plays, the emphasis on clarity and plainness as verbal objectives, the tendency to use repetition, the concern with verbal/visual links. One aspect of all this which is particularly relevant to this chapter is the concern to achieve clarity of articulation in poem or speech.

At its simplest this structural clarity can be seen in a minor lyric called 'A Nymphs passion'.[13] This is the second stanza:

> I'le tell, that if they be not glad,
> > They yet may envie me:
> But then if I grow jealous madde,
> > And of them pittied be,
> > > It were a plague 'bove scorne,
> > > And yet it cannot be forborne,
> Unlesse my heart would as my thought be torne.

Much of the poem's strength lies in the working out of the argument over its five stanzas, but the process can be seen here in epitome, in the care Jonson takes with the little connective words—'that if . . . yet . . . But then . . . And of . . . And yet . . .' This is not a matter of logic for its own sake, for the pattern of connectives works to map out the movement of the nymph's mind and gives both clarity and quiet drama to the psychological tension between the desire to tell the name of her lover, the fear that this may expose her to unbearable pity if things go wrong with the affair, and the feeling that she will nevertheless have to tell to gain some relief of tension. This is not an important poem, but there is impressive intelligence in the writing in that Jonson works towards maximum clarity without betraying the tensions in the mind of his persona.

This ability to organize material with decorous logic is often united with Jonson's creation of a conversational voice for his poems. He has several conversational manners at his disposal and they cannot all be examined here, but one of them occurs in that 'Epistle to a Friend' which starts 'They are not, Sir, worst Owers, that doe pay Debts when they can . . .' [14] It is a quiet poem and we know little of the occasion which gave rise to it, but it still has considerable life and this is because Jonson has created an interesting voice which says interesting things, both facts being very much bound up with the technical achievement of controlling the argument. The voice is, in the best sense of the word, 'manly': it admits the debt and offers explanation of the delay in paying, without becoming cringing or flattering. It offers a compromise based on the premise that debtor and creditor are both men and that the acts of lending and borrowing are both part of humane contact—or should be:

> Nor should I at this time protested be,
> But that some greater names have broke with me,
> And their words too; where I but breake my Band;
> I adde that (but) because I understand
> That as the lesser breach: for he that takes
> Simply my Band, his trust in me forsakes,
> And lookes unto the forfeit . . .

The connectives are again working to make clear distinctions, to follow faithfully the mind's movements and to define variations of tone. This kind of control is essential for a poet who relies as much as Jonson does on unobtrusive effects, and it is an ability which seldom fails him in his epistolary poetry.

In the plays and masques examples of careful organization are legion. One could point again to the articulation of the opening speech in *Volpone*, or examine the way in which Jonson creates the confusion of the quarrel which sets *The Alchemist* going while simultaneously conveying basic information about character and situation, or analyse the organization which maximizes the impact of the exposure of Busy in *Bartholomew Fair*. But a more ordinary moment in a lesser play will serve to indicate the fundamental competence of Jonson's verbal structures. Cupid is answering Mercury's inquiry about Philautia, early in *Cynthia's Revels*:

O, that's my lady and mistris, Madam Philautia. Shee admires not her selfe for any one particularity, but for all: shee is faire, and shee knowes it; shee has a pretty light wit too, and shee knowes it; shee can dance, and shee knowes that too; play at shittle-cock, and that too; no quality shee has, but shee shall take a very particular knowledge of, and most lady-like commend it to you. You shall have her at any time reade you the historie of herself, and very subtilely run over another lady's sufficiencies, to come to her owne. Shee has a good superficiall judgement in painting; and would seeme to have so in poetry. A most compleat lady in the opinion of some three, beside her-selfe.[15]

The positive qualities of this are obvious enough to need little comment: the movement from identification of Philautia to definition of her; the careful marking out of the elements of this definition; the reiterated 'shee knowes it' to drive home the subject's complacency; the withholding of the main satiric jab until the end of the speech so that it can draw on what goes before to make the impact as strong as possible, while also rounding off the portrait.

But another aspect of the speech is worth noticing. It is typical of the manner of *Cynthia's Revels* that the account is so formally organized and that it fixes Philautia verbally from the outside instead of allowing her to reveal herself by word and action. This is consistent with Jonson's general concern to make his viewpoints as clear as possible and with the demonstrative rather than exploratory nature of his art, but the tightness with which he controls Cupid's speech (and thus the way we see Philautia) once again suggests both determination to communicate with precision and an anxiety that such communication is extremely difficult to achieve.

So Jonson's sense of language as society's instrument leads him to emphasize and exploit words and their organization in ways which are designed to produce 'good superficial judgment'. Cupid's words are satirically intended, but they can be applied to what seem to be Jonson's artistic ends. A concern with the nature of society as a whole, when linked with a desire to communicate this concern to that society, almost inevitably means concentration upon the superficial —in the sense of 'that which deals with surfaces'. This is really two points: the pattern and operation of society are reflections of what the species has in common at a particular time and in a particular place; and what a set of individuals has sufficiently in common to allow them to live in societies is usually of the surface, in the sense that it involves reduction of uniqueness in favour of the generic. Secondly, an attempt to communicate widely involves an artist in decisions about how far he can work with understood conventions to transmit his own vision—and any artist who exists to transmit his vision for the purpose of making society at large realize its potential and its follies is likely to be much concerned with artistic vehicles which offer him the best chance of getting over what he wants to say as widely as possible, while losing as little as possible of the integrity of his vision. But here Cupid's other words become relevant, for the 'superficial' concentration will only have value if it is 'good' (squares with integrity) and if it leads to 'judgment' (the evaluation of the vision honestly in relation to experience).

I have suggested that Jonson's drive towards sharp definition may spring as much from lack of confidence as from excess of it, and have indicated in passing some possible reasons for the tension between confidence and uncertainty. The drive itself could be illustrated further. It can, for example, be linked with Jonson's interest in using words of classical origin, often with their root meanings; Latin especially being a language which, because of its inflexions and strict word-order, conveys clarity and precision more easily than a less closely organized language such as English. Jonson was also very interested in native slang and dialect, using these for many purposes, but one aspect of this interest is that it enlarges the word-hoard available to Jonson and thus increases his chances of finding the exact word for a particular need or situation. There is reason to think that the tension of which I am speaking has subconscious roots, but Jonson's thinking about and use of language indicate that he was consciously aware of the difficulties of adequate communication, so that there is an aggressive side to his handling of words. I mean by this that Jonson often uses language to show how easily man may break or abuse the communication-contract which Jonson sees as an important aspect of the social order and unity which he admires and wishes to see realized.

Some aspects of this aggressive use of language are obvious enough to need little comment. In several plays, for example, characters play word-games which Jonson introduces to indicate trivialization of language and associated trivialization of character, an obvious example being the game of 'vapours' in *Bartholomew Fair* [16] and another the 'jeering' at the start of Act IV of *The Staple of News*.[17] For Jonson such abuse of language represents both breakdown of communication and deficiency of character, and so Marston's type of verbal grotesquerie cannot go unpunished: the point of the vomiting scene in *Poetaster* is not just that Marston must be purged of his ugly vocabulary but that we see his vocabulary as antisocial because obscure and redundant in relation to the needs of the vernacular, hampering social communication rather than facilitating it. In *Discoveries* Jonson shows himself well aware of the difficulty of striking the right balance between importing or coining words 'when wee either absolutely want a word to expresse by . . . or when wee have not so fit a word' and the introduction of new words for reasons of fashion or ostentation: the formula is that such introduction is justified if 'wee avoid losse by it . . . escape obscurenesse, and gaine in the grace and property, which helpes significance'.[18] The Marstons of this world must be kept in line because they foster 'obsceneness' and hinder 'significance'. Another clear instance of Jonson using language to indicate abuse occurs when characters misuse words or use special vocabularies to deceive others: Cob's shaky grasp of his native tongue in *Every Man in his Humour* is basically a common comic device but it also serves to make it difficult for others to understand him, while in the same play Bobadilla is one of many Jonson characters who seek to achieve and exploit social position by technical vocabulary.

This type of abuse of language is extended on other occasions for weightier reasons, when characters use moral terms for immoral or self-deceiving reasons. One instance of this has already been touched on: Volpone's use of gold as the standard for all things involves his using moral terms defined by that standard and his vision of experience is accordingly circumscribed. Just how spiritually impoverished Volpone is is brilliantly shown in Act III. Celia, pleading not to be raped, says that if she is spared she will kneel to Volpone, 'pray for you, pay downe / A thousand hourely vowes, sir, for your health, / Report, and thinke you vertuous', whereupon Volpone breaks in with, 'Thinke me cold, / Frosen, and impotent, and so report me?'[19] His mind cannot understand the word 'vertue' except in sexual terms: his blindness is self-deception and it is this which makes his exit line ('This is called mortifying of a fox') so effective—the scorn grows from the fact that he has learnt nothing about himself and the First Avocatori's remark, 'Now, you begin, . . . To thinke what your crimes are'[20] is almost wholly meaningless. Like Volpone, Mammon in *The Alchemist* sees moral goodness in material terms: for him the 'great med'cine', 'can confer honour, love, respect'.[21] In Mammon's mouth the words change meaning—love shrinks to lust, while honour and respect are external commodities with no internal substance. Blinded as he is by lack of 'grace' he is a natural victim for Face and Subtle. Elsewhere characters use language to confuse and deceive others. In *Bartholomew Fair* Busy and Overdo use their respective professional vocabularies to convince others that they are what they are not.

Language can also be used antisocially in other ways. Much of the middle acts of *Cynthia's Revels* is taken up with backbiting expressed through precise stabs of language, but stabbing is destructive and verbal stabbing is a sign of social disruption. The famous opening of *The Alchemist* makes use of a blaze of vivid vituperation to indicate how frail are the bonds of the 'venter tripartite', and although Subtle and Face go on to use words brilliantly to deceive others they have already shown that they are vulnerable because of the vanity and greed indicated in their quarrel. In *Epicoene* Truewit torments Morose in Act II with his pictures of the horrors of marriage, but the comedy goes beyond this, for the length of Truewit's speeches is itself agony to Morose, who can only bear to hear his own voice; and on this occasion communication is being achieved all too efficiently—from Morose's point of view—but it is communication designed to hurt another and in this sense is again antisocial.

The kinds of aggression in language discussed so far may be at times subtle in articulation, but the purpose is clear enough—to indicate ways in which words can be used to deceive oneself or others. But perhaps the most interesting aspect of this area of Jonson's way with words is how they are used to manipulate his audience. Our response to Volpone and Mosca is partly defined by their delight in using words to deceive others and to express their pleasure at doing so. As Celia and Bonario come into the play we are reminded of another standard than Volpone's and we begin to see that our enjoyment of Volpone and Mosca is based on self-indulgence. But because the lines which Celia and Bonario are given are, on the whole, so vapid our responses are confused. We know that the values they hold are admirable but the vigour of Volpone and Mosca continues to appeal even as it appals, and this vigour is very much tied up with their mastery of language. The avocatori should prove another refuge for us in our confusion, but are so incompetent and venal that their sentences and moral pronouncements at the end are empty echoes of the morality of justice. If we shelter under the confidence of those closing pronouncements we have hidden ourselves from the sight of ourselves as having been again wrong-footed by Jonson, whose strategy in the play is to draw us towards Volpone and Mosca, to keep our responses to them mixed, to insert the expected counter-worlds of virtue and to indicate that these worlds are either impotent or deceptive, leaving us with a comic bleakness equivalent to the tragic experience of *Sejanus*.

This strategy, whereby audience response is deliberately confused so that the moral complexity of the vision in the major plays can be adequately represented, is an extension of the use of language to deceive spoken of earlier. When, for example, the disguised Wittipol in Act IV of *The Devil is an Ass* piles up technical cosmetic vocabulary and foreign terms he is doing so to convince Tailbush and Lady Eitherside that he is indeed the Spanish lady he is disguised as, and we enjoy the way in which this shows up the folly and superficiality of these characters, while simultaneously enjoying the virtuosity of Wittipol's use of language. But the same technique of deception is expanded in *Volpone*, *The Alchemist* and *Bartholomew Fair* to include us as audience. We have seen this already in *Volpone*. In *The Alchemist* the virtuosity of Face and Subtle with words is an important part of their attraction for us, and leads us to undervalue the truth of what Surly sees. When Lovewit returns, his urbanely witty use of language encourages us to see him as representing that return to norm which we expect in comedy. He does, in a sense, represent such a norm but it is only when we realize that his manner disguises a world-view which is essentially the same as that of Subtle and Face that we realize that the norm is little else than a continuation of the same world, or, to put this another way, an indication that the apparently extraordinary happenings in Lovewit's house during his absence are a comic heightening of the ordinary 'way of the world' as Jonson sees it in this play.

Bartholomew Fair is, linguistically, a packed play. The greatest verbal energy lies once again with characters who are either clearly dishonest or, like Busy, Overdo and Wasp, deluded about themselves. In this play, however, the verbal energy does not lead directly to quite the same kind of audience manipulation as in the other two comedies, for while the vitality of the rogues and self-deceived figures is attractive we are more constantly aware in this instance that the characters in question are rogues and self-deceivers. None the less, this disposition of energy is disturbing because the exposure of Busy, Wasp and Overdo involves their reduction to at least temporary silence and because those characters who most clearly see what is going on—Quarlous and Winwife—follow Lovewit in indulging the follies and blindnesses of others so long as they can capitalize on them. The commentaries of Quarlous and Winwife may seem to present a standard by which to judge others, but once again attachment to them as a way of escaping the implications of the play is self-deception by us as audience. As in *The Alchemist* we find that what seems like clear-sighted moral language covers blemishes. Paradoxically, in both plays, Jonson uses language to draw us into his comic worlds, to invite identification of various kinds, and thereby to suggest that his art-world has connections with our real world, but at the same time traps us within his world—a world in which the norms are expediency, hypocrisy and the survival of the fittest. The trap is such that we are left to consider whether we have misunderstood the nature of reality by sentimentally believing that positive values eventually reassert themselves.

I do not want to spend time on the matter of Jonson's realism of language, since the topic has been discussed often enough elsewhere. But it is perhaps worth noting that the realistic element in Jonson's vocabulary—the use of slang, dialect, strongly physical words—and the tendency to make use of language-piles operate to increase this drawing in of an audience to the play-world. But these factors also suggest once again an anxious concern to communicate: detail is piled up and repetition is common because Jonson is so concerned to communicate his visions. This linguistic density is not really an alternative to the technique of tight definition spoken of earlier, partly because the piling up of language in speeches like those of Wittipol in *The Devil is an Ass* or in such satirical poems as 'An Epistle to a Friend . . .' [22] is usually firmly controlled through Jonson's mastery of rhetoric and syntactical organization. Also, the two tendencies share a common objective—the desire to communicate—and a common psychological basis—uncertainty and anxiety about the possibility of communication. This basis relates also to Jonson's use of classical material, the subject of the next chapter.

Chapter 6

Jonson and Classicism

Edmund Wilson, lively but not always accurate, once summed up and endorsed a common view of Jonson's use of the classics by saying that his 'reading of Greek and Latin . . . has served him very insufficiently for the refinement and ordering of his work, and usually appears . . . as either an alien and obstructive element or, when more skilfully managed, as a padding to give the effect of a dignity and weight which he cannot supply himself'.[1] Wilson has little sympathy for Jonson and it would be hard to find another statement which is more triumphantly and confidently wrong. Its view of how creative writers may use borrowed material is remarkably naïve and Wilson reveals both ignorance of the facts about Jonson's use of classical material and blindness to his motives in using it.

Wilson's view is expressed with some exasperation, but classicism has often been suspect in English literature and a casual glance at the notes to the Herford and Simpson edition of the *Works* can easily create the suspicion that pedantry is close at hand. In recent years critics have become more tolerant of Jonson's classicism, more inclined to accept that it may have helped him and less willing to generalize from one or two examples of 'alien and obstructive' elements in *Poetaster*, say, or *Catiline*. Yet comparatively little detailed work has been done on what happens when Jonson makes use of classical material and until such work has been done the chances of our understanding what his classicism amounts to and what it indicates about his personality and achievement will be limited.

If Wilson had had even minimum curiosity he might have paused before committing his confident indiscretion. Had he checked—even in a fairly superficial way—on the sources, proportions and disposition of Jonson's classical borrowings he would have noticed, for example, that the amount of borrowing varies considerably. It is quite heavy, for instance, in *Cynthia's Revels* and *Poetaster* and substantially lighter in *The Alchemist* and *Bartholomew Fair*, but any pat theory that Jonson relied less on such material as he became more experienced is destroyed (even if we ignore the Roman tragedies) when we notice that borrowing is slight in *A Tale of a Tub*, *Every Man in his Humour* and *Every Man out of his Humour* (all written in some form before *Cynthia's Revels*), substantial in *Epicoene* (one of the mature comedies), but slight again in later plays such as *The Devil is an Ass* and *The Magnetic Lady* (although one might expect a tiring dramatist to lean more heavily on secondary material than in his prime). It might be possible to produce a tortuous—and tenuous— biographical theory to account for this inconveniently uneven pattern, but it seems more sensible to believe that Jonson had some artistic idea of when to borrow and when not to do so. Giving Jonson this minimal benefit of the doubt becomes more justified as we look more closely, for (staying with the plays for the moment) we notice interesting variety among the loans. In *The Case is Altered*, for instance, loans from Plautus dominate, while borrowings of this kind have largely vanished from the quarto of *Every Man in his Humour*; and if we look at *Every Man out of his Humour* we find that there Jonson's chief classical debts are to the Roman satirists, but also that he makes fuller use of Erasmus than he does of them and that the classical loans are minuscule when compared with the mass of local detail. Or we might turn to *The Alchemist* for further evidence of selectivity. The play doesn't make great use of classical material, except on two occasions: in Act II there is a sudden cluster of borrowings, while three scenes in Act V are based on Plautus' *Mostellaria*. I am not concerned at this stage to discuss why there are these two outcroppings, but only to make the point that they suggest purposive rather than mechanical activity and to hint that generalization about classicism in Jonson has its dangers.

This is not, however, to deny that Jonson did make extensive use of classical material and that, in the course of his career, he drew upon a considerable variety of Roman and—less frequently—Greek authors. What needs to be examined now is how Jonson uses the material he borrows and how well. It will only be possible within a single chapter to indicate some of the ways in which such material is used, and here again the poems are a useful starting point since they provide variety within limited bulk.

One small but well-known poem might have given Edmund Wilson food for thought: the song 'Drink to me, onely, with thine eyes',[3] which is constructed from passages in the Greek prose epistles of Philostratus. These epistles convey, through ingenious and often overworked conceits, a kind of tired sensuality. Jonson takes over the bantering tone of the original and something of Philostratus' ingenuity, but shows no sign of subservience to his material. Although the two final quatrains are almost literal translation the second is a free adaptation and the first a rearrangement of two passages in the Greek; but the important point is that the resultant English poem shows such full assimilation of the Greek that it reads like a single unit and is so thoroughly English in diction, syntax and rhythm that its highly derivative nature is virtually impossible to detect by internal analysis (in fact the basis in Philostratus was not noticed until the nineteenth century). Two other songs show the same ability to absorb classical material, 'Come my Celia, let us prove . . .' and 'Kisse me, sweet',[4] both of which are based on Catullus. 'Kisse me, sweet' includes three lines from the famous 'Vivamus mea Lesbia' but they are merged with a passage from another Catullus lyric—'Quaeris, quot mihi basiationes'—and Jonson's ending fuses the conclusions of the two Latin poems. The 'translation' is as perfect as in the mosaic from Philostratus.

With 'To Sir Robert Wroth'[5] we come to a more complex situation, one in which several sources are used and where the poem has as its general background a major Roman *topos* which compares the active, or urban, life unfavourably with the contemplative, or rural, one. Jonson's poem shows awareness of Virgil's second *Georgic*, Horace's second *Epode* and Martial's epigram 'Vir Celtiberis non tacende gentibus', but there are also more specific borrowings: free adaptations of Tibullus and Statius and two loans from Juvenal.[6] The range of authors used suggests both a broad and a detailed knowledge of classical Latin literature, while the exactness of some of the borrowings indicates conscious exploitation of this knowledge —yet the poem's local detail is fully English, as are the diction and rhythms of the whole. 'To Sir Robert Wroth' could scarcely be bettered for tactful use of the poetry of another country and culture: not only has Jonson avoided importing Latin material which might disrupt his English setting, but he has borrowed positively, in that he has established his poem in the richly suggestive context of the Latin genre.

Such assimilation of more than one source is common in Jonson. 'An Epode',[7] for example, opens with a passage based on Plato's *Gorgias*, borrows from Lucian, and also contains reminiscences of St Luke, Horace, St Matthew and Seneca. The nature of the loans varies from what looks like a semi-conscious memory of Satan's temptation of Christ

> Who . . .
> Would, at suggestion of a steepe desire,
>   Cast himselfe from the spire
> Of all his happinesse . . .   (ll. 62–5)

to an epigrammatic version, used as Jonson's last line, of Seneca's 'tuta scelera esse possunt, secura esse non possunt'.[8] Another good example is the 'Epistle to Sir Edward Sackvile',[9] which is mainly interesting here because of the extensive borrowing from Seneca's *De Beneficiis*, although use is also made of Plato, Horace and Plutarch. Jonson's first 110 lines include a dozen loans from Seneca, drawn from seven different sections of the Latin text. Here again Jonson varies from close translation to free adaptation, constantly making small alterations and additions, the net result being more direct and aggressive than Seneca's prose. This example is also important because—typically—Jonson uses Seneca not as a source for images or allusions but for basic ideas and details connected with his argument about 'benefits'. The issue of the morality of giving and accepting presents was a live one in Seneca's Rome and Jonson has seen the relevance of Seneca's discussion not merely to his own financial position but to the wider matter of place and patronage in Elizabethan England. But Jonson does not force a Roman view: instead Seneca is used to help him articulate strongly held opinions about human dignity and moral values in society. In so far as the poem depends upon Seneca it is a piece of creative imitation of a high order.

The high quality of imitation is a characteristic of much of Jonson's work (although, oddly, it scarcely ever appears in his formal translations) and is manifested in the smoothness with which borrowed material is integrated and in his preference for drawing upon ideas and attitudes compatible with his strongly English fabrics, rather than using the classics for historical, mythological or illustrative references. The same sensitivity is also shown in Jonson's feeling for when to borrow; for the poems, like the plays, are marked by varying densities of classical borrowing, and there are many cases where an occasional loan is drawn into an essentially original composition. A simple example is in the epigram 'On Chev'ril',[10] where the second line—'And threatens the starre-chamber and the barre'—uses fully English legal terms which are nevertheless adapted from Horace's line 'Servius iratus leges minitatur et urnam'.[11] A general similarity of context may have suggested the adaptation to Jonson, but the subjects of the two poems are not really close and the loan looks the result of memory rather than of formal decision to borrow. A more important case is the end of the great epitaph 'On my first Daughter':[12]

> This grave partakes the fleshly birth.
> Which cover lightly, gentle earth.

This is closely related to Martial:

> mollia non rigidus caespes tegat ossa nec illi,
> terra, gravis fueris: non fuit illa tibi.[13]

The paganism of the Latin poem has not touched Jonson's epitaph, however. The sentimentality of Martial's 'mollia . . . ossa' has given way to 'fleshly birth', which gives the adaptation a distinctly Christian connotation, setting the physical birth against spiritual rebirth through death. Also, Jonson's use of Martial's idea of the earth lying lightly on the corpse is not exotic—the idea is commonplace, both in classical and Elizabethan contexts.[14]

One other example will have to be enough. In 'To Heaven' [15] there is a loan which indicates the thoroughness of Jonson's classical memory. Speaking of his unworthiness to approach God Jonson says, 'there scarce is ground, / Upon my flesh t'inflict another wound', which is a close rendering of Ovid:

> sic ego continuo fortunae vulneror ictu
> vixque habet in nobis iam nova plaga locum.[16]

It seems likely that Ovid's expression of the grief of exile from Rome was brought to Jonson's mind by the sense of his own alienation from God, but the slightness of the contextual link indicates real familiarity with Ovid, and the use of a classical poet in one of Jonson's most personal poems is interesting evidence of how close he is to his classical learning, of how much it is alive to him as part of his reaction to experience. The loan is also a good example of poetic tact, for Jonson has suppressed Ovid's 'fortunae' and the lines he has assimilated have a natural affinity with Christian use of the imagery of physical wounds to express spiritual suffering and remorse.

Jonson's use of classical material in his poems, in fact, shows his mind moving easily from original statements to borrowed ones, adapting the latter where necessary to fit the new context. The unobtrusiveness of most of the loans also needs to be noticed: care is consistently taken to make the loan fully part of the total fabric and it is very seldom that either the material which is borrowed or the original expression of it is allowed to stand out from its English context. The very high level of assimilation should be enough to free Jonson from charges of pedantry or of wishing to show off, for pedantry is an attitude of mind, a failure of mental proportion, rather than the inevitable result of erudition and love of accuracy. Borrowing is clearly central to Jonson's poetic method and the nature of this borrowing clearly provides the basis for possible pedantry—Jonson knew a great deal of classical literature in detail and willingly makes use of minor authors (Ausonius, Claudian, Pausanius) as well as of major ones. But the bulk of Jonson's poetry shows no concern to make the poet's learning obvious and none to make loans literal translations. His classicism is something finer than this and more subtle: an attempt to show how classical attitudes and ideas could be relevant to Renaissance England. The tendency is to draw upon Roman ethical ideas and Jonson largely avoids classical mythological allusions and specifically classical local detail; he is willing to alter what he borrows and is anxious to make it fully English.

As I have argued elsewhere, Jonson sees experience in ethical terms. But his ethical attitudes are seldom distinctly classical in content (partly because there is a large area of common ground between classical and English ethical attitudes [17]). So there is no necessary incompatibility between Jonson's detailed use of Roman statements of ethical belief and a lively awareness of his native social and cultural environment. This being so there is no reason why Jonson's loans should fit awkwardly into the English contexts which they are given—unless Jonson should fail to re-create what he borrows in the rhythmical, syntactical and linguistic terms of his 'original' or native manner. The opening lines of the 'Epistle to Sir Edward Sackvile' [18] provide a good example of that manner at its most confident:

> If Sackvile, all that have the power to doe
> Great and good turns, as wel could time them too,
> And knew their how, and where: we should have, then
> Lesse list of proud, hard, or ingratefull Men.
> For benefits are ow'd with the same mind
> As they are done, and such returnes they find.

This is fully Jonsonian in thought and manner, with its poised phrasing and confident movement between abstract and concrete. Yet the passage is taken from Seneca.[19] Here is another extract, from 'On Lucy Countesse of Bedford': [20]

> I meant the day-starre should not brighter rise,
> Nor lend like influence from his lucent seat.
> I meant shee should be courteous, facile, sweet,
> Hating that solemne vice of greatnesse, pride;
> I meant each softest vertue, there should meet,
> Fit in that softer bosome to reside.

The fourth line quoted has a direct Latin source,[21] but nothing internal gives a clue and the line expresses one of Jonson's firmest convictions—that empty pride is worthless show.

It should be clear from such examples that Jonson at times finds classical loans an aid to articulation; but they have a more important function than this. The bases of Jonson's ethical thought are com-

monplaces of classical and native thinking, but they are commonplaces which, instead of being superficial responses to experience,
sum up the ethical speculations and conclusions of many men across
many centuries. Jonson's frequent use of classical expressions of such
commonplaces adds to the authority and weight of his social analysis.
We may instinctively prefer individual insight to collective wisdom
but we gain nothing by imagining that Jonson did: his effort is
obviously to muster and organize the 'best thoughts' of the past in
the service of the present. When Sackville is told that 'Where any
Deed is forc't, the Grace is mard' [22] and Vere that 'Humanitie, and
pietie are / As noble in great chiefes, as they are rare',[23] it is the
whole rhythmical and contextual fabric of the poems which must
convince us of the truth of these remarks, and this truth cannot be
proved or disproved by tracing the comments to their sources in
Seneca. But the Senecan sources may have increased Jonson's
confidence that he was saying something true: they help to lift the
remarks from the particular to the general. It is partly in this sense
that Jonson's habit of translation and adaptation is creative: his
conception of the poet's rule is public and he seeks to present moral
truths and to analyse society in terms of these truths. To Jonson truth
is not primarily individual perception, but rather a summary and
synthesis of human experience over centuries.

Yet again we find ourselves apparently facing an unfamiliar Ben
Jonson. The evidence of the poems does not support the view that his
classicism is pedantic or that it is another element of his arrogance.
The use of classical material to buttress his ethical analyses is certainly consistent with his desire to be the sort of counsellor defined in
Discoveries, but it indicates also a kind of humility—a willingness to
accept that the quality and weight of ethical perception necessary
for this role of counsellor/analyst require more than the insight of a
single man. In this sense the habit of borrowing may, indeed, be
meant 'to give the effect of a dignity and weight which he cannot
supply himself', but Wilson's remark can now be thought of not as
the belittling observation it is meant to be but as touching acci-
dentally upon Jonson's sensible awareness of the difficulties of his
task. We may once again feel that beneath the confidence of manner
lies uncertainty in his own powers—and I hope to show in the final
chapter that Jonson's massive effort to preserve the standards he
believed in was scarcely a matter of fighting ghosts. For the moment
it can simply be suggested that Jonson's use of the wisdom of the past
is his equivalent to Eliot's shoring up of fragments at the end of
The Waste Land.

So far I have concentrated on the poems because they provide a convenient microcosm of some aspects of Jonson's use of the classics, and this should provide a context for looking at a few features of classicism in the plays. It will only be possible to touch on a few plays and a few moments of importance: what follows is meant to be suggestive and makes no pretence to exhaustiveness.

Volpone draws upon several classical texts for general analogues to its world of legacy-hunting and fraud, particularly—as Herford and Simpson point out—two of Pliny's epistles (II.20 and IV.2), Petronius' *Satyricon* and Lucian's *Pluto and Mercury* and *Simylus*. The play makes use of classical material across a range which extends from such broad influences to small matters of detail: Jonson, for example, makes use of a particular author for particular passages of his play—the speeches of Lady Politic Would-bee in III. iv use the treatise *De Muliere Loquaci* by Libanius of Antioch, while Diogenes Laertius and Lucian are raided for the account of the soul's transmigration in Nano's speech in the opening scene. There are also interesting differences in the extent to which different authors are used. Some, like Persius, Pindar and Tacitus, are apparently used only once, while some are drawn upon fairly consistently throughout (notably Juvenal and Martial) and others influence one part of the play more than another—thus the ten or so borrowings from Horace are almost exclusively confined to the introductory matter and the first two acts, whereas the Plautus loans come, with one exception, in Act II or later. Horace, Juvenal and Martial (social, moral, satiric writers) are the most important classical influences so far as detail is concerned, but the overall range of borrowing is impressive: six different Horace poems are used and five of Juvenal, while over thirty authors are drawn on in the course of the play.

Volpone's opening speech has already been discussed in an earlier chapter: it is unified, carefully organized and very important. In organizing it Jonson has made use of three classical borrowings. The first is the image 'Show'st like a flame by night', which is taken from Pindar's first Olympian ode (1-2). Jonson's praise is an almost exact translation and there is a contextual link in that Pindar is also speaking of gold. The appropriateness is obvious enough, Jonson making the image another pointer to Volpone's excess (gold, among his other treasure, is like a flame in darkness) and ultimately crude hyperbole.

A few lines later Volpone is praising 'wise poets' for calling the golden age golden and is explicitly setting gold beyond 'children, parents, friends'. The lines involved (14-21) are adapted from Seneca,[24] who is at this point quoting from Ovid and Euripides and satirizing their attitudes to gold. Volpone, as we should expect, presents the Ovidian and Euripidean views (which are favourable) seriously, while Jonson's valuing of his character's response corresponds to Seneca's view. We should also notice the confidence with which Jonson adapts and develops his source. This is the end of the fragment from Euripides which Seneca quotes:

> And if the sweetness of the lover's glance
> Be half so charming, Love will rightly stir
> The hearts of gods and men to adoration.

Jonson writes

> Thy lookes, when they to Venus did ascribe,
> They should have giv'n her twentie thousand Cupids;
> Such are thy beauties, and our loves! [25]

Jonson's 'they' ties this detail up with the wise poets of 1.14; his 'Venus . . . Cupids' draws Euripides' reference to love into the fully personified world of Renaissance iconography and also provides one of the play's early associations of gold with sex; the 'twenty thousand' is a detail added by Jonson and characteristic of Volpone; and the rest of the last line just quoted ('Deare saint') leads us back into the specifically religious area of Volpone's outlook.

This provides the link with the third borrowing in this speech. Volpone concludes with a list of gold's attributes:

> Thou art vertue, fame,
> Honour, and all things else! Who can get thee,
> He shall be noble, valiant, honest, wise . . .

—and here the source is Horace who, in *Satires* II. iii. 94–8, tells us that worth, repute, honour, things human and divine, are all 'slaves to the beauty of wealth', and that he who is rich will be famous, brave, just, wise. The detail of Jonson's lines is close to Horace's discussion of Staberius' wealth, but the loan is controlled to achieve a double context. The list of attributes which, in Volpone's eyes, gold comprises or obtains echoes into classical morality, but at the same time the context is Christian, for immediately before the lines just quoted Volpone has called gold 'The price of soules' and has said that 'even hell, with thee to boot, / Is made worth heaven!' Jonson's assimilation of Horace's idea gives Volpone's blasphemy maximum significance: once again we see that even detailed borrowing can be an organic process.

'Organic' perhaps calls for some definition here, for anyone who has studied Shakespeare's use of Plutarch and North or who has read

Middleton Murry's classic *Road to Xanadu* has probably got some idea of organic borrowing as a process of more or less unconscious absorbing and transformation, with the creative pressure shaping and fusing the borrowed and the original without deliberate contemplation of the former. This kind of process connects with Coleridge's idea of the 'plastic' quality of poetic imagination, but in Jonson's case 'organic' refers to something more cerebral and less instinctive. The loans in Volpone's opening speech are clearly conscious ones. The Pindar borrowing might be a memory, involving no research or checking, but the other two are detailed, and—being 'moral' rather than 'image'—involve more than half-conscious processes of memory. They look, in fact, like fully conscious workings out, part of a deliberate, calculated artefact. But this sort of integration involves a sensitive simultaneous awareness of the borrowed detail and the overall purpose of the play. A balance is struck between the loan and the local and general dramatic contexts. Nothing is ostentatiously imported: Jonson is not showing off.

How acutely Jonson can work on a narrow margin between borrowing and creation (how close, in fact, these two processes are for him) can be shown in another loan from Horace. At I.i.52 Mosca begins a speech ('And besides, sir . . .') describing his view of Volpone's activities, and his words are again based on Horace's satire used in the opening speech.[26] Horace speaks of hoarding as madness and provides three images of the miser, who is like (1) a man lying hungry and watching a heap of corn with a cudgel while feeding off herbs; (2) the owner of many jars of Chian and Falernian wine drinking vinegar; (3) an old man lying on a straw bed while worms and moths devour the rich coverlets in his chest.

Mosca uses these images and in the same order, but each is slightly changed. Horace's man-with-cudgel becomes a man with a flail and the image is made more active by delaying the detail 'hungrie', by the sharp contrast of 'huge flaile' with 'smallest graine' and by the specific 'mallowes'. Horace's Chian and Falernian become contemporary Romagnia and Candian wines, the vinegar is made specific and the contrast extreme by 'lees'. The third image is followed closely, but 'soft beds' is added by Jonson and is a good example of how carefully he is working: this detail is a significant foreshadowing of the luxurious Volpone who will try to seduce Celia later. It is also important to notice how Horace's lines are integrated to Jonson's dramatic purposes, both in the pushing of Horace's contrasts to extremes and in the way in which Mosca turns praise into begging.

Three further examples will underline how sensitive and confident the controlled and creative borrowing in *Volpone* is. Here, first of all, is Mosca speaking to Corvino about Volpone's need of a woman:

> . . . it must be one, that ha's no trickes, sir,
> Some simple thing, a creature, made unto it;
> Some wench you may command . . .[27]

This is again derived from Horace. In Satires II. v. 75–6 Tiresias speaks about flattery for gain and stresses that if the old man who is being flattered is a libertine, the flatterer should freely hand Penelope over to him. What happens here is that a detail in Horace's poem is made into a motif of Jonson's dramatic plot, for the basic idea in the Latin lines affects more than just the lines quoted, informing, in fact, the Mosca/Corvino dialogue to the end of the scene.

But the matter is more complicated than it may at first seem. For the immediate purpose of the play-in-performance what matters is the motif itself, made strikingly perverse because Celia is Corvino's wife and because he has just been seen as insanely jealous: we are at extremes again, where greed turns jealousy into wife-prostitution. All this is fully present in the play and we need no knowledge of Horace to be aware of it. Such knowledge, however, increases our awareness of how carefully Jonson works and also sharpens our sense of how solidly he creates his artefacts. Wanting a pure heroine Jonson ignores the lines in Horace about Penelope, but when we make the Jonson/Horace link the Tiresian attitude not only echoes that of Corvino, Mosca and Volpone but acts as a contrast to Celia's purity.

This loan is particularly interesting, however, because another text is at work, contributing to the precise complexity of Jonson's motif. This is the incident of Abishag the Shunammite in I Kings. The Bible echo parallels Horace in its juxtaposition of an aged man with a young woman and adds the health/sickness contrast which Jonson uses, together with the idea that the woman may give heat to the sick man. But it is Horace who provides both the flatterer figure and the idea of an intimate relationship between the flatterer and the woman. Also, in the Bible, the woman is a virgin and is willing to lie with David in what is seen as a good cause. Becoming aware that Jonson is drawing upon both I Kings and Horace is a process of seeing how fully merged the two sources are. But once again awareness of the Old Testament passage, while not essential to Jonson's main dramatic point, underscores his dramatic purpose, for the pure self-sacrifice of Abishag makes an ironic contrast with the perverted plotting of Volpone, Mosca and Corvino. But the final emphasis must be upon Jonson's mastery of his material, for the motif in question is one of the most brilliantly executed pieces of callous cynicism in English drama—and it depends ultimately upon the habit of creative borrowing.

This example suggests why *Volpone* exists in two closely linked and interdependent dimensions, that of the immediate impact and that of the reinforcing awareness of the loan-context. It is perhaps necessary to add that this does not mean that the play is study-bound: the reinforcement I speak of is only a particular version of the process which makes any play great—that process of creation which produces depth of a kind which emerges fully as our knowledge of the text increases. Here again, also, is evidence of a desire to build solidly, a desire which is partly architectonic but partly also the sign of Jonson's determination to give his fictions maximum authority. Similar points emerge from another of the play's loans, this time from Act III. Mosca, defending himself from Bonario's accusations of sloth and flattery, says

> You are unequall to me: and howere
> Your sentence may be righteous, yet you are not,
> That, ere you know me, thus proceed in censure . . .[28]

The lines are part of an episode where we see Mosca at his perverted best. We know that Bonario is right, but Mosca outfaces him, turning defeat into victory and integrating victory with plot with a confidence and sureness of touch which is as admirable as it is abominable. The cool insolence of Mosca's mind is fully present in the lines quoted, in the logic and poise of 'howere . . . yet . . . That, ere . . . thus', and in the confident deceitfulness with which he makes logical rightness outflank Bonario's morally correct instinct about Mosca's parasitic nature. So the lines are fully Mosca—but they are also fully Seneca. Lines 199–200 of his tragedy *Medea* read

> Qui statuit aliquid parte inaudita altera,
> aequam licet statuerit, haud aequus fuit . . .

which Miller translates

> He who has judged aught, with the other side unheard,
> may have judged righteously, but was himself unrighteous.[29]

Jonson has carefully fitted Medea's dignified appeal to Creon to Mosca's dissimulating appeal to Bonario. But here again we have a situation in which the loan is both so fully absorbed as not to need recognition for the immediate point to be clear, and one where such recognition adds a further and satisfyingly relevant dimension; for the words of Medea are debased in the mouth of Mosca and, by extension, Seneca's tragic world is debased to the treachery and corruption of Jonson's Venice.

My final example from *Volpone* concerns Juvenal. In Act III Lady Pol is preparing to talk with Volpone. She is concerned about her appearance and her maid's apparent inability to do her job properly. She asks four questions: (1) Is this curl in place? (2) Have you (the maid) not yet washed your eyes? (3) Do you squint? (4) Where is the other maid? At this point Nano comments that soon Lady Pol will 'beate her woman / Because her nose is red'. Jonson is drawing on Juvenal's sixth satire (lines 492–4): Juvenal has the detail of the curl, the idea of beating and that of the nose. But there are changes. Jonson dramatizes Juvenal by dividing the Latin-based lines between two characters and he draws the Juvenal material into the character of Lady Pol. Thus Juvenal's question as to how the maid would be blameworthy if the mistress disliked the shape of her own nose is coarsened into the idea of the nose being red, while the abuse in the English passage ('you ha' not wash'd your eies, yet? / Or do they not stand even i' your head?') is an addition, implied perhaps in the Latin, but made explicit and revealing by Jonson. He is controlling and exploiting Juvenal, not being dominated by him.

Enough has, I hope, been said to make it clear that the classicism in *Volpone* is a triumph of creative assimilation. Direct loans from the classics (which affect only about a tenth of the play's lines) are far from alien or obstructive. On the contrary, they are important reinforcements of Jonson's vision. But *Volpone* tells only part of the story and I now want to look at isolated moments from other plays to fill the picture out a little.

Jonson, as everyone knows, often makes use of elaborate prefatory material to his plays. In *Cynthia's Revels* he uses the Induction and Prologue to define the formal nature of the drama he has written, but he does so without letting this prefatory material itself become static and he also uses it to make a bridge between the real world and that of Gargaphie, the play world, with its deities and sub-deities. The first scene of the play proper shows Jonson's concern to keep the two worlds in contact, with the Cupid/Mercury quarrel echoing that of the actors in the Induction (the point being, of course, underlined by the actors of the Cupid/Mercury quarrel being children themselves). The brisk exchange at the scene's opening gives way to domination by Cupid's speeches and Jonson several times draws upon Lucian's *Dialogues of the Gods* in organizing his material. The basic idea of Mercury (Hermes) as a thief is common enough but Lucian provides a number of details and suggestions. The first of these comes at lines 14–17:

> You did never steale Mars his sword out of the sheath, you? nor Neptunes trident? nor Apolloes bow? no, not you? [30]

where Jonson uses Lucian's seventh dialogue. In Lucian Hermes is the subject of the dialogue between Hephaestus and Apollo, and is a baby. Jonson takes over the specific examples of Hermes' thieving but uses them as ironical exclamations by Cupid, directed at an older Mercury. More strikingly, when Jonson uses Dialogue 24 in Cupid's next speech he takes the complaints made *by* Lucian's Hermes to his mother and transfers them into a satirical attack *on* Mercury. Also Jonson reduces the number of classical references and the Greek prose is recast in a thoroughly English idiom. Then, after assimilating a single Lucian phrase from the sixth dialogue ('made the whole body of divinity tremble'), Jonson turns back to Dialogue 7 for further examples of Mercury's thefts, the last of which (that of Vulcan/Hephaestus' tongs) is carefully worked into the linking of Gargaphie with the worlds of the playhouse and contemporary London. First the action is made internally contemporary ('the other day'), then it is specifically located on earth, and finally moves to prophecies about possible Mercury-thefts in London:

> S'light, now you are on earth, wee shall have you filch spoones and candle-sticks, rather then faile: pray Jove the perfum'd courtiers keepe their casting-bottles, pick-toothes, and shittle-cocks from you; or our more ordinarie gallants their tabacco-boxes; for I am strangely jealous of your nailes. [31]

Cynthia's Revels is not immediately attractive to modern taste, but the evidence of Jonson's use of Lucian here suggests that the play's classical material may not be to blame. Lucian is not used inertly: Jonson selects, adapts, and adds details, while the Greek prose is transformed into lively and idiomatic English. It is true that the Cupid/Mercury exchanges are formal (although the long speeches are verbally active and separated by Mercury's brief interjections) but this is consistent with the kind of play *Cynthia's Revels* is, and certainly is not the result of using Lucian, who, if anything, is a model to help Jonson towards lively writing. Given that the play is basically a debate written for child-actors Jonson's use of Lucian is discreet and sensitive.

A rather more complex piece of borrowing—one already touched on [32]—occurs in Act III of *Poetaster*. The use of Lucian was primarily a matter of selecting details and dovetailing them, but in *Poetaster* Jonson takes one of Horace's most famous satires (I.ix) as basis for the whole of the opening part of his act—and, of course, has to try to find dramatic form for Horace's poetry.

Basically Horace helps Jonson with this problem, because his satire contains a lot of dialogue and a strong sense of action (being in this respect rather like Donne's first satire). Yet much of the success of Horace's poem depends upon the anecdotal reflections of the poet-figure, or, more specifically, upon Horace's projection of himself as comic victim caught up in a complex of his own courtesy, his own exasperation, and the tenacious insensitivity of the 'man I knew only by name'. Jonson had to decide how much of this projection he should retain and how to dramatize it, considering both in relation to his presentation of Horace in the play as a whole.

Structurally, Jonson fails to cope fully with the problems of dramatizing the element of interior monologue in Horace's poem. For example, the modest, casual opening of the satire gives way in Jonson's version to a more solemn, slightly pretentious note:

Hm'm? yes; I will begin an ode so: and it shall be to Mecaenas.[33]

The need to make verbal/visual what Horace can leave purely verbal has produced an obviousness and seeming self-assertion in Jonson's Horace which is both a bit clumsy and somewhat ambiguous. Crispinus (the tormentor) must be overt about attaching himself to Horace, whereas in the satire the leech is more comically troubling because so unmotivated. Similar awkwardness leads to an over-reliance on asides to convey thoughts which are natural parts of the Latin anecdote-poem, but it is also this problem of adaptation which leads to the differences between Jonson's characters and Horace's. Crispinus emerges as more assertive and more insensitive than his Latin counterpart, for while the bland, courteous exasperation of Horace's poet-figure certainly calls for, as foil, a leech who lacks perception and self-awareness, the subtlety of Horace's presentation is broadened and coarsened by Jonson. His Horace attacks Crispinus directly and the latter's obliviousness to what is happening therefore necessarily seems more extreme in its insensitive egocentricity than anything in Horace's poem. Horace too is changed, and in ways which raise interesting questions about the whole play. Jonson's Horace refers to his 'tame modestie / (which) Suffers my wit be made a solemne asse / To beare his fopperies'.[34] Inevitably, since this is *spoken*, the 'tame modesty' emerges as something like complacency and one can hardly avoid wondering if Horace is revealing pride while claiming modesty. Also, there is a lack of self-knowledge in the remark, for although in Jonson's scenes Horace fails to find a way of shaking Crispinus off it is not because of modesty. Jonson's

Horace tries tricks taken over from the Latin poem, but also uses sarcasm, impatience and direct attack in his efforts to get free. The figure which emerges is not uninteresting—but it is not Horace's poet-figure nor the modest victim it claims to be. Neither is it confidently assimilated to the play as a whole.[35]

This is not to say that Jonson has failed ignominiously: the discreet selectivity of the Lucian loans in *Cynthia's Revels* is not wholly missing here. Jonson again merges borrowed detail with extension of it in a confident manner, and his scenes have moments of real vitality, such as this brief exchange:

Horace: Pray, sir, give me leave to wipe my face a little.
Crispinus: Yes, doe, good Horace.
Horace: Thanke you, sir . . .[36]

Jonson catches nicely Horace's ironic desperation, Crispinus' condescension and Horace's mock-gratitude.

This, then, is an example of an adaptation which does not succeed, but it is not a failure because of pedantic literalism. Jonson is quite willing to alter his material, but he has not managed to dramatize it fully, using worn and rather clumsy stage techniques as equivalents for Horace's poetic strategy, and showing himself less than fully aware of how his Horace comes over in these scenes in relation to the rest of the play.

By the time he came to write *Epicoene* Jonson was at the height of his powers and this means that we should expect to find there a very high level of control over the material he uses. The play is a fine piece of stagecraft and a remarkable example of the creation of great comedy from a single idea. Even if one regards *Epicoene* as 'pure' comedy any decent production impresses one with the confident wit and beautiful architectonics of the play—and yet it is shot through with borrowed material. Jonson moves from Seneca to Ovid, from Plautus to Horace, with a sureness of touch which leaves scarcely a trace of where he has gone for an idea or detail. Dryden said one sees the footprints of the classics everywhere in Jonson;[37] granted modern standards of classical knowledge it is more accurate to say that the prints are revealed by dusting powder and not otherwise. But one scene is particularly interesting as a test of Jonson's creative assimilation. This is the second scene of Act II and Jonson there draws upon Juvenal's sixth satire. As with the Horace adaptation discussed above Jonson here faced problems in adapting his source. Juvenal's poem is a long and bitterly detailed attack upon women and marriage, marked by brutal sarcasm, obscenity and a pressure at times almost frenetic in its reduction of woman to a shrewish, utterly ruthless fucking-machine, similar to Procopius' Theodora in *The Secret History*. The tone is one which Jonson was quite capable of reproducing in English (perhaps most notably in *The Under-wood*, XV), but it is not an appropriate tone for *Epicoene*, a play of sly, poised, often oblique effects. The scene I am concerned with here is the one in which Truewit comes to taunt Morose about his plans to marry, and all the Juvenal loans come in Truewit's long speeches. Dramatically the scene is a fine blend of verbal and visual effects. Truewit dominates on the verbal level, the comedy here being, of course, twofold: Truewit's great outpouring of words is agony to Morose simply at the level of noise, while the content of the speeches is agony because designed to rend Morose's idea of a silent wife. The visual dimension prevents any possibility that Truewit's long speeches might seem dramatically static or excessive, for on stage Morose's reactions, which can appropriately find only fleeting verbal expression, take an equal share of our attention: we listen to Truewit and watch Morose.

But Truewit is playing a role, and it is not equivalent to the 'voice' of Juvenal's poem. His approach is at times aggressive—as at the start of the scene—and at times that of a reasonable man who only wants to help ('I but tell you, what you must heare'). He argues with Morose—although it is a one-sided argument—and his use of vivid detail to terrify him is controlled by the terms of the argument, so that his speeches have a poised and seemingly dispassionate quality which is quite unlike the rush and frenzy of Juvenal's tirade. In drawing on Juvenal, therefore, Jonson has the problem of reorganizing the loans in a native context and also of re-creating what he borrows in terms of Truewit's role; it is also relevant that Jonson's scene is less than a quarter of the length of Juvenal's poem. It would be tedious to examine each of the loans,[38] but three examples should be enough to show how completely Jonson solves his problems. A striking case occurs at the end of Truewit's first long speech:

... if you had liv'd in King Ethelred's time, sir, or Edward the Confessors, you might, perhaps, have found in some cold countrey hamlet, then, a dull frostie wench, would have been contented with one man: now, they will as soone be pleas'd with one leg, or one eye ...

Here Jonson runs together two short passages from Juvenal:

> Credo Pudicitiam Saturno rege moratam
> in terris visamque diu ...

and

> unus Hiberinae vir sufficit? ocius illud
> extorquebis, ut haec oculo contenta sit uno.[39]

Two passages, separated by some fifty lines, have been linked, made to follow each other logically, and neatly anglicized. Juvenal speaks of a (somewhat tentative) belief that chastity lingered in Saturn's golden age: Jonson conveys, in English terms, the idea of a similar distant past with the reference to 'Ethelred's time' and reinforces it by mentioning Edward the Confessor, the latter slyly chosen to indicate a time of exceptional piety. He then catches Juvenal's tentativeness by linking the placing in time with the idea of chastity being both rare and unnatural ('some cold countrey hamlet . . . dull frostie wench') and completes his transplant by doubling Juvenal's 'oculo . . . uno' into 'one leg, or one eye'.

A simpler example occurs in this passage:

If, after you are married, your wife doe run away with a vaulter, or the Frenchman that walkes upon ropes, or him that daunces the jig, or a fencer for his skill at his weapon . . .[40]

Jonson has taken Juvenal's long passage (line 60 ff.) about the dangers posed by actors, gladiators and the like to Roman husbands and condensed it into a brief and thoroughly contemporary parallel. But a final instance will show just how creatively Jonson is working. The first borrowing from Juvenal in the scene coincides with Trucwit's indication to Morose of the purpose of his visit: 'They say, you are to marry? to marry! do you marke, sir?'—going on to explain that Morose's 'friends' cannot understand why he is choosing this form of 'death', concluding a series of alternative ways to die with 'or, if you affected to doe it neerer home, and a shorter way, an excellent garret windore, into the street; or, a beame in the said garret, with this halter' would serve. Jonson takes from Juvenal the idea of the basic absurdity of marriage and the suggestion that suicide is preferable. Two or three of the suggested ways of suicide are taken from the Latin, but others are dropped as inappropriate to an English context; those which are retained are thoroughly anglicized; substitutions and additions are made; while the whole passage based on Juvenal is carefully integrated both to Truewit's role as messenger for Morose's 'friends' and to Jonson's own terse English style ('or, take a little sublimate, and goo out of the world, like a rat; or a flie (as one said) with a straw i' your arse: any way, rather, then to follow this goblin matrimony'[41]). The last of the ways of suicide taken from Juvenal is hanging. The Latin reference is brief, whereas Jonson links it to the preceding idea of jumping from a garret window, neatly uses the English word 'halter' for the more pallid 'rope', and—with the 'halter . . . wed-lock nooze' wordplay— fits the idea into Truewit's character. This is impressive work, but not all the story. Truewit's 'halter' is not just a verbal suggestion, for he enters carrying a rope—and Truewit's final touch, his way of completing his performance in this scene, is to leave the noose with the shaken Morose:

God b'w'you: I'll be bold to leave this rope with you, sir, for a remembrance.[42]

As Truewit rounds off his part in the scene, Jonson completes his use of Juvenal with a splendidly theatrical 'remembrance': Juvenal's few words have been made into a fine visual moment.

The complexity and variety of Jonson's use of the classics are such that it is almost embarrassing to leave the topic with so many aspects completely untouched, but a whole book would be needed to do the subject justice. I have said nothing about the use of classical and neo-classical material in the masques, but some excellent work has already been done on this. Nor have I concerned myself with the use of Latin material in *Sejanus* and *Catiline*: if I had space I should seek to show that in the former Jonson masters his material but fails to do so in the latter. What I have tried to do, however, has both a negative and a positive aspect. The former is to indicate by specific examples that Jonson was capable on many occasions of making creative use of what he borrows, that it is far from alien or obstructive. Positively I have tried to show that Jonson's imagination was often fired, or at least stoked up, by his awareness of classical literature, that it is his particular version of the process of assimilation which is common to most—probably all—creative writers. But the version *is* peculiar, in that instead of, say, formal imitation of the type represented by Samuel Johnson's 'Vanity of Human Wishes' at one extreme, or subconscious assimilation as in Coleridge's 'Rime of the Ancient Mariner' at the other, we have a persistent habit of borrowing pieces of varying lengths and with varying degrees of freedom, these pieces being absorbed into the original framework of the play, poem or masque on which Jonson is working.

Two aspects of this process, both of which have already been touched on, merit further comment: the tendency to borrow ideas (either ethical commonplaces or ideas for images) rather than decorative material, and the tendency to keep the loans well hidden—a practice which sets Jonson apart from most of his contemporaries. Both aspects suggest that to Jonson the classics were something other than raw material for allusion and a display of learning. Clearly there are occasions when a loan would be recognized by an educated spectator or reader, but Jonson seldom does anything to encourage such recognition, and although this diffidence may be part of his sense of writing for 'the few but fit' it is also indicative of a view of the classics as providing nourishment of a wider and richer kind than decorative or self-advertising usage could do. Jonson, it would seem from what we know of his early life, gained his classical education the hard way, and he would have been less than human if he had never shown pride in having got this education. But what is interesting, and much to Jonson's credit, is that in his writings themselves there is so little sign of this pride. Psychologically, what seems to have happened is that the role of public poet which Jonson was so keen to play led him to use the classics to buttress his analysis of society, to give the weight of massed authorities to the perceptions and beliefs of the individual man; and it seems to me that it is this sense of the poet's role as analyst/counsellor to society which decides the nature of Jonson's classicism. This is what I would substitute for Wilson's much more personalized perversion. It is not unreasonable to feel that Jonson may have depended more on his learning than other men did, because of his background and the effort of attaining that learning, and it is also not unreasonable to view the habit of borrowing as a sign of ultimate insecurity, uncertainty about his own creative powers. If we stress this point we discover a fine paradox, for Jonson's creative powers are often shown at their fullest when he is working with, or close to, classical material. But the final point is that if the root of the habit lies in uncertainty rather than arrogance (and the two are not necessarily antithetical) it remains true that the habit was turned to good use as a means of strengthening the poet in the social task to which he chose to devote his career. This social task and its context are to form my final chapter, but before turning to it I want to say a little about Jonson's reputation and about the theatricality of his drama.

Chapter 7

Reputation and Theatricality

Richard West, one of the contributors to *Jonsonus Virbius*, the volume published in 1638 to memorialize Jonson's death, wrote that

> Shakespeare may make griefe merry, Beaumonts stile
> Ravish and melt anger into a smile; . . .
> But thou exact'st our best houres industrie;
> We may reade them; we ought to studie thee . . .[1]

Shakespeare is associated with the arousing of emotions, while Jonson is a writer who should be studied. Behind this distinction there seems to lurk a feeling that Shakespeare is entertaining but not really suitable for serious attention, whereas Jonson is implicitly placed with the classics. There may also be a ghost of the idea that Shakespeare was a popular dramatist and Jonson more of a coterie taste, an idea which is given a more personal form in the famous comment attributed to Kemp in the Cambridge play *The Returne from Pernassus* (part two) which was acted at St John's College and printed in 1606:

O that Ben Jonson is a pestilent fellow, he brought up Horace giving the Poets a pill, but our fellow Shakespeare hath given him a purge that made him beray his credit.[2]

We shall return to the matter of Jonson and Shakespeare later, but for the moment I want to look at some aspects of Jonson's reputation in his lifetime, to see what sort of writer his contemporaries felt him to be—we shall find that contemporary response did much to fix the image of Jonson which has come down to us.

Jonson himself often claimed that his work was for a small judicious circle, or at least that only members of such a circle could judge what he wrote, and this exclusiveness is emphasized by a number of his contemporaries (who, incidentally, by stressing this appeal to a minority are—at least implicitly—claiming to be part of it), particularly when they are commending plays which were not popular successes. Thus Ev. B. (who is conjecturally identified as Edward Bolton by Herford and Simpson) says of the failure of *Sejanus*:

> . . . when I view'd the Peoples beastly rage,
> Bent to confound thy grave, and learned toile,
> That cost thee so much sweat, and so much oyle,
> My indignation I could hardly 'asswage . . .[3]

and Francis Beaumont, commenting on *Catiline*, makes a distinction which probably pleased Jonson:

> If thou had'st itch'd after the wild applause
> Of common people, and had'st made thy Lawes
> In writing, such, as catch'd at present voyce,
> I should commend the thing, but not thy choyse.
> But thou hast squar'd thy rules, by what is good;
> And art three Ages yet, from understood . . .[4]

T.R. (probably Jonson's friend Thomas Roe) provides a neat twist to this idea of exclusiveness in his commendation of a more successful play, *Volpone*, when he addresses the reader:

> If thou dost like it, well; it will imply
> Thou lik'st with judgement, or best company . . .[5]

—if you don't like the play the implications are obvious!

As Ev. B. and Beaumont indicate, this emphasis on judgment by minority is linked with the recognition of Jonson as a learned, painstaking writer who is concerned with the nature of art. So, rather clumsily, Thomas Bancroft praises Jonson's 'messe of Learning'[6] and, more gracefully, Aston Cockayne makes the obvious connection between the learning and Jonson's classicism:

> . . . great Jonson, he
> Who all the ancient wit of Italy
> And learned Greece (by his industrious Pen)
> Transplanted hath for his owne Countreymen . . .[7]

while Richard James sums up the interwoven strands of learning, care and classicism:

> Your rich Mosaique workes inled by arte
> And curious industrie with everie parte
> And choice of all ye Auncients . . .[8]

(James's phrase 'rich Mosaique workes' is genuinely revealing.)

Cockayne, when he refers to Jonson 'transplanting' the classics, touches on another important feature, and Jonson's function of anglicizing classical models and material is close to his position as arbiter of taste, the 'elaborate English Horace' as Sir Thomas Smith called him.[9] To men like these Jonson was admirable because he was regulating English literature, bringing discipline to the stage, and enriching our culture by adapting the classics. The fact that these tributes were designed to please Jonson does not rob them of all value: they *select* labour, concern for rules, and classical learning as worthy of praise, with no suggestion that Jonson is either plagiary or pedant.

However, the world of dedications (like that of epitaphs) is unreal or—at best—partisan, and the emphasis upon exclusiveness, cosy though it is, reminds us that Jonson was often embattled with authority, the public and other writers. If the commendations we have been looking at are seldom models of close critical analysis or intense response to Jonson's personality, neither do contemporary attacks on him often transcend personal abuse or laboured wit. Drummond's story about *Epicoene* which is tagged on, rather oddly, at the end of *Conversations* [10] adequately represents the latter, and we have seen something of the former in the nastiness of Alexander Gill.[11] The anonymous author of 'The Cuntrys Censure on Ben Johnsons New Inn' shares Gill's lack of generosity to the sick and weakening poet and his comments are very much *ad hominem*: Jonson is 'decaying Ben', 'steept In sack'; his muse is 'Crazye' and he is a 'pore Cracktbraine elfe'.[12] Jonson's behaviour over the *New Inn* fiasco had scarcely been a model of restraint and dignity, but he had a long and honourable record of literary achievement behind him, and even if he was often his own worst enemy in matters of personal and private relationships it is sad to see his enemies making no effort to confront his work. Those comments which do touch on his creative habits and talents are usually infiltrated with responses to his personality. This happens in Dekker's *Satiromastix*—mentioned in Chapter 1—and also in *The Returne from Pernassus* when Judicio refers to Jonson as 'The wittiest fellow of a Bricklayer in England' and Ingenioso comments:

A meere Empyrick, one that getts what he hath by observation, and makes onely nature privy to what he endites, so slow an Inventor, that he were better betake himselfe to his old trade of Bricklaying, a bould whorson, as confident now in making of a booke, as he was in times past in laying of a brick.[13]

Except for the suggestion here that Jonson was simply a recorder of 'nature' and the claim that he was a slow creator, there is little in the hostile comments on his work to indicate any coherent challenge to his methods on aesthetic grounds: the normal line of attack is directed at his personality and behaviour. But the contemporary record does include some serious efforts to come to terms with Jonson's achievement, and John Selden has some remarks which indicate such effort. He writes of 'my beloved friend that singular Poet M. Ben: Jonson, whose speciall Worth in Literature, accurate Judgment, and Performance (is) known only to that Few which are truly able to know him . . .' [14] What is interesting here is that Selden seems to recognize (although his syntax is ambiguous) that Jonson was not an easy character to understand, but he feels the effort is worth while and in this reminds us of the friendship communicated in poems by men like Sir John Roe and Francis Beaumont, and also of the more critical response of writers such as George Chapman and Thomas Carew.

Chapman's long poem on *Sejanus* [15] touches on a number of themes already mentioned, but it rises from the ruck because of the sense it communicates of a fellow artist who is aware of considerable affinity between himself and the man he is addressing. He feels that they share the same concern with morality—'we, that would with Vertue live secure, / Sustaine for her in every Vices anger'—and he writes to Jonson as his equal, concerned with such matters as the partnership of ignorance and moral wrong, the distrust of art when it is deceptive decoration, and the way in which poetry is abused and misunderstood. Later (in 1633 or 1634) Chapman wrote 'An Invective . . . against m^r Ben: Johnson',[16] which the Oxford editors describe as 'unpleasant'. It is certainly sarcastic and at times roughly satirical, but it is something more than the nasty attack of Gill. Jonson's relationship with Chapman was complicated and uneven, but Chapman's 'Invective' seems to me to contain some real concern for Jonson and it has a context (an anxiety about what constitutes good art and the function of the artist) which makes it other than merely a personal attack. Chapman seems to feel that Jonson's pride is likely to prevent him fulfilling himself creatively—and if I am right in sensing this concern it links Chapman's verses with the more measured criticism of Carew's poem, written as part of the *Now Inn* furore. Like Chapman, Carew is willing to chide Jonson, referring [17] to his 'immodest rage' and 'itch of prayse', but he understands the pressures on the older man and recognizes his past achievements even while facing (and trying to make him face) his decline:

> . . . yet 'tis true
> Thy commique Muse from the exalted line
> Toucht by thy Alchymist, doth since decline
> From that her Zenith . . .

Throughout his poem Carew is thinking as poet, friend and critic, and he is more generous than Owen Felltham was when the latter wrote on the same topic. Yet Felltham, rougher and less a Jonson-man than Carew, is no Gill. He will admit that Jonson had ability:

> 'Tis known you can do well,
> And that you do excell
> As a translator . . .[18]

but he baulks at Jonson's sensitivity to criticism:

> Yet if men vouch not things Apocryphal,
> You bellow, rave and spatter round your gall,

and he, like Chapman, sees aspects of personality which may damage Jonson's work:

> Leave then this humour vain . . .
> Where self-conceit and choler of the bloud
> Eclipse what else is good . . .

Even while Jonson was alive, then, his character and writings provoked a variety of response, and this is scarcely surprising when we think of the complexity and power of that character and these writings. There seems to have been general agreement as to what most characterized his work—learning, devotion to the classics, concern with standards—but there is also a sense of the personality informing, threatening to dominate, responses to the work, and men like Chapman and Carew seem to have felt that there was danger that Jonson himself would allow his pride and hot temper to damage his writing. One can certainly sense that Jonson's character must have made things difficult for even his best friends. One of these, the generous James Howell, gives us an anecdote which catches this nicely. Howell is writing to Sir James Hawkins:

I was invited yesternight to a solemne supper by B.J. where you were deeply remembred, there was good company, excellent chear, choice wines, and joviall wellcome; one thing interven'd which almost spoyl'd the relish of the rest, that B. began to engrosse all the discourse, to vapour extreamely of himselfe, and by villifying others to magnifie his owne muse; T. Ca. busd me in the eare, that though Ben had barreld up a great deale of knowledge, yet it seemes he had not read the *Ethiques*, which among other precepts of morality forbid self commendation . . . But for my part I am content to dispense with this Roman infirmity of B. now that time hath snowed upon his pericranium . . .[19]

The memorial volume *Jonsonus Virbius* (1638) need not detain us long. Although several competent poets (Beaumont, King, Waller,

Cartwright) contributed to it, the circumstances of such a volume scarcely encourage good critical writing and most of the poems simply repeat attitudes already touched on. It is, however, worth noticing the emphasis put upon Jonson as legislator; by James Clayton, for example, to whom Jonson is the man 'Who first reform'd our Stage with justest Lawes', or by Shackerley Marmion:

> He fram'd all minds, and did all passions stirre,
> And with a bridle guide the Theater.[20]

The obituarists also comment frequently upon the dead poet's concern with ethics. Falkland—with a touch of wish-fulfilment which Jonson might have smiled grimly at—tells us that spectators

> With thoughts and wils purg'd and amended rise,
> From th'Ethicke Lectures of his Comedies . . .

and Hawkins, with similar optimism, would have it that

> Thy Pen so on the stage doth personate,
> That ere men scarce begin to know, they hate
> The Vice presented, and there lessons learne,
> Virtue, from vicious Habits to discerne . . .[21]

Hawkins's lines—which describe in brief the view of art's function presented by Sidney's *Defence of Poesie*—reflect one of Jonson's main concerns accurately enough, but he had come to know the difference between aim and effect, so that the coincidence of the two in such lines is amiably glib.

The outlines which were to define most later writing on Ben Jonson were clear by the time of his death. He was seen as a careful writer who was concerned with ethical issues, with the need for standards in composition, with the artist's need to be learned—especially in the classics. At the same time criticism of the art tends to run close to response to the personality of the man, and here the evidence is that Jonson irritated and at times outraged both his public at large and his friends as well as his enemies. Much of what was written about him in the decades and centuries after his death was to be centred on, or strongly conditioned by, personality rather than the art itself. We have seen an extreme example of this in Chapter 1, with the remarkable statement by Charles Macklin, and we also saw there some reason to feel that even as distinguished a modern critic as Edmund Wilson could hardly see the art for the bulky personality. A lighter, better-tempered version occurs in the anonymous poem 'The Great Assises' (1645),[22] where Jonson is presented as

> the sturdy Keeper then
> Of the unhospitall Trophonian Den,
> . . .
> For sterne aspect, with Mars hee might compare,
> But by his belly, and his double chinne,
> Hee look'd like the old Hoste of a New Inne.
> . . . sowre Ben . . .
>
> And since the Tubbe of which he told the tale,
> By splitting, had deceived him of his ale;
> And since his New-Inne too had got a crack,
> He bids him take the Sugar loves, and sack,
> To make his lov'd Magnatick Lady glad,
> That still (for want of an applause) was sad.

Jonson, who in this poem is not among the judge/critics or poet/jurors but is relegated to the position of a middle-range court official, interests the author mainly because he can be presented as a comic character.

But Jonson continued to be seen as the main alternative or challenge to Shakespeare. Even in Jonson's lifetime Francis Beaumont was alluding to Shakespeare as a kind of model of what could be achieved by 'the dimme light of Nature' alone:

> . . . heere I would let slippe
> (If I had any in mee) schollershippe,
> And from all Learninge keepe these lines as [cl]eere
> As Shakespeares best are . . .[23]

In Beaumont's lines the Jonson = Art / Shakespeare = Nature formula is already accepted as established. It is a formula which echoes down the years, but the contexts in which it is used reflect various attitudes to the two writers. When Leonard Digges, for example, writes his poem 'Upon Master William Shakespeare' he refers to Shakespeare as 'the pattern of all wit' and as the example of 'Art without Art unparaleld as yet', going on to compare audience response to Shakespeare and Jonson:

> So have I seene, when Cesar would appeare,
> And on the Stage at halfe-sword perley were
> Brutus and Cassius: oh how the Audience
> Were ravish'd, with what wonder they went thence,
> When some new day they would not brook a line
> Of tedious (though well laboured) Catiline . . .[24]

Digges does not denigrate Jonson (or at least not directly) but feels that Shakespeare has an immediate and emotional appeal which Jonson lacks: his position is not dissimilar to West's but he sees the same things in a rather different perspective. This balanced contrast is commonplace for quite a long time and can be seen in Fuller's famous anecdote (in which Jonson is 'a Spanish great Gallion' and Shakespeare 'the English man of War, lesser in bulk, but lighter in sailing' [25]), in the lines of Margaret Cavendish which appear in the 'General Prologue to all my Playes', and in Flecknoe's *Short Discourse*, where Shakespeare's 'natural Vein' is set against Jonson's 'Gravity and ponderousness of Style'.[26] Often one detects a hint that the commentator secretly prefers the 'natural' Shakespeare but, formally at any rate, the scales are usually kept even, although Dryden admitted to loving Shakespeare while admiring (relatively cool word) Jonson, and Charles Gildon calls Shakespeare 'the greatest Poet that ever trod the Stage'.[27]

The extraordinary story of the assassination of Jonson's character —and thus of his literary reputation—has been summarized entertainingly and well by Jonas Barish [28] and I don't want to waste space in covering the ground again. As Barish says, during the eighteenth century, 'The well-authenticated tradition of Jonson's conviviality gave way to a fraudulent countermyth: that Jonson, throughout his life, harbored an envenomed dislike of Shakespeare . . .' and, 'The eighteenth-century critics . . . competed with each other in ascribing ignoble motives to Jonson. They charged him not only with parody but with plagiarism, with scurvy attacks on his fellow players, with a want of decency and decorum.' The point I want to make is that although Jonson's reputation among academics has slowly recovered since Gifford's glorious counterattack, to the point where in the last few decades his work is better understood, and appreciated with fewer nervous glances at Shakespeare, he is still honoured at a distance by many who enjoy not only Shakespeare but also the work of many other Elizabethan and Jacobean writers. One reason for this (and it is not the only reason) is that Jonson has not been given a fair run in the modern theatre, and so I want to use the rest of this chapter to look briefly at the question of his theatricality.

Of course it is not unknown for some of Jonson's plays to be produced on the contemporary stage: without thinking too hard I can recall Wolfit's *Volpone*, Nottingham Playhouse productions of *The Alchemist*, *Bartholomew Fair* and *The Devil is an Ass*, another version of the latter at Edinburgh and a student production of *Epicoene*. Doubtless there have been others which I have missed or simply forgotten, although it is also relevant to remember that a number of non-Shakespearean/non-Jonsonian plays have also been produced in recent years. There is even some reason to think that such productions are becoming more frequent—and Jonson may (or may not) benefit from this.

I don't for a moment want to be ungenerous towards the producers of these plays, but I do think that the situation I have outlined can only be seen in its proper perspective if we include Shakespeare, and as soon as we do this we should be led to ask questions about tradition; to ask, for example, whether any relevant non-Shakespearean play has a modern stage tradition comparable with any of Shakespeare's. Perhaps *Dr Faustus* has, and perhaps one or two of the others are produced as often as Shakespeare's *Henry VIII* (which is probably not wholly Shakespeare's anyway), but the situation is certainly very heavily weighted in Shakespeare's favour. Of course Shakespeare is incomparably our greatest dramatist, but there is a blatant fallacy in believing that because his finest work represents the greatest drama our culture has produced therefore everything he wrote deserves frequent revival, and that even his least impressive work is better than the best of Marlowe, Webster, 'Tourneur' and Jonson. There is such a thing as Shakespeare-tyranny and it has at least four adverse effects. It is incestuous in that producers sometimes seek frenetically for an 'original' approach to a Shakespeare play; it has prevented the growth of any theatrical tradition of presenting non-Shakespearean drama of the period; it has at times led producers of non-Shakespearean plays to underestimate the individuality of the dramatist with whom they are concerned, and to show a lack of confidence in the text they are presenting, as was clearly seen with the Nottingham Playhouse *Alchemist* (where the producer seemed convinced that Jonson's verbal activity had to be replaced by stage business) and with the Stratford *Revenger's Tragedy* (where the producer could not quite convince himself that the dramatist's blend of comedy and horror would work).

These difficulties are perhaps most acute when we are thinking of Jonson, because he is the most consistently unlike Shakespeare in dramatic method and the most important of his contemporaries: a Shakespeare-dominated tradition of producing Elizabethan and Jacobean plays cannot be adequate for a Jonson play, but even Jonson's finest plays are not produced often enough for a relevant tradition to be established.

It can, of course, be argued that this is a merely academic grumble because Jonson is simply not really theatrical, but this rapidly turns into a circular argument: is Jonson not produced more often because he is not theatrical, or is his theatricality in doubt because he is not produced more often?

One answer to this conundrum might emerge from looking back.

Jonson's plays were frequently produced up to the closing of the theatres, and Noyes [29] has shown that when the theatres reopened at the Restoration Jonson was again often acted. This is not perhaps surprising, partly because neo-classicism in the Restoration court would favour Jonson and partly because in the early years after the Restoration managers had to make extensive use of old scripts because of a shortage of usable contemporary material. But Noyes has also shown that several of Jonson's plays continued to hold the stage until toward the end of the eighteenth century: this is especially true of *Every Man in his Humour*, *Volpone* and *The Alchemist*, but also applies to *Epicoene*, *Sejanus* and even *Catiline*. Yet this is only evidence that for a long time in the past Jonson was considered theatrical, and the almost complete absence of nineteenth-century productions might be taken as indicating that his theatrical inadequacy was then finally and permanently exposed. But this won't carry much weight if we remember the general level of nineteenth-century dramatic achievement and taste and if we also recall the extraordinary campaign of vilification of Jonson as allegedly an envious ingrate towards Shakespeare, a campaign which built up in the eighteenth century and produced some fine editorial infighting in the nineteenth. (Readers with a taste for such fireworks are referred to the splendid commentary in Gifford's edition of Jonson.) But, at best, this looking back is inconclusive: it may prompt us to consider the possibility that Jonson is theatrically viable now, but it doesn't prove this. The same is true of evidence such as Dryden's examen of *Epicoene* and Coleridge's comments on *The Alchemist*, although Dryden's long practical experience of the professional theatre means that his response should command respect in this context. In fact, however, the lack of a Jonson tradition in the modern theatre means that one cannot *prove* that such a tradition can or should be established. Beyond a certain point one can only use one's general theatrical experience to supplement imagination, and offer some opinions out of the amalgam.

I suppose that in so far as there is a view of Jonson in terms of putative production it is that he had a talent for comic structures and for acute observation of human absurdities, and that this talent was most fully realized in *The Alchemist* and *Epicoene*. On this view *Volpone* and *Bartholomew Fair* are seen as less fully successful, the former because it is too bleak, the latter because its structure is less obviously satisfactory. The tragedies scarcely get thought of at all, while the early comedies (after a promising start with *Every Man in his Humour*) are seen as progressively hag-ridden by theory and the later ones by that most evasive of qualities, 'decline of creative powers'. The masques, of course, are never taken into account. It is interesting that the stress on structural ability and on observation of folly reflects views which are in some ways old-fashioned: Jonson's ability to organize material has seldom been in question and, in a rather vague way, can be tied in with his reputation as a classicist; while the 'observer of human folly' aspect can be made to fit both with the nineteenth-century idea of Jonson as thwarted romantic and with the bugbear of the theory of humours (basically, the idea that Jonson's characters each represent an individual 'humour'—trait of character or affectation: an idea which has done considerable harm to Jonsonian criticism).

I am not suggesting that these factors are unimportant, but I do think that the emphasis that has been given to them has made it difficult for producers (and often critics) to make the most of what really is important in Jonson's work. So I want to look, at this point, at examples of Jonson's writing which are thoroughly out of contact with traditional ideas about what might be stageable.

Cynthia's Revels and *Poetaster* are two serious attempts to find ways of making moral analysis of society effective. As indicated above the usual view is that the plays are failures; that Jonson moved away from the vitality of *Every Man in his Humour* towards increasingly clogged and static anti-drama; and that he was only saved from dramatic self-immolation because he had enough sense to accept (not very gracefully) public repudiation of these experiments. But it is not clear that the plays were in fact repudiated,[30] and our view of *Cynthia's Revels* and *Poetaster* tends to be distorted by preconceptions about what Elizabethan audiences wanted and about what effective drama is, as well as by blurring of ideas about the audiences of public theatres with those of private ones and by our limited knowledge of the private companies and their acting methods. Renewed academic interest in Jonson's masques, together with the work of such scholars as Frances Yates and Roy Strong, has begun to break up some prejudices and preconceptions about court entertainments, while other scholars have improved our understanding of the relationship between public and private theatres and of their contact with the court. Such work provides the background and justification for looking again at the sort of drama Jonson provides in *Cynthia's Revels* and *Poetaster*.

It would be helpful to know exactly what the acting texts of these plays were, but even if we assume that both were slimmer in production than in printed versions it remains true that they are very verbal plays. Yet it is a mistake to assume that long speeches are necessarily undramatic (Beckett, for one, has called that cliché into question) or that 'drama' must mean 'filled with action and/or internal psychological tension'. I want to make three points here about theatricality in *Cynthia's Revels*. First, there is evidence that Jonson made capital of his child actors. I have already claimed [31] that the Induction is lively and communicates a real sense of childish behaviour—but this is not an isolated effect. The children squabble about which of them should provide the Prologue, and when this is finally delivered it seems to me that although Jonson's statement of purpose is wholly serious it is given a comic tinge by coming from an actor who has just been seen involved in the quarrel and general high spirits of the Induction. Aspects of Act I are also affected by memories of the Induction: the satire of self-loving fools is strengthened by the actors being 'diminutives' and underscored by the fact that the behaviour of these characters is not dissimilar to that of the children in the Induction. There are moments later in the play where this kind of link again seems part of Jonson's purpose, an obvious instance coming at the opening of Act II, when Mercury says to Cupid 'since we are turn'd cracks, let's studie to be like cracks'.[32] The word was used in the Induction when the third child called the second 'crack' (glossed by Gifford as 'a sprightly forward boy' [33]). The joke of a child actor playing an adult speaking of behaving like a child is given an additional twist, since the addressee is Cupid, a child actor playing the part of a child god noted for his 'forward' behaviour.

Secondly, in speaking of plays such as this we are (despite the renovatory work mentioned above) still handicapped by having virtually no live contact with masque-like drama, and so tend to read the play 'flat', as if only the words existed, whereas spectacle—in the sense of costume, formal grouping and movement—can produce a type of drama in which the patterned and highly artificial acting out of an emblematic sequence can create its own sort of satisfaction. We may get a glimpse of the possibilities of this in plays for which we do have a live tradition—in the casket scene of *The Merchant of Venice*, the statue scene at the end of *A Winter's Tale* and in much of *The Tempest*. Or we might find modern analogues in films like *Last Year at Marienbad*, with its extremely enigmatic formal patterning. How effective *Cynthia's Revels* could be on stage is impossible to imagine without sympathetic test-productions, but it is obvious that it operates through formal groupings which change, shape and reshape, with the central symbol of the fountain of self-love providing a constant focus and the suggested power of Cynthia/Elizabeth a formal counterpull. Ballet retains the sort of formal articulation which is perhaps closer than any other live tradition to the sort of effect *Cynthia's Revels* would make on stage: we should at least not dismiss the play out of hand for not being like *Volpone* or *The White Devil*. Thirdly, it is easy to overstate the play's rigidity, particularly if we are reading the folio text with its much enlarged fifth act. Even without considering the animation which production could properly add it is worth noticing that Jonson is careful to provide some variety of rhythm and manner. We have, for example, by the end of Act I, had four contrasting movements: the childish humour of the Induction; the witty exchanges of Cupid and Mercury; the elegiac-didactic Echo episode, with its lovely song 'Slow, slow, fresh fount'; and the satiric self-exposure centred on Amorphus and Asotus, which is crossed with commentary from Crites. There are, of course, long passages of direct comment, but these are usually framed by episodes of folly in action and the writing is normally far from monotonous. Jonson is also good at using dialogue to convey, with sharpness and economy, his sense of the petty backbiting of his fools, as when Phantaste and her companions 'run over' the male characters.[34]

This is not to claim that *Cynthia's Revels* has more plot-interest than is normally admitted, nor that its methods are less formal than earlier remarks suggest. The basic method is that of tableaux, but the pictures are varied and often animated, and this is true even of scenes which are longer than their point requires. The long challenge scene in the folio Act IV, for example, is certainly over-extended, but it is also amusing, as are the word-games of Acts IV and V. Also, Jonson continues to use the framing devices of *Every Man out of his Humour* to provide varied perspectives. Thus the backbiting already mentioned is used partly to place the characters being attacked and partly to reveal the attackers, while the use of Crites, Arete and Cynthia as commentator/judges does not exclude situations in which they themselves are commented upon, although such situations are, of course, not meant in this case to throw doubt upon their credentials as judges. *Cynthia's Revels*, in fact, strikes me as an unusual play rather than as a dramatically turgid one, and its limitations spring less from the methods Jonson uses than from the shallowness of his vision in this case. Much of the satirical detail is in itself acute and funny (the Palinode, for example, is an amusing, mildly sacrilegious parody), but the play as a whole lacks resonance and depth. Jonson can see folly very clearly but what emerges is his irritation at its surface manifestations as such: there is not yet the sense of the profound dangers for society which Jonson was to show in the later plays, and so points seem laboured because they have not been made to seem important; they signify only their local selves. But this does not prove that there was anything fundamentally wrong with the method—and it is a mistake to assume that Jonson abandoned the formal basis seen in this play when he came to write his finest ones.

Poetaster is known mainly as a document in the so-called War of the Theatres, and a natural curiosity about playing literary detectives in the context of the quarrel between Marston and Dekker, on the one hand, and Jonson on the other, has led to a strong tendency to concentrate upon the figures of Horace, Crispinus and Demetrius, a tendency which distorts the proportions and balance of the play as a whole. It is surprising how much more lively and impressive *Poetaster* is if we approach it without preconceptions and with an open mind as to what Jonson may be trying to do. One result of such an approach is that we notice that the movement towards highly formalized drama in *Every Man out of his Humour* and *Cynthia's Revels* begins to give way to a blend which makes the play more fluid in method and more oblique in its handling of audience response.

If we look first of all at Acts I and II we can concentrate upon what kind of play Jonson is trying to write, because the question of the Marston/Dekker/Jonson quarrel scarcely arises (which in itself suggests that to treat the play merely as personal satire may be too narrow an approach). Because Ovid is a poet—and particularly because of his famous eulogy of poetry ('O, sacred poesie, thou spirit of artes' [35])—it is often assumed that the character is to be approved of, whereas it seems to me that in the early part of his play Jonson adopts a distinctly ambiguous attitude, not only to Ovid but also to Gallus and Tibullus. I should hesitate to suggest that we are meant to take Ovid senior as a direct adverse criticism of his poet-son, but the father's concern, although it comes over as fussy and exaggerated, none the less has some weight (reminiscent of Lorenzo in the quarto *Every Man in his Humour*) and this is increased by the impact of Ovid junior's erratic behaviour, his fixation on love and the 'ecstatic' element in his attitude to poetry. The impression is that poet-Ovid's personality is immature: he may have the right seeds in him (in the play's terms this means the potential of Horace and Virgil) but he is, as yet, irresponsible and unreliable, an impression confirmed in the second act.

Jonson begins this by establishing, with considerable care and precision, the folly of Albius and Chloe and then brings Ovid back on stage, together with the other poets of his group—Gallus, Tibullus and Propertius. Propertius stands rather aside from the others and his grief over the death of his mistress may be meant as a comment upon the folly of poetic love, but the main point here is that the other poets treat Chloe with a gallantry which suggests that they fail completely to see her lack of substance: there is no indication in the text that remarks such as Ovid's 'I see, even in her lookes, gentrie, and generall worthinesse' and Tibullus' 'I have not seene a more certaine character of an excellent disposition' [36] are to be taken ironically: Ovid and Tibullus are not just playing the game of love but are doing so in relation to a person whom we know to be unworthy of attention and whose behaviour should make them as aware of this as we are, if (that is) they were able to see beyond the surface conventions of the game.

So up to this point in the play it is possible to argue that Jonson is concerned to set up an inquiry into the nature of poetry, at least in some of its forms, and that his handling of this inquiry is deft and nicely balanced. The humour up to this point is certainly neither laboured nor diffuse : Hermogenes, for example, is a good illustration of Jonson giving a minor character comic life by a few verbal touches, while his control over his material is shown on other levels also, in the way in which Albius and Choe are made to reveal their personalities through their speech mannerisms and in the adroitness with which Jonson works in the song 'If I freely may discover' to make use of the musical talents of his young actors. As with *Every Man out of his Humour* and *Cynthia's Revels* there is little sense that plot is going to be important, but the opening acts of *Poetaster* show a gain in tightness : the variety and vitality of the writing suggest that the dramatist of *Every Man in his Humour* is closer to hand than is usually realized.

The Horace/Crispinus meeting which opens Act III has been discussed in detail elsewhere, but it is worth mentioning here that—read without preconceptions—it fits quite well into the way the play has been developing up to this point : that is, it reads as if Jonson is writing a comedy in which no one is exempt from humorous glances and which is concerned to examine social behaviour and the pretensions of poetry coolly but neither bitterly nor with personal vindictiveness. As the act proceeds personal satire of Crispinus and Demetrius becomes more obvious but the vitality of Tucca keeps the play lively and the tone is neither savage nor complacent, although the balance is, of course, altered if we take account of the Dialogue between Horace and Trebatius which, in the folio, Jonson added to conclude the act (but which seems not to have been performed). In the last two acts things do begin to go wrong, but even there Jonson achieves admirable effects. For example, he makes good use of Tucca's blunt manner to 'place' Chloe : to him she is 'punke' and 'cockatrice' [37]—the language is authentic Tucca but has a brutal accuracy in undercutting and defining what Chloe's aspirations really mean. Similarly Tucca is given one or two remarks about Horace which throw a comic light on that figure, and I think that Tucca's real (if unworthy) vitality is such that these remarks work comically—they are not extensions of the envy of Demetrius and Crispinus. The purging of the latter is cruel comedy, but it is funny and its edge seems less spiteful if we assume that performance by child actors could give the whole set-up of the trial scene a mildly parodic tone.

Too much stress has often been put upon the Dialogue and Apologetical Dialogue and the play has been further distorted by the attention paid to the personal element, at the expense of characters like Tucca and Lupus. In many ways *Poetaster* has a lightness of touch and economy of method which make it less necessary to defend it in terms of a special kind of formal drama. But in the final analysis the play certainly falls apart: not because Jonson is failing to find a defensible theatrical form, but because in two important instances he seems to have lost his grip on his overall design. It is possible to argue that Ovid deserves his banishment for his misuse of poetry and for his affair with Julia, but the specified offence is his involvement in the gods-game. Various questions arise: whose view of the game are we to take—the severe one of Caesar or the more lenient one of Horace? [38] If Ovid is justly banished how are we to respond to his long farewell scene with Julia? Is his view of what he is to lose to be seen as a sign that his eyes are now open, or is he still blinded by show? If, as Caesar feels, the gods-game is the major offence, why are Gallus and Tibullus let off so easily? [39] They are rebuked, but Caesar sees potential good in them and so admits them to his inner circle— yet we have seen nothing to suggest that they are significantly superior to Ovid. There is the same blurring with Horace: he is more of an agent than is usually realized, clearly less the representa- tive of the true poet than Virgil, and some humour is directed at him —but the Horace who is admired by Caesar is hard to reconcile with the figure who is routed by Crispinus in Act III.

It is therefore difficult to claim that *Poetaster* is a coherent critique of true and false views of poetry, and the play's social analysis is again witty rather than deep. But there are clear indications that Jonson realized that the complex machinery of formal analysis worked out in the two previous comedies was overloading the signifi- cance of the analysis itself (which is quite different from saying that the method was of itself misbegotten). *Poetaster* fails because of weak- nesses of focus, but much of the play is confident without being either rigid or arrogant—and much of it remains distinctly amusing.

But, of course, this is highly speculative, for whatever one may think of the theatrical possibilities of plays like *Cynthia's Revels* and *Poetaster*, the chances of their getting a major production are, to put it mildly, slim, and the same is true of the masques, even though the best of these are extremely beautiful and often also contain comedy of a very high order. Obviously it is easier to retreat to plays like *The Alchemist* and *Epicoene*, which are superbly articulated to provoke the laughter which comes from complex plotting controlled by masterly feeling for theatrical rhythm and timing: obvious examples are the opening scene of *The Alchemist* and the way in which Jonson organizes the plot-strands of *Epicoene* to create the maximum cumu- lative torment for Morose. Such quality of timing and rhythm should provide a strong attraction for producers and actors and such tests of their craft can produce great amusement for an audience—and this is without mentioning the linguistic richness of the plays or the opportunities they offer to good character actors.

It is easy to work outwards from emphasis on the comedy-as-entertainment potential of these two plays to make similar claims for several other of Jonson's comedies. *Every Man in his Humour* is a good example of a well-handled intrigue plot, while both *The Devil is an Ass* and *The Staple of News*—although they lack the firmness of structure and sharpness of focus of the greatest of Jonson's comedies and both need trimming for production—contain fine comic passages and characters (and indeed *The Devil is an Ass* has worked well on the stage at least twice in the last decade). *Bartholomew Fair* is a trickier problem. At first sight its structure looks looser than that of *The Alchemist* or *Epicoene*, but the richness and range of its content mask what is in fact another tightly organized artefact, with a firm controlling vision, and this control, abetted by a remarkable variety of fine acting parts (how can Ursula and Overdo *not* be part of the great tradition of English comic characters?) should challenge producers more often than it has : it would repay them.

Yet, in the end, I do not want to base my claims for Jonson's theatricality upon any simple statement of their laughter-potential, for it could be argued that such a statement admits that his plays make good once-off theatre and that if they became again established in our classic repertoire (in so far as we have one) it would be by stressing their superficial theatricality while leaving most of Jonson's artistic originality and vision back in the study. The sort of theatrical tradition which I should wish to see established for Jonson would be one which released his comedy without losing his bite, and this would best be achieved by investigating the stage potential of two other plays—*Volpone* and *Sejanus*. Critic after modern critic has pointed to the 'blackness' of the comedy in *Volpone*, and some can even be caught using other words with a strong twentieth-century ring ('absurd', 'alienation'), so it seems odd that a comedy which has such strong affinities of mood and tone with modern black comedy and the Theatre of the Absurd has not become a regular part of the theatre tradition of the past twenty years. It is true that the rhythm of *Volpone* does not have the initial speed of *The Alchemist*, but the more deliberate and sombre establishing of the vicious world of the play creates a threatening theatrical depth which, when allied with the force of Volpone and Mosca, the ambiguities of the Avocatori and the enforced weakness of Celia and Bonario, produces a world which is thoroughly modern in its evocation of corruption, moral uncertainty and loss of positive values.

Sejanus probably seems an almost insane suggestion, but it is at once less so if we can bring ourselves to contemplate the possibility that there might be valid ways of treating Roman history other than those of *Julius Caesar* and *Antony and Cleopatra*. *Sejanus* shares the bleakness of *Volpone* and defies any idea that tragedy must hold out hope. Without the comic filter of *Volpone* its vision is crushingly depressing, its world one of splintered virtue and cyclic evil. Production would have to realize this vision, would have to recognize the way in which Jonson works between violent action and sardonic or bewildered commentary, and would have to create the intensifying atmosphere of corruption, of lights going out, which accumulates, first around Sejanus and then through our growing awareness of Tiberius. And anyone who thinks that a scene dominated by words cannot be dramatic need only make a genuine attempt to imagine the potential stage impact of the great Senate scene.

The establishment of these two plays in my hypothetical stage tradition for Jonson could create the climate in which the others could be staged in a way which would enrich our theatre as well as making an audience laugh. For Jonson was, at his best, a great and original manipulator of audiences, as I have argued earlier. We are made to laugh with Subtle and Face of *The Alchemist* as they outwit the gulls and the would-be-exposer Surly, but we are not allowed to forget that this alliance of ours with Subtle and Face is at the expense of the harmless as well as the dangerous; that it is ultimately parasitic upon weakness; that Surly is basically right. Yet we don't like him, and when Lovewit arrives we expect him to be the exposer who will comfort us by arranging punishment and comic harmony. But Lovewit only does this by joining the world of the play—and in so far as he represents us we are left with the uncomfortable feeling that we can only have harmony by joining a world of gulls and gullers. In *Bartholomew Fair* the treatment of audience is, if anything, still more subtly subversive of comic norms, but the final position is much the same—we are left feeling distinctly compromised, thoroughly uneasy about our status as human beings.

In the various modes of Jonson's plays there is always this exploration of what is, finally, doubt about the possibility of human communication and uncertainty as to whether life has meaning at anything above animal level. The greatness of his drama comes from Jonson's reluctance (he being basically a strong moralist) to admit the disturbing possibility that his doubts and uncertainties may be justified. It is a greatness which has its individuality, but which has affinities with such great moderns as Zola, Sartre and Beckett (as well as with the visions of lesser men such as Pinter and Stoppard) and which, I believe, can work powerfully on the modern stage.

Jonson and Society

I started this book by speaking of Jonson as one of the great characters of English literature, but—granted this—it is surprising that relatively little real investigation of his connections with the society and age to which he belonged has been done. There has been biographical comment upon various aspects of his life, some of which has risen above the charming inadequacy of the summary in *Chambers' Cyclopaedia*, where we are told that, 'Inured to hardships and to a free, boisterous life in his early days, Jonson contracted a marked roughness of manner and habits of intemperance . . .' [1] There has been some discussion of Jonson as social critic, but this has usually concentrated upon his analysis of particular vices and follies in the context of the history of satire rather than of the early decades of the seventeenth century itself. It is only Professor Knights who has made a real effort [2] to examine Jonson in relation to major social and economic changes, and even Knights restricts himself to selected plays and a limited historical perspective. Although Jonson is widely seen as preoccupied with ethical issues there has been an odd reluctance to look at this preoccupation in an historical light and to see where Jonson's account of society in an ethical context places him in relation to that society, something which is particularly important since it is obvious that Jonson's artistic concern was very much with the welfare of man in society, specifically in Jacobean society.

Considerable attention has of course been paid to Jonson's 'realism', which has often been seen as a force operating to mitigate the blight of his didacticism and classicism. The strength and range of his command of English are usually admitted, as is his use of local detail, whether in the sense of local colour or of technical detail appropriate to the particular material he is working on. This realistic concern has various extensions. One of these is Jonson's interest in articulating and manipulating the links between play or masque and audience so as to make art seem an extension of nature and nature an expansion of art, an interest perhaps most fully worked out in the masques, where the form itself depends upon some merging of performer with audience—we have seen something of how complex Jonson's exploitation of this merging can be. Another clear implication of Jonson's mastery of idiom is that he was deeply interested in the society to which he belonged.

To say this is partly only to state the obvious: Jonson is very much an urban writer (like many of his contemporaries) and he lived an active life, marked (as we have seen) by frequent clashes with authority in its various forms,[3] so that it is possible to take evidence from his life, from *Conversations*, plays, masques and poems, and to create a picture of Jonson as a rough, aggressive, 'involved' writer whose strength lay chiefly in accurate recording of how people spoke and acted during his lifetime—the view, in fact, taken of him in *The Returne from Pernassus*.[4] But such a picture, superficially plausible, is—because incomplete—distorted and misleading.

One reason why this is so is that to concentrate upon this Jonsonian realism may suggest that he had something of the 'scientific' approach to art which Zola claimed,[5] but mercifully could not carry fully into practice (Zola, incidentally, once adapted *Volpone*), or else the finally inartistic accumulation of information which makes and mars Defoe's work. Either suggestion would be misleading because the 'realistic' Jonson can only be shorn from the ethical and didactic Jonson if we are willing to throw away a very large part of his achievement; and such a shearing is not only unnecessary but blinds us to the individuality of Jonson and his work. In this chapter, therefore, I want to outline where Jonson stands in relation to his society and why his stance is instructive and important; this requires us to remember the types of realism mentioned above, but it goes beyond them. The use of realistic language, of local detail and of sophisticated manipulation of audiences is undeniably there in Jonson's work, and is vital to an understanding of it, but needs to be seen in the context of Jonson's overall concerns about society rather than as a phenomenon in its own right.

This means, in effect, that the starting point for any discussion of Jonson's relationship with society has to be recognition that he works outwards from a set of fixed beliefs about what man should be able to achieve, both individually and socially, and that these fixed beliefs lie behind even Jonson's most distressed questioning of their viability. He may doubt that man can or will learn the lessons he wishes to teach, but he does not doubt that the lessons are necessary to a fulfilled life for both individual and state. But Jonson's ideals are not pragmatically based in any normal sense: instead of being assembled from patient observation and analysis of how contemporary man actually behaves, they are the codification of the 'best thoughts' or wishes of past centuries.[6] This suggests two things—that Jonson believed that man was essentially the same whatever culture he came from or whatever point in time, and that his analysis of contemporary society will be in terms of ideals derived from time past. Neither suggestion makes it very likely that Jonson's art will be flexible in its response to social change: if change is towards the ideals he holds it can be welcomed, but if it is away from these ideals it will be condemned. In fact there is a very strong bias in Jonson's art against welcoming change, and this emerges, of course, as the strong satirical element in his work. As a satirist working from a clearly defined positive moral position Jonson is acutely aware of deviations from that position, and it is the clarity and power of the positive position which give Jonson's best satire more focus than that of men like Marston and Hall.[7] Politically Jonson's ideal is of a responsible hierarchy. Such an ideal, of course, depends upon belief that some men are born with greater ability to govern than others and that this ability is closely linked with social status. But it also stresses the importance of government as the art of fostering the common good—it is a paternalistic view, but we shall never understand Jonson unless we are willing to suspend our automatic sneer at the word 'paternal'. Because of this concept of responsible hierarchy Jonson fears both tyranny and democracy: the former because it is socially irresponsible and the latter because it gives power to people who cannot know how to use it for a common good which includes them.

Immediately, though, any sense that this position was one of unthinking acceptance by Jonson of a traditional view of society has to be checked, and the easiest way of providing the necessary check is by drawing attention to the need felt by Jonson—particularly in *Discoveries* and *Sejanus*—to attend to what Machiavelli is saying (instead of merely turning him into a figure to frighten babies with) and the need to rebut him. His intelligence and integrity force him to try to understand the Italian, while his sense of what society could be like—under certain circumstances—led him to animate a Machiavellian world in *Sejanus*, and his belief that only through full acceptance of hierarchic ideals could social fulfilment come meant that he continues throughout his career to labour to present an alternative to the world of *The Prince*.[8]

If we glance at another, rather more specific, theme of Jonson's art we see the same process of mind. It has often been noted that Jonson was anti-puritan, and his dislike of puritans is often linked with the fact that many of them were hostile to the stage. Puritans, in Jonson's art, are often presented as paradigms of hypocrisy. This vice, of course, is a common target of satire (Jonson was not the discoverer of the gap between appearance and reality) but is of particular concern to Jonson because his whole vision of what society should be depends upon men knowing themselves and being open to others: society is only possible, in any meaningful sense, if men co-operate, and they cannot do this unless they are honest with themselves and in their relationships. But Jonson's persistent satirizing of puritans has, I think, deeper roots than this. Jonson caricatures puritanism in a way in which he does not caricature Machiavelli, and this happens because he fears puritanism even more than he fears the ideas of Machiavelli. There is little evidence that Jonson allowed himself to contemplate the virtues of puritan thought, even though he claims to have been interested in theology [9] and was sufficiently religiously minded to be stubborn about his own religious practices. It is fair to say that Jonson was pretty blind to the goodness in puritanism and individual puritans, and there are probably a number of contributory reasons, but the one which seems to me the most important is that puritanism would seem to Jonson hostile to the hierarchical organization of society which he considered essential to social health. The puritan emphasis upon the individual's right to interpret scripture was potentially anarchic (although dialectically not necessarily so) and this anarchy would affect State as well as Church, since—broadly speaking—puritan thinking accepted no division of the two.[10] Oddly, both Jonson and puritan thinkers place considerable emphasis upon self-analysis, but for the former such analysis is ultimately necessary for the maintenance of a particular social order. You analyse yourself in order to maximize your responsible contribution to the state, and although it is possible to read puritan emphasis upon self-scrutiny in a similar way the results—to a mind like Jonson's—would be too horrible to contemplate, for the puritan impulse was to call into question the whole hierarchical structure of established Catholic Church and State. We may feel strongly that Jonson's refusal to show generosity to puritan thought is a mark of inflexibility and of blindness to the possible benefits of change. This may be true, but what is important at the moment is to recognize that the fundamental reason for Jonson's caricature of puritanism was probably fear, and to note that from Jonson's angle of vision events were to prove his fear justified.

But although Jonson's use of self-analysis is ultimately for different purposes than those of puritan self-scrutiny it remains true that his examination of society is conducted in terms of the individual good man as outlined in Chapter 2, a figure marked by self-knowledge and humane reason. Because Jonson has a clear vision of the good man and—by extension—of the good state his satire can be very acute (the terms which define his attacks being seldom in doubt) and this satire, however local it may at first seem, is always relevant to issues beyond the purely particular. A key word is irresponsibility, Jonson being much concerned with the sort of aspiration which is both a betrayal of self and of the social good, with confusion of roles, denial of duties, the elevation of appearance at the expense of inner truth. Behind all this there lies the kind of conservatism innate in a satirical outlook, a conservatism based on fear of change. Jonson was too intelligent and too sensitive to shamble through his life happily believing that all was well in the worlds of Elizabeth, James and Charles: the very clarity of his vision of what should be made him extremely aware of what was, and of differences between the two. But Jonson seems to have felt that what was—at least on the national scale—was modelled on what should be, and that reform (pressingly necessary) depended upon men stripping themselves of new-fangled ideas and opening themselves to the truths which would render the actual a model of the ideal. This is again conservative (in the sense that the ideals are substantially models from the past) but we can only regard Jonson's responses to society as simply programmatic if we ignore the tensions within his work: he can create pictures of a world where all seems well and he can also create pictures of a world at breaking-point. But we have to realize that both sets of pictures are versions of, or selections from, reality and we have—if we want to do justice to Jonson—to relate the two sets. Beyond this we also have to recognize that the pictures are often less simple than they seem, that there are often tensions within individual works which make relating pictures of different emphasis a complicated business, and that Jonson's work is best seen as a continuing struggle to come to terms with the gaps between what his ideals tell us about the society he wished to see and what his sensitivity to what was actually going on indicated about what society really was or was becoming. It is this tension which makes Jonson's relationship to his society so interesting.

This is not the case because of anything idiosyncratic about Jonson's beliefs. I have argued elsewhere [11] that the various strands which go to make up Jonson's ethic are largely commonplaces of native, as well as classical thought. The objects of his satire are very often the same as those of the formal satirists of the 1590s; the concerns of his social comedies are usually similar to those of Middleton and Massinger; his emphasis upon degree and responsibility is no more conservative than Shakespeare's; his ethical positives—humaneness, generosity, honesty—are secular equivalents to the religious emphases of George Herbert. Jonson is a conservative in ethical attitudes—but who, in this period, was not? There were, of course, creative writers who were anything but conservative in their aesthetic positions—but in this area Jonson was one of the chief revolutionaries. Ethically, however, his worlds are at base defined by much the same positions as those of Chapman, Webster and the author of *The Revenger's Tragedy.* If we look for contemporaries who took a positive view of change we can get little further than the intermittent and often muddled outbursts of Marlowe and the complex inner world of John Donne.

Yet Jonson does stand out as the most awkwardly challenging of Jacobean writers in relation to the history of the decades which lead up to the Civil War. There are various reasons for this: his close contact with the court for a long period means that he is in some ways and at some times apparently an establishment voice; his ethic is clearer and more coherent than that of most of his fellows (and is insisted on more); his position amounts to a philosophy, in the sense that it accounts for all aspects of human life (again the difference from Shakespeare strikes one, it being impossible to speak of Shakespeare as having a philosophy); his anxiety about man and society is more persistently and directly located in the world around him than the anxieties of writers like Middleton and Massinger (whose 'realism' seems to me to be pretty superficial). This last point is particularly important. There is no reason to believe that Jonson's pessimism (when he was pessimistic) was more deeply rooted in his nature than the pessimism of Shakespeare or Webster. But Jonson is unusual in expressing his pessimism in comedies firmly located in contemporary London, and the pessimistic elements of civic comedy in writers like Middleton and Massinger seem comparatively superficial because the realistic dimension which conveys their pessimism does not seem to be connected with any body of firmly held ethical beliefs about, and desires for, man and society, such as we find implied in *The Alchemist* and *Bartholomew Fair.*

The poles of Jonson's art, perhaps, are ethics and realism, and even if the two are not antithetical it is at least likely that they will create tensions within the art itself (let alone within the artist). Jonson's social ethic is basically simple and traditional. Society is hierarchical: the monarch is supreme (under God) and is supported by the nobility, to whom he delegates local power and to whom he turns for advice. Below the nobility are further ranks, each with its own function in the state. The system, paradoxically, is both static and dynamic—static in that changes in the social order are theoretically unthinkable; dynamic in that the stasis can only be maintained if there is a constant flow of mutual responsibility. The monarch has great power but also the burden of total responsibility for the welfare of the commonwealth. At the other extreme the peasant has 'feudal' duties and severely circumscribed freedom, but he also has (in theory) rights and fosterage, and this mixture of privilege and duty applies to everyone in society. If this concept of mutual responsibility is actualized, hierarchy will work, and everyone will be sustained, everyone will be receiving as well as giving. Psychologically, the strength of the concept is that this hierarchy is clearly defined and hence comforting—particularly if the alternative seems to be anarchy. Granted the idea of mutual concern, it becomes in everyone's interest to maintain hierarchy and to ensure that he or she gives as well as receives, because the two are part of the same process and safety depends upon the process being maintained. An obvious corollary of the hierarchical idea is that place becomes vitally important: men must 'know their place', both in the sense of knowing what it is and of knowing how important it is for society and themselves that they remain in it, fulfilling its responsibilities and accepting its benefits. In theory no one in his right senses will seek to change his place because that will cause a gap in the vertical structure, and in the consequent collapse he will suffer as much as anyone.

All this is commonplace, but basically it is what Jonson seems to have believed and to have accepted in common with most of his contemporaries: it was, at least, the starting point of social thinking. But if tension means anything in Jonson—and if it doesn't I've wasted my time—we have to accept that this body of belief was real to him and important. The shades of doubt and admissions of other truths in the masques, for example, can best be understood if we accept that a play like *Sejanus* was written as a genuinely felt discussion of the nature of authority. The very nature of the hierarchical model puts the greatest pressure upon the king and his nobility: Jonson's conviction that that model was the best one possible accounts not only for those poems and masques which may seem sycophantic but also for the effort in a number of the *Epigrammes*, in several of the masques, and in poems as famous as 'To Penshurst' to demonstrate the possibility of achieving virtue in reality. It also explains—as soon as we take the word 'conviction' seriously—the distress behind Jonson's satire. The failures of Lovewit and Winwife are not comic in the manner of the follies of third-rate imitations of Chaplin: they are absurd, in the modern theatrical sense of the word, because they represent the abnegation of responsibility which prefigures exactly the collapse of the hierarchical ideal in the decades of and before the Civil War, a collapse which, as we shall see, was more real than apparent. Authority, as represented by such figures, and, in a more extreme fashion, by Mammon and Overdo, has lost sight of the responsibility which Jonson felt vital to social health, and it is this which unleashes the forces of stupidity and petty but socially enervating vice—forces which are germane with the brutal inhumanity of *Volpone* and *Sejanus*. This inhumanity has vitality in itself, but Ursula is a comic Macro and the life is perverse—because those who have the authority abuse it. Jonson's worlds are hard ones and he is no crypto-socialist. In mass men are animals but they are *rationis capax* (or at least the genus is) and the belief that we are capable of organizing society in terms of humane reason is what keeps Jonson going. It also explains his dual stress, upon the need for responsibility among the rightful rulers and upon the threat of those who challenge place-concept or who opt out of the system of hierarchy. Jonson has little sense that the ordinary man may be oppressed by the system: we distort artistic facts in the name of dogma if we present the Dappers and Druggers of Jonson's art as sad products of incipient capitalism. To Jonson they are examples of what necessarily happens when rulers forget their responsibilities—in a word, what happens is anarchy and the rule of the opportunists.

Where, then, does this put Jonson in terms of history? Satirists always (an occupational hazard) notice change and fear it, but that is not to deny that the changes which Jonson was aware of were real. If we grant his perspective we then have to grant that he was alert to the real challenges to the model in which he believed. Jonson, in other words, was not wrong to identify puritanism, the seeming-pragmatism of Machiavelli, the venality of the mercantile class and the neglect of the traditional function of the aristocracy as sources of danger to the established state. In fact the history of England for centuries after Jonson's death suggests that he was right to sense that the values in which he believed were under real threat in the early decades of the seventeenth century. The hierarchical model was progressively undermined (perhaps by what men did more than by what they said) in the course of that century, and what I now want to suggest is that Jonson's views as to the desirable shape of the state, far from being exotic, were basic to social and political thought in England even after the outbreak of civil war. Jonson was certainly conservative in his thinking, but his reliance upon tradition was so normal that regicide is miraculous. Yet what matters is not the fact that Jonson's lines of thought are close to those of contemporaries and successors so much as awareness that discussions about how society should be organized and the commonwealth ruled were matters of vital importance to the men involved in these discussions and to those whose lives could be—and were—profoundly affected by decisions made and conclusions reached. We insult our ancestors if we regard them as naïve precursors of modern thought or if we imagine that Harrington or Filmer, Hobbes or Milton, Marvell or Winstanley were just playing games. In tract and pamphlet, speech and action, the sort of issue which preoccupied Jonson dominated the lives of preachers and Members of Parliament, of monarchs, lords and lesser men. The issues were real—even if many ordinary people had only scant idea of what was happening.

It is easy with seventeenth-century theorists to imagine that they are only concerned with structures of argument and the apparatus of citing authorities against their opponents. But it takes only a few moments with one of Milton's pamphlets to be made aware that rhetoric need not be a way of insulting reality by padding it with pretty prose, and what is true of Milton is also true, if not so strikingly, with such writers as Filmer and Harrington. Filmer is perhaps the sanest and most persuasive defender of monarchy in the seventeenth century, a man of moderation and honesty, and it is not surprising that his views have affinities with Jonson's. What is interesting, however, is that Filmer is nobody's fool, that he wrote close to the actualities of the mid-century, and that his appeal to traditional authority emerges in the texture of his prose as far more than just a rehash of old arguments. But, having granted Filmer the due which his intelligence demands, it remains true that his views are essentially held within the traditional framework of hierarchy. When, for example, he writes that 'the relation between King and people is so great that their well-being is reciprocal' [12] or that 'the King, as Father over many families, extends his care to preserve, feed, clothe, instruct and defend the whole commonwealth' [13] the appeal seems almost one to myth—the 'ought' has become the 'is' it seems, and the facts of Charles's reign have either vanished or been transformed. What is striking is that Filmer uses traditional imagery and concepts: the king as father ('There is no nation that allows children any actions or remedy for being unjustly governed. And yet for all this every Father is bound by the law of nature to do his best for the preservation of his family' [14]) and the idea of the mass as inevitably unstable ('the nature of all people is to desire liberty without restraint' [15]). Writing in the 1640s Filmer cannot see that there is any alternative framework except anarchy, but the rhetorical effects which seep into his prose strike me as genuinely felt: 'the common people everywhere tenderly embrace it [the view of monarchy as a contract] as being most plausible to flesh and blood, for that it prodigally distributes a portion of liberty to the meanest of the multitude'.[16]

Filmer cannot see any alternative except anarchy to the traditional view he puts forward, but the man's prose tells us that he was far from stupid, far from a prosaic Cleveland, and so he is useful here in that he represents a version of a very common seventeenth-century phenomenon. The urgency of his prose indicates his awareness that the relationship between king and subject had gone badly wrong, while his offered solutions indicate that the only concepts realistically to hand were traditional ones.

What had gone wrong can only be touched on here and a remark of Christopher Hill's offers a useful line into a terrifyingly complex subject. The remark comes in Hill's introduction to his *Intellectual Origins of the English Revolution*:

For as long as history recorded there had been kings, lords, and bishops in England. The thinking of all Englishmen had been dominated by the Established Church. Yet, within less than a decade, successful war was levied against the King; bishops and the House of Lords were abolished; and Charles I was executed in the name of the people. How did men get the nerve to do such unheard-of things? (p. 5)

The answer to Hill's question is, as all good historians of the seventeenth century realize somewhat ruefully, mindbendingly difficult, and it would be absurd to suggest that Englishmen in the decades leading to the Civil War were consciously seeking to 'get the nerve' to overturn the traditional pattern of society. But many of the most prominent features of early seventeenth-century thought and action can be seen as contributing to breaking up, or seeking to maintain, this pattern—and so we are dealing with a very restless period.

This restlessness took many forms. In the book just mentioned Hill describes the vitality and questioning which mark scientific thought and practice in a period roughly coterminous with Jonson's life, and it is easy enough to demonstrate that creative writing in the period was also marked by an equivalent desire to find new modes of expression, a desire which marks Jonson as much as anybody. But this restlessness is clearly not exclusively an intellectual matter: indeed it could be argued that it is the product rather than the cause of a much wider social disturbance, and it is certainly the case that writers like Jonson himself, Middleton and Massinger, considered their society to be marked by social upheaval—the question of how far this upheaval was more extreme than at earlier times is not of primary importance here, for what really matters is that men felt that something unusual was happening.

One good, if generalized, example of what men felt was involved concerns the role and behaviour of the country gentry. In 'To Penshurst' Jonson articulated his vision of how the gentry should live, stressing their responsibility to the country and people around their great houses. In creating this vision Jonson was touching on an aspect of social organization which both Tudors and Stuarts felt vital to the wellbeing of the commonwealth. Both Elizabeth and James were aware that national administration depended, at the local level, upon the willing and responsible co-operation of the gentry in organizing and enacting the operation of law, in the broad sense of that word, and both monarchs found it necessary to legislate in an effort to prevent nobility and gentry from abandoning their local responsibilities in favour of a life based on London.[17] Jonson animates a picture of the responsible local gentry, and 'To Penshurst' has the kind of fidelity to experience which convinces a reader that the ideal held in the poem is not impossibly distant from the conceivable reality; but the crisis of the mode of thought which lies behind Jonson's poem is made acutely present if we remember that at much the same time Overbury published his 'character' of 'A Country Gentleman'. Overbury's sketch of this type anticipates the Restoration comedy view of the country gentleman as a man of severely limited experience and *savoir faire*:

His travell is seldome farther then the next market towne, and his inquisition is about the price of corne: when he travelleth, he will goe ten miles out of the way to a cousins house of his to save charges; and rewards the servants by taking them by the hand when hee departs . . .[18]

On the surface Wye Saltonstall, writing about two decades after Jonson and Overbury, seems to present the same sort of view as the former when he says of 'A Gentleman's House in the Country' that such a house is 'the seat of hospitality, the poore mans Court of justice, . . . and the onely exchequer of charity, where the poore goe away relieved, and cry, God blesse the founder'.[19] But when we read Saltonstall's pamphlet as a whole it is clear that his outlook is strongly conditioned by facetiousness: what Jonson saw as an ideal which could be considered attainable has, by 1631, been so cut away that the ideal can only be seriously used to mark its deviation from reality.

Behind Jonson's poem is the contemporary belief that the country gentry were betraying their traditional role; while behind Overbury's prose there is a sense of a court and/or city view that the country can represent no more than the quaintly amusing failure to match the sophistication of the court and city. What matters is not the difference between Jonson and Overbury but the fact that both attitudes indicate that there was the possibility that traditional values were being attacked or ignored—a possibility which is reflected again at the level of the king's relationship with his traditional advisers. The fact that George Villiers was 'the second son of a simple knight' [20] but became earl, marquis and duke of Buckingham in 1614, 1617 and 1623 respectively points to a fairly dramatic rise, and although this was not in itself unique (by any means) there was both a feeling that the natural order was being disturbed and that Villiers' talents were not such as to justify the influence which he was allowed to wield. One aspect of such feeling was the concern that private interest was taking precedence over public, a concern which manifests itself also in the anxiety over the movement of the gentry and in the preoccupation of Parliament and individuals with the careers of such men as Sir Francis Mitchell and Sir Giles Mompesson, whose involvement with monopolistic practices was seen as a form of selfishness. Monopolies, in fact, were one of the factors which contributed to the War—like usury they were felt to indicate concentration upon the individual at the nation's expense.

The long verbal battle between monarch and the House of Commons which led up to the Civil War can be seen as another manifestation of the restlessness of which I have been speaking. In a sense it is misleading to use the word 'battle': J. P. Kenyon has made the point that there was little disagreement about the theoretical relationship between monarch and Parliament—'in the sphere of practical politics the disagreement essentially lay in how to operate a constitution of whose nature few had any doubts'.[21] Yet this disagreement was such as to produce collision after collision in the early seventeenth century, even though there seems to have been genuine concern on the part of many men to proceed by discussion rather than threat, and although the issues which produced conflict were, for the most part, around the edges of a theory of rule which most accepted. James spoke of his view of monarchy in a speech to Parliament (21 March 1610) in which, having said that, 'The state of monarchy is the supremest thing upon earth', he went on to speak of the king as 'truly *parens patriae*, the politic father of his people' and then to underline his sense of the grave responsibility of his office: 'a king governing in a settled kingdom leaves to be a king, and degenerates into a tyrant, as soon as he leaves off to rule according to his laws . . .'[22] The image used by the king at the opening of Parliament in February 1624 shows much the same concern: 'it is a very fit similitude for a king and his people to be like to a husband and wife . . .'[23]

Such sentiments and images are all very well, however, until actual issues press upon them, as had happened as early in James's reign as 1604, when the king had had to back down over the election in Buckinghamshire of the outlaw Goodwin.[24] The Goodwin case was one where James came to accept that his prerogative could not overrule the House: on the other hand the same Parliament admitted defeat in an attack on the system of wardship, was admonished by James and came back with the 'Apology of the House of Commons', which stood firmly to the position that the privileges of the House were 'the general liberties of England' and which claimed that those privileges had been 'more universally and dangerously impugned than ever (as we suppose) since the beginnings of parliaments'.[25]

There is no space here to trace the process whereby the gap between king and Parliament widened into war, a process marked by declarations such as the 1610 Petition of Grievances, the 1621 Protestation and the 1628 Petition of Right. The essence of the argument did not involve any necessary departure from a moderate presentation of the theory of rule which James had articulated in 1610, but as Parliament examined its view of its privileges it came increasingly to feel that these extended to almost any aspect of government, in the sense that—having responsibility for proper use of the wealth of the nation—it had the right to comment upon how monies voted to the Crown were used, and indeed to withhold such monies if it doubted that they would be properly handled. This pressure upon the royal prerogative inevitably led to tighter definition of it, and hence (particularly with Charles) to an increasing intransigence. By 1625 when Laud, in a sermon at the opening of Parliament, referred to the king as 'God's High Steward' and to other officials as stewards under the king, going on to state that, 'for inferior governors of all sorts the King is the sun' he was saying nothing new, but the 'inferior governors' in question were no longer prepared to accept the practical application of this doctrine at the hands of Charles and Laud himself.[26]

The evidence that the nation was moving towards crisis can be drawn from other sources as well. There was trouble over the relationship between the courts and the Crown, Sir Edward Coke being particularly concerned at what he felt was increasing erosion of the independence of the law. There was—concurrently with the decline of the king/Parliament marriage—a feeling that the court was becoming increasingly alienated from the nation at large. There were scandals such as the Overbury case and irritation with such things as the sale of honours, the La Rochelle fiasco and the shambles of the proposed Spanish marriage. And there were major religious tensions, with bitter suspicion that the Crown was secretly papist in sympathy and anger at England's failure to offer effective help to continental Protestant countries in peril from Catholic sources.

The point at which event can be distinguished from discussion is not always easy to find. I have already claimed that the type of political and social view which Jonson holds should not be seen as purely intellectual; there are few if any seventeenth-century theorists who are operating in ivory towers, and theory in this instance must be seen as distillation of experience or as an attempt to impose a pattern upon it.

We have already seen something of kingship theory in the early seventeenth century and I have quoted Professor Kenyon's remark that there was little or no disagreement at the theoretical level about the desirability of monarchy as the proper constitutional form of government, a point recently reinforced by William Lamont and Sybil Oldfield, who have argued that 'king worship' was as marked among followers of Parliament in the pre-Civil War years as among 'Cavaliers'.[27] There was, however, room for plenty of disagreement as to how the theory should work in practice.

There is no reason to assume that James's view of his role was self-aggrandizing nor to regard his state-pronouncements cynically: it is fairer to the evidence to accept that the king believed what he said and tried to live and act accordingly. Overbury's *Crumms fal'n from King James's Table* may contain its fair share of apocrypha but the James he reports is interestingly consistent with the public James quoted earlier. Overbury cites James as saying, for example, 'I came not to the crown of Scotland by conquest, to give it what laws I list, but by descent, and if I do not governe it accordingly, I should be a tyrant'; and again, 'A King ought to be a preserver of his people... 'tis true when he commands they must obey; yea, and if it be in an ill quarrell, he must answer that to God alone, and is not accountable to any; but shame befall that King that warrs wrongfully'.[28] Much of the disputation which led up to the War can be tied to this idea of accountability: James registers the sort of awareness of the monarch's responsibility which Jonson caught in 'Panegyre', but Stuart credibility fell as the century progressed, while puritan ways of thought encouraged men to wonder whether God always conveyed his desires through the monarch rather than directly to his subjects. But the most interesting fact that emerges as one reads theorists of the period is that the terms of the discussions are almost always the same. Gunn quotes Edward Frost, writing early in the century, as saying that 'the Prince's contentment must be the happiness of the subject and the subject's welfare the security of the Prince',[29] while Filmer extends this idea of fostering, his emphasis being on what the king does (seemingly by nature to Filmer) for his people:

... the King, as Father over many families, extends his care to preserve, feed, clothe, instruct and defend the whole commonwealth...

and

... the prerogative of a King is to be above all laws, for the good only of them that are under the laws, and to defend the people's liberties...

For Filmer 'the relation between the King and people is so great that their well-being is reciprocal', a concept which is presented less as theory than as a statement of inevitable fact.[30]

If we look at the statements of men less closely tied to the Stuarts than Filmer we find the same ideas but with a different emphasis. So Raleigh stresses the king's dependence upon his traditional advisers—'the King is to believe the general Council of the kingdom, and to prefer it before his own affection'—while Coke says starkly that, 'The King has no prerogative but that which the law of the land allows him', a view which can be linked with Sir Edwin Sandys's and Sir Roger Owen's belief that kingship was originally elective 'with reciprocal conditions between king and people'.[31] Milton provides a useful way of underlining the point that these various statements have a common basis. In 'Of Reformation in England' he says that 'the most sacred and lifeblood laws, statutes, and acts of parliament . . . are the holy covenant of union and marriage between the king and his realm . . .' [32] The imagery is such as James himself used, but Milton's definition of the relationship between monarch, Parliament and the state reminds us not only of Filmer's view of fostering but also of Coke on prerogative. Finally in this context it is worth quoting Hill's reminder that before 1629 'there was no republican political theory . . . there were none who said that sovereignty should reside in Parliament to the exclusion of the King',[33] and we may remember that when Marvell wrote his 'First Anniversary' on Cromwell's protectorate the only images of rule which he could find led straight back to monarchic theory. Even after Charles's head had fallen and after the varied possibilities of forms of rule which the Civil War and its aftermath had produced Marvell could only conceive of responsible rule in terms which were highly conservative.

One thing which is constantly emphasized in seventeenth-century discussion of monarchy is responsibility and this emphasis applies not just to the king but also to the subject. Professor Gunn has argued that the subordination of private good to public weal was unanimously accepted as desirable in thinking before the Civil War: '*Pars pro toto* was the rule, and it admitted of few exceptions.' Gunn goes on to make the point that Parliament men such as Parker developed a view of the public weal as something which might be better served by Parliament than by the monarch,[34] but whether the viewpoint is parliamentarian or royalist the ideal remains much the same. It is fundamental to Jonson's view of the good man as responsible servant of the state; it clearly underlies James's view of his own role—but equally the Leveller belief that, 'Men ought to seek the public good, and by their nature were bound to do so.' [35] We find it again in Harrington—for whom 'a wise legislator' is 'one whose mind is firmly set, not upon private but the public interest'—and in Milton's image of the commonwealth as 'one huge Christian personage, one mighty growth and stature of an honest man, as big and compact in virtue as in body . . .' [36]

But when we start to consider who is being thought of when the matter of public and private interest is mentioned we find ourselves again facing the conventional hierarchic ideas, as well as the realities of power in the seventeenth century. One extension of the view that public interest is paramount is that it is best served by everyone staying in the place decreed for him or her by God. But seventeenth-century theorists did not waste much time on detailed discussion of how cowherds were to subordinate private interest to public—they were, reasonably enough, more concerned with real power and who should have it, some such concern obviously underlying the dialogue between Crown and Parliament mentioned earlier and the discussion of the extent and nature of the monarch's independence. But the most striking feature of discussions of political power at this time is the very close link between power and land. During the Putney Debates Ireton argued that Members of Parliament with a 'permanent fixed interest', 'do comprehend whatever is of real or permanent interest in the kingdom', and Cromwell's definition of those with a 'permanent fixed interest' was 'a nobleman, a gentleman, a yeoman'. [37] So royalists had no exclusive option on the identification of the right to a voice in government with the possession of property: it is self-evident to James Harrington, for example, that 'servants' should have no voice, for 'the nature of servitude', 'is inconsistent with freedom, or participation of government in a commonwealth'. [38] Even the groups to the 'left' of Ireton and Cromwell thought in terms of property: Gunn tells of John Warr, a man of Fifth Monarchist tendencies in bent and language, who yet thinks of power as property, [39] while Winstanley refers to 'the gentry of England assembled in Parliament' and seems to accept that it is right and proper that the populace should be represented by these gentry: 'We looked upon you to be our chief council . . . though you were summoned by the King's writ, and chosen by the freeholders' [40]—and this comes from a man who was profoundly (if that's the word) concerned with the rights of the mass of people who were what Harrington would call 'servants'.

Behind this adherence to the idea that the franchise should be confined to male property-holders lies a deeply felt distrust of democracy, and this is something which is as true of those who went against Charles as of those who clung to his cause. James was concerned that a distinction be understood between a king and a tyrant, but he was equally sure that good government was not demo-cratic: 'Good lawes must be made by a few men and reasonable, and not by a multitude.' [41] This may remind us of Jonson's suspicions of democracy, mentioned in Chapter 2, but it might also be seen as echoing the Elizabethan Archbishop Whitgift's opinion that 'the people are commonly bent to novelties and to factions, and must be ready to receive that doctrine that seemeth to be contrary to the present state, and that inclineth to liberty' [42] (for Whitgift 'liberty' seems to mean something akin to anarchy). It is an attitude which was often expressed: by William Gough—preaching in the 1620s—who claimed that Anabaptists (a useful smear term of the time) 'teach that all are alike and that there is no difference betwixt masters and servants'; by Sir John Potts in 1642—'Whenever necessity shall force us to make use of the multitude I do not promise myself safety'; by Cromwell in 1649—'Did not the levelling principle tend to reducing all to an equality . . .?' [43]

Words like 'liberty' and 'equality' may have developed different associations since the seventeenth century, but we need to develop the ability to understand that men like Whitgift and Cromwell are genuinely perturbed by egalitarian ideas and that their motives are not necessarily therefore selfish. We also need to be clear how closely this response is connected with the feeling for property already mentioned—in fact, remarks about the 'multitude' are often in contexts which specifically involve property. Charles, in the 'Answer to the Nineteen Propositions' of June 1642, warned supporters of Parliament that 'at last the common people' may 'set up for them-selves, call parity and independence liberty . . . destroy all rights and properties, all distinctions of families and merit',[44] and some seven years later a Leveller manifesto found it necessary to claim that Levellers 'never had it in our thoughts to level men's estates'.[45] Few theorists would have disagreed with Filmer that it is 'the nature of all people . . . to desire liberty without restraint' and that 'there is no tyranny to be compared to the tyranny of a multitude'.[46] The sensitivity of the whole issue of property, and thus of the relation-ship between public and private interest and of the danger of demands for a wider franchise, is well indicated by Cromwell's protest in 1650 that, 'We cannot mention the reformation of the law but they presently cry out, we design to destroy property.' [47] And as a reminder of how far the metaphors of rule applied to gradations within the social hierarchy as well as to the king's position there is Edward Brerewood who, in the 1630s, regarded servants as 'their masters' living instruments. If the master gave wrong commands, the sin was his, not the apprentice's: the latter's duty was to obey without question' [48]—which position is very close to some of the remarks of King James and which again requires us to remember that orthodox theory demanded power with responsibility.

It will be obvious from the above that a number of the concerns of politicians and theorists in the seventeenth century are close to major preoccupations of Ben Jonson. His views on kingship, on responsibility, democracy, hierarchy and the importance of putting consideration of the commonwealth above private interest fit closely with the views of contemporaries and of men who were born or came to maturity after his death. One evident conclusion is simply that Jonson's thinking was mainstream, and that in so far as his direct sources were classically based they were not so in a way which makes them exotic. More important is to see that the genuineness of Jonson's involvement with a conservative view of social organization is reflected by men who were (like James and Cromwell) directly involved with running the commonwealth and by men whose concern is, at least ostensibly, more theoretical (like Filmer and Harrington). Jonson's 'fictions' are no less involved with contemporary social issues than the rhetoric of Milton's pamphlets is— and neither is ultimately less relevant than the actions and statements of Charles and Laud or Fairfax and Pym.

But, of course, art does not stand in the same relation to society as action or theory. An artefact may comment directly upon the society in which it is produced, but if it is to be more than propaganda its comments will be defined through the art itself. 'To Penshurst' is not a statement about Jacobean ideals of the gentry's social roles—it is a poem which creates Jonson's sense of how these ideals feel in operation and part of its social function is to make, through art, this operation desirable. *The Alchemist* is 'about' certain aspects of Jacobean city life and its realistic element is such as to preserve some interesting information about that life, but Jonson's social analysis depends upon our responding to his art, to the 'meaning' of the exaggeration and distortion of people like Mompesson in the figure of Mammon and the comic dynamism of Subtle and Face as a rendering of energies which, in Jonson's eyes, were threatening to destroy the social model in which he believed. Beyond this, however, there is a sense in which art may well tell us much about society even when it is formally located elsewhere in space and/or time than the author's own period.

When we look over Jonson's literary output certain recurrent motifs emerge, motifs which have been touched on or analysed repeatedly throughout this book. I am thinking of such things as Jonson's constant concern to experiment, to investigate and develop different ways of communicating his visions; his preoccupation with the necessity to communicate; his reliance upon tradition as the basis for analysis; the tendency to break experience down into blacks and whites; and the concurrent tendency to express parts of his total view in separate works, with the resultant tensions within and between these works. In an earlier chapter I argued that Jonson often presents different—even flatly antithetical—views of society in works written very close together. This tendency, along with the urge to analyse and the drive to define, almost certainly owes a lot to Jonson's personality and to the particular circumstances of his life. So I do not want to suggest that Jonson's view of society is transparent or anonymous: such a suggestion would be absurd with so forcefully idiosyncratic a writer as Jonson. Clearly, such factors as his position in society and his financial situation at given times are important in a discussion of his art. But it does seem to me that the tendency to compartmentalize and juxtapose reflects something of the situation of Jacobean society and of the dilemma of intelligent members of that society. When we note the schism in Jonson's work between his ideal social order and his images of social anarchy, and when we respond to Jonson's attempts to make sense of this schism, we are dealing in microcosm with a problem which many other men felt. Jonson's sense that things were changing, his fear that the old models were proving inadequate or irrelevant, and his inability to envisage an alternative that was not anarchy—these are the fears and limitations of most men who tried to understand their society in the early seventeenth century. We do not need to accept De Luna's thesis that *Catiline* is an allegory of the Gunpowder Plot [49] to see that play's relevance to contemporary discussions of power in the state and we do not have to allegorize *Volpone* to understand that the patterns in it make perfect sense as an account of social pressures in Jacobean England. Jonson's need to analyse and define is, I think, more than an idiosyncrasy and more even than an equivalent in art to Baconian attitudes to science. It is just one example, but a particularly powerful one, of a widespread social need which grew out of uncertainty and doubt.

It may be as well to finish by commenting briefly upon the line taken recently by Raymond Williams in *The Country and the City*. Williams's book is only briefly concerned with Jonson but it is relevant here in that its standpoints make Jonson (and many other writers) an example of an art dominated (and diminished) by capitalism. Williams's position would be made more complex if he were to take account of how far Jonson's position in 'To Penshurst' is modified by works which Williams ignores and how far his concerns are similar to those of other writers in the seventeenth century. There is something faintly ridiculous about a condemnation of Jonson which in effect blots out most of the seventeenth century. But what interests me most is that Williams's position means that he is unable to make sense of either Jonson or the seventeenth century. It may be descriptively accurate to speak of Jonson as articulating in 'To Penshurst' 'the familiar hyperboles of the aristocracy and its attendants' [50] but the prescriptive bias of Williams's book (and, to be fair, he makes it quite clear that his book is a very personal one) means that he tends to berate the seventeenth century for not being able to think like the nineteenth and the twentieth, a tendency which insults the long struggle which led to men being able to think as socialists. For Jonson and for most men of his time (including most of the most intelligent) the only social order which avoided chaos was hierarchic. Thus when Williams comments that the society celebrated in 'To Penshurst' was 'at best the gentle exercise of a power that was elsewhere . . . mean and brutal' and that, 'The morality is not, when we look into it, the fruit of the economy; it is the local stand and standard against it' [51] he speaks truth but misunderstands it. He fails, for example, to notice how troubled Jonson was himself about the decay of the values in which he believed (and the literal truth of their past existence is not, as Williams seems to believe, vitally important to their value) and he fails to understand how far men still were from thinking backwards from economy to morality. Similarly he is unable to make the imaginative leap which would allow him to grasp that the concept of hierarchy need not entail oppression: the fact that it did is, of course, part of the guilt we inherit from our past, but that does not dehumanize the fosterage and responsibility which the theory advocates and which Jonson so desperately wanted to believe could come about.

I am, as I mentioned at the begining of this book, aware of at least some of its omissions and simplifications, but I hope that the questions I have raised will do something to encourage more and better reading and production of Jonson's work.

Notes

For full details of works cited, see Select Bibliography, p. 175.

CHAPTER I

1. H/S III, p. 301.
2. *The Under-wood*, LVII.
3. H/S XI, p. 348.
4. Quoted in J. A. Barish (ed.), *Ben Jonson. A Collection of Critical Essays*, p. 3.
5. Originally published in *The Triple Thinkers*; reprinted in Barish, op. cit.
6. Quoted by S. Schoenbaum, 'The Humorous Jonson', in *The Elizabethan Theatre* IV, ed. Hibbard, p. 8.
7. See 'Of Dramatic Poesy', *Selected Criticism*, p. 58.
8. 'Ben Jonson' in Barish, op. cit., p. 14.
9. *Lord Herbert of Cherbury*, p. 1.
10. *Sowing*, p. 11.
11. Parfitt, *Poems*, p. 467.
12. Ibid.
13. *Poems*, p. 468.
14. Ibid., p. 467.
15. *The Under-wood*, XLIV.
16. See 'An Execration upon Vulcan' (*The Under-wood*, XLIII) lines 102–104, and H/S I, pp. 41–3.
17. *Lives*, p. 327.
18. *The Worthies of England*, p. 382.
19. Gill's comments have been quoted above. R. G. Noyes says (*Ben Jonson on the English Stage*, p. 10) that in 1753 an allusion to Jonson's bricklaying was still good for a laugh. When Henslowe calls Jonson 'bricklayer' in a letter to Alleyn which laments the death of Gabriel Spencer he may merely be alluding to some formal connection between Jonson and the guild or he may be venting his anger at Spencer's killer (*Diary*, p. 286). G. E. Bentley prints an anonymous poem of 1674 which takes a more favourable line: 'Good lines, and brick and verse do well agree, / Jonson did famous grow for all the three' (*Shakespeare and Jonson*, p. 164).
20. *Epigrammes*, CI, XCVIII, XCIX; *The Under-wood*, XLVII.
21. *Poems*, p. 467.
22. *The Worthies of England*, p. 382.

23. *Poems*, p. 467.
24. *Epigrammes*, XIV.
25. H/S argue that Camden may well have taught Jonson throughout his time at Westminster (I, p. 3).
26. On Jonson and Camden see J. B. Bamborough, *Ben Jonson*, p. 10 ff. Professor Trevor-Roper speaks of Camden's 'quiet methodical scholarship' ('Queen Elizabeth's First Historian', *Neale Lectures in English History*, p. 16) and his account of Camden suggests several points of contact with Jonson, some of which are touched on in later chapters.
27. *The Worthies of England*, p. 382; Gildon quoted from Bentley, p. 257.
28. *Poems*, p. 467.
29. H/S I, p. 3.
30. *Brief Lives*, p. 177.
31. *The Worthies of England*, p. 382.
32. *Poems*, p. 467.
33. H/S XI, pp. 571–3.
34. H/S (I, p. 6) are inclined to follow Fleay's view that the 'Flemish adventure' came later (1596), but they accept that the chronology is difficult, and I find their argument unconvincing.
35. H/S I, p. 6. (But on p. 8 H/S do suggest that Jonson's studies probably did include the classics.)
36. *Poems*, p. 467.
37. Ibid.
38. Ibid. G. E. Bentley (*The Profession of Dramatist in Shakespeare's Time*, p. 31) quotes the famous remark from Manningham's *Diary* that 'Ben Jonson, the poet, now lives upon one Townshend and scornes the world'.
39. H/S I, p. 8 ff.
40. *Epigrammes*, XLV, XXII. (The son died in 1603, the daughter perhaps in 1593.)
41. Swinburne reacted quite violently to this duality (*A Study of Ben Jonson*, p. 107) and could only explain it by regarding Jonson as a woman-hater who flattered individual women for dubious reasons. The basis of the split is not at all hard to trace in medieval and Renaissance literature, however, and it goes back to a dichotomy of attitude whereby woman is associated with Eve, but also with the Virgin Mary. Jonson's duality can be matched by Donne's or by contrasting Ralegh's view of woman as 'for the greatest number . . . but Idolls of vanitie' with his tender letters to his wife.
42. *Diary*, p. 52.
43. *Dramatic Works*, ed. Bowers, London and New York, 1953, I, pp. 326, 351.
44. H/S I, pp. 13–14.
45. Ibid., p. 351.
46. *Brief Lives*, pp. 177, 275.
47. 'I have begun the induction and the first act of it . . .' (*Works*, ed. McKerrow, III, p. 154).
48. H/S I, p. 15.

49. Ibid., p. 217.
50. Ibid., p. 16.
51. *Diary*, pp. 73, 85.
52. Ibid., pp. 96, 100. (These two quotations have been modernized for the sake of clarity.)
53. But Jonson was quickly out of the apprentice stage if Meres's judgment means anything (which is arguable), for in *Palladis Tamia* (1598) Jonson is cited as among 'our best for Tragedie'.

CHAPTER 2

1. See, for example, J. A. Symonds, *Ben Jonson*, pp. 6–7: 'it would not be impossible . . . to regard Jonson's genius as originally of the romantic order, overlaid and distorted . . . by a scholar's education.'
2. H/S print this after their text of the play (VI, pp. 492–4); editors of the poems usually print it in the miscellany section.
3. I quote here the 1640 quarto text. H/S, using a revised text, omits the specific reference to Brome.
4. *The Under-wood*, II. 2.
5. Ibid., LII.
6. Ibid., IX.
7. *The Forrest*, XV.
8. *Epigrammes*, XLV.
9. *The Under-wood*, LXXI.
10. *Poems*, p. 479.
11. E. B. Partridge writes well on how we should see *Conversations* (*The Elizabethan Theatre* IV, pp. 146–7).
12. *Poems*, p. 461.
13. Ibid.
14. Drummond's MS does not survive. The earliest printed version is Sage and Ruddiman's, in their edition of Drummond's *Works* (1711) but, like most other writers, I refer to a text based upon Sir Robert Sibbald's transcript of Drummond's MS. The editorial problem is, of course, relevant to what conclusions we try to draw from the way the text is arranged, and here Sibbald seems much the better authority.
15. *Poems*, p. 461.
16. Ibid., p. 461 f.
17. *Epigrammes*, CXXXII.
18. *The Elizabethan Theatre* IV, p. 24.
19. *Poems*, pp. 463, 466.
20. Ibid., p. 394.
21. *Ungathered Verse*, XXVI.
22. e.g. in *Epigrammes*, LV.
23. H/S VIII, p. 561. D. C. Boughner (*The Devil's Disciple*, p. 139 ff.) has some interesting remarks on *Discoveries*.
24. See Chapter 4.
25. H/S VIII, p. 563 (and cf. *Epigrammes*, XCVIII).
26. Ibid., p. 604.
27. Ibid., p. 597.

28. *Epigrammes*, XCVIII.
29. H/S VIII, p. 563.
30. Ibid., p. 608.
31. Ibid., p. 592.
32. The fact that Bacon was impeached and admitted guilt on corruption charges may suggest to a modern reader that Jonson is idealizing a tarnished public servant. But Bacon's guilt seems to have been that he participated moderately in the widespread practice of taking gifts. There is no evidence I know of that he allowed his judgment to be influenced by these gifts, and his merits as thinker and public servant far outweigh his crime. Jonson is standing by a man who deserved support.
33. *The Rise of Puritanism.*
34. H/S VIII, p. 563.
35. Ibid., p. 588.
36. Ibid.
37. Ibid., p. 565.
38. Ibid., p. 563.
39. Ibid., p. 580.
40. Ibid., p. 595.
41. Ibid., p. 597.
42. See my 'Ethical Thought and Ben Jonson's Poetry', S.E.L., ix, 1969.
43. H/S VIII, p. 594.
44. For fuller discussion of Jonson's socio-political thinking and its context see the final chapter.
45. H/S VIII, p. 593.
46. Ibid., p. 579.
47. Ibid., p. 613.
48. Ibid., p. 565.
49. Ibid., p. 592.
50. Ibid., p. 601.
51. Boughner (p. 139 ff.) shows that Jonson probably read Machiavelli in the Italian and indicates his detailed understanding of *Il Principe*.
52. H/S VIII, p. 565.
53. Ibid., p. 566.
54. Ibid.
55. Ibid., p. 564.
56. Ibid., p. 569.
57. Ibid., p. 571.
58. Ibid.
59. Ibid., p. 576.
60. Ibid., p. 607.
61. Ibid., p. 565.
62. Ibid., p. 564.
63. Ibid., p. 573.
64. Ibid., p. 592.
65. Ibid., p. 593.
66. Ibid., p. 595.

CHAPTER 3

1. J. A. Barish has recently reminded us of Miss Ellis-Fermor's extra-ordinary remark that 'at no time did [Jonson] dramatize himself and it was only with some difficulty that he dramatized anything else' (quoted in *A Celebration of Ben Jonson*, ed. Blissett, Patrick and Van Fossen, p. 27). J. A. Bryant is much more sensible when he says that Jonson 'regularly dramatized, both singly and in a variety of permutations and combinations, the public roles that he saw the poet as being obliged to assume . . .' (*The Compassionate Satirist*, p. 2.)

2. J. E. Savage's view that Jonson thought of himself as embodying the sort of figure Savage deduces from these texts seems to me to be non-sense (*Ben Jonson's Basic Comic Characters*, p. 126).

3. See Chapter 5.

4. *The Prelude* (1805–6 text), I. 60–3.

5. *The Under-wood*, LVI.

6. Ibid., LXXI.

7. Ibid., II, IX.

8. I have written more fully about this in 'The Poetry of Ben Jonson', *Essays in Criticism*, January 1968.

9. *The Under-wood*, XV.

10. *The Forrest*, XII, XIII. Jonson knew both these ladies well: the Countess of Bedford (Lucy Harington) was a famous patron of writers and took part in several of Jonson's masques, while Jonson lived with Lord Aubigny for some while.

11. *The Under-wood*, VII.

12. It would be arrogant and inaccurate to pretend that my ideas about this complicated matter are wholly new, untainted by contact with other writers. I don't want to clutter up the argument with debates with other critics: the ones I have found most stimulating here are Bryant, Dessen, and Barish and McKenzie in *A Celebration of Ben Jonson*.

13. See above, p. 165, n. 53.

14. *Discoveries*, H/S VIII, p. 567.

15. H/S III, p. 203. (The journey is the visit which Prospero wants Lorenzo junior to make to him.)

16. Ibid., p. 198.

17. Ibid., p. 201.

18. Ibid., p. 308.

19. Ibid., p. 201.

20. Ibid., pp. 208, 210.

21. Ibid., p. 287. It is interesting to compare quarto and folio for an insight into how Jonson's feeling for personality develops during his career.

22. *The Compassionate Satirist*, p. 7. Lorenzo and Prospero, of course, provide one of the links between Roman and Restoration comedy, but this does not show that Jonson endorsed this kind of hero, who always seems too self-centred and superficial to represent Jonson's good man with his strong sense of responsibility and social standards.

23. See H/S I, p. 20 and W. D. Kay, 'The Shaping of Ben Jonson's Career', pp. 226–7.

24. e.g. Asper's 'I had not observ'd this thronged round till now', and 'a mirrour / As large as is the stage, whereon we act' (H/S III, pp. 430, 432).
25. H/S III, pp. 428–9.
26. Ibid., p. 423.
27. Ibid., p. 427.
28. Ibid., p. 436.
29. Ibid., p. 597.
30. Ibid., p. 423.
31. Ibid., p. 575 ff.
32. Ibid., p. 565 ff.
33. Ibid., pp. 596–7.
34. H/S I, p. 24 ff.
35. 'Jonson's *Cynthia's Revels* and the War of the Theatres', p. 4 ff.
36. 'Tragedy at the Children's Theatres after 1600' (*The Elizabethan Theatre* II, ed. Galloway).
37. See e.g. A. Gurr, *The Shakespearean Stage*, p. 69 ff.
38. On the audiences see W. A. Armstrong, 'The Audience of the Elizabethan Private Theatre', p. 234 ff.
39. H/S IV, p. 43.
40. *The Works. With notes by William Gifford*, ed. F. Cunningham, I, p. 152.
41. H/S IV, p. 74.
42. Quoted by Cunningham, *The Works* I, p. 152.
43. Ibid., p. 223.
44. Jonson's adaptation of Horace's poem is discussed more fully below (p. 117 f.).
45. H/S IV, p. 266.
46. Ibid., p. 269.
47. Ibid., pp. 284, 292.
48. Ibid., pp. 320 ff., 317 ff.
49. Ibid., p. 324.
50. H/S I, p. 30.
51. Ibid., p. 31.
52. H/S IV, p. 355.
53. Ibid., pp. 356–7.
54. Ibid., p. 358.
55. Ibid., p. 359.
56. Ibid., p. 419.
57. See especially H/S IV, pp. 423–4.
58. Ibid., p. 428.
59. It is interesting in this context that Professor Trevor-Roper (op. cit., p. 24) regards Camden's *Brittania* as seeing English history in the 'continuing physical structure of Roman Britain', which perhaps indicates the relevance of Jonson's Rome to seventeenth-century discussions of power.
60. Jonson (despite his friendly relationships with the Inns of Court) seems to have had a fundamentally suspicious view of the law, which is perhaps hardly surprising granted his brushes with it. His poems praise

individual lawyers but references to the profession in the plays are usually satirical.

61. I. iii. 52 ff. (H/S V, p. 34.)
62. Ibid., p. 132.
63. Ibid., p. 105.
64. *Miscellaneous Criticism*, p. 55.
65. H/S V, p. 383.
66. Ibid., p. 316.
67. *Jonson and the Language of Prose Comedy*.
68. *The Devil is an Ass* complements this by showing how hell is rendered impotent by human folly.
69. *Poems*, p. 469.
70. H/S VI, p. 139.
71. Ibid., p. 33.
72. Ibid., p. 35.
73. Ibid., p. 139.

CHAPTER 4

1. '... since the Comick Muse / Hath prov'd so ominous to me, I will trie / If Tragoedie have a more kind aspect. / Her favours in my next I will pursue, / Where, if I prove the pleasure but of one, / So he iudicious be; He shall b'alone / A Theatre unto me ...' (H/S IV, p. 324.)
2. H/S VIII, p. 599 ff.
3. H/S VII, p. 130.
4. Ibid., p. 131.
5. Ibid., p. 113.
6. Ibid., pp. 113–15.
7. *Patriarcha* (*c.* 1640), *passim*.
8. By, for example, George Buchanan in *De Jure regni apud Scotus* (1580).
9. See, for a striking example, the epigram 'On Spies' (*Epigrammes*, LIX).
10. Dryden's examen in *Of Dramatic Poesy*; Coleridge's *Miscellaneous Criticism*, pp. 47, 417, 437.
11. On this see *Jonson and the Language of Prose Comedy*, especially on Jonson's use of language with regard to Mammon.
12. H/S VII, p. 343.
13. Ibid., p. 344.
14. Ibid., p. 348.
15. Ibid., p. 349.
16. Ibid., p. 350.
17. Ibid., p. 351.
18. Ibid., p. 282.
19. Ibid., p. 299.
20. Ibid., p. 302.
21. Ibid., p. 329.
22. Ibid.
23. Ibid., p. 377.
24. Ibid., p. 378.
25. Ibid., p. 381.

26. Ibid., p. 382.
27. *The Works* III, p. 78.
28. H/S VII, p. 368.
29. Ibid., p. 370.
30. Ibid., p. 367.
31. H/S VI, p. 140.
32. H/S VII, p. 411.

CHAPTER 5

1. Tom Stoppard has two remarks in his play *Jumpers* which sum up quite a lot of contemporary thought about language : 'Language is an approximation of meaning and not a logical symbolism for it'; and 'Language is a finite instrument crudely applied to an infinity of ideas' (pp. 24, 63).
2. I. iii.
3. H/S V, p. 44.
4. H/S IV, p. 375 ff.
5. H/S VI, p. 263 ff.
6. *The Under-wood*, XIII.
7. *The Forrest*, XIV.
8. *The Under-wood*, XLIV.
9. H/S VIII, p. 621.
10. Ibid., p. 620.
11. Ibid., p. 621.
12. H/S I, p. 89 ff.
13. *The Under-wood*, VII.
14. Ibid., XVII.
15. H/S IV, p. 78.
16. H/S VI, p. 96 ff.
17. Ibid., p. 345 ff.
18. H/S VIII, p. 621.
19. H/S V, p. 85.
20. Ibid., p. 136.
21. Ibid., p. 315.
22. *The Under-wood*, XV.

CHAPTER 6

1. 'Morose Ben Jonson', in *Ben Jonson. A Collection of Critical Essays*, p. 62.
2. I am using Herford and Simpson as my basic guide to Jonson's loans, even though they tend at times to see borrowings where none exist.
3. *The Forrest*, IX.
4. Ibid., V, VI.
5. Ibid., III.
6. Jonson, lines 67–72/Tibullus, I. x. 29–32; Jonson, lines 53–5/Statius, *Silvae*, I. vi. 43–5; Jonson, lines 85–8 and 95–106/Juvenal, III. 49 f. and X. 347–59.
7. *The Forrest*, XI.
8. *Epistulae Morales*, XVII.
9. *The Under-wood*, XIII.

10. *Epigrammes*, LIV.
11. *Satires*, II. i. 47.
12. *Epigrammes*, XXII.
13. *Epigrams*, V. xxxiv.
14. It is found, for example, in several poems in *The Greek Anthology*, and T. W. Baldwin (*Shakespeare's Small Latine and Lesse Greeke* 1, p. 322) has shown that it was a school theme at Westminster.
15. *The Forrest*, XV.
16. *Ex Ponto*, II. vii. 41–2.
17. I have discussed this more fully in 'Ethical Thought and Ben Jonson's Poetry'.
18. *The Under-wood*, XIII.
19. *De Beneficiis*, I. i. 1.
20. *Epigrammes*, LXXVI.
21. Claudian, *On Stilicho's Consulship*, ii. 160–2.
22. *The Under-wood*, XIII, line 24.
23. *Epigrammes*, XCI.
24. *Epistulae Morales*, CXV, 12–14.
25. H/S V, p. 25.
26. The passage relevant here is II. iii. 111–21.
27. H/S V, pp. 63–4.
28. Ibid., p. 67.
29. *Tragedies*, I, p. 247.
30. H/S IV, p. 44.
31. Ibid., p. 46.
32. See above, p. 51 f.
33. H/S IV, p. 233.
34. Ibid., p. 237.
35. See above, p. 51 f.
36. H/S IV, p. 237.
37. *Selected Criticism*, p. 28.
38. Herford and Simpson record the fourteen obvious loans, but more of Truewit's attack is coloured by Juvenal than these references suggest.
39. H/S V, pp. 179–80; *Satura* VI, 1–2, 53–4.
40. Ibid., p. 180.
41. Ibid., p. 179.
42. Ibid., p. 183.

CHAPTER 7
1. H/S XI, p. 468.
2. Ibid., p. 364.
3. Ibid., p. 317.
4. Ibid., p. 325.
5. Ibid., p. 319.
6. Ibid., p. 357.
7. Ibid.
8. Ibid., p. 332.
9. Ibid., p. 374.

10. *Poems*, p. 480. ('When his play of a *Silent Woman* was first acted, there was found verses after on the stage against him, concluding that the play was well named *The Silent Woman*, there was never one man to say "plaudite" to it.')
11. See above, p. 1.
12. H/S XI, p. 344 ff.
13. Ibid., p. 364.
14. Ibid., pp. 383–4.
15. Ibid., p. 309 ff.
16. Ibid., p. 406 ff.
17. Ibid., p. 335.
18. Ibid., p. 339.
19. Ibid., pp. 419–20.
20. Ibid., pp. 450, 464.
21. Ibid., pp. 432, 439.
22. The Luttrell Society, no. 6. My quotations are from pp. 7 and 18, and my attention was drawn to this poem by my friend and colleague, Mr Robin Simon.
23. H/S XI, p. 378. Samuel Schoenbaum has an interesting article, 'Shakespeare and Jonson: Fact and Myth', in *The Elizabethan Theatre* II.
24. Ibid., p. 496.
25. Ibid., p. 510.
26. Ibid., pp. 511, 512.
27. G. E. Bentley, *Shakespeare and Jonson*, p. 263.
28. In his introduction to *Ben Jonson. A Collection of Critical Essays*.
29. *Ben Jonson on the English Stage*.
30. See especially W. D. Kay, 'The Shaping of Ben Jonson's Career', p. 224 ff.
31. See above, p. 49.
32. H/S IV, p. 63.
33. *The Works* I, p. 146.
34. H/S IV, p. 100.
35. Ibid., p. 216.
36. Ibid., p. 227.
37. Ibid., p. 267.
38. Ibid., p. 280 ff.
39. Ibid., p. 289 ff.

CHAPTER 8
1. 1901 edn, vol. 1, p. 403.
2. In *Drama and Society in the Age of Jonson*.
3. Such clashes continued into Jonson's last years. The actors of *Magnetic Lady* were in trouble with the Court of High Commission in 1632 because of 'offensive' material in the play, and in 1633 Inigo Jones successfully complained to the Lord Chamberlain about 'personal injury' to him in the revived *Tale of a Tub*.
4. See above, pp. 124, 126.

5. See, for example, the preface to *Thérèse Raquin.*
6. Jonson would, I think, have agreed with Pope: '. . . to say truth, whatsoever is very good sense must have been common sense in all times; and what we call Learning, is but the knowledge of the sense of our predecessors. Therefore they who say our thoughts are not our own because they resemble the Ancients, may as well say our faces are not our own, because they are like our Fathers . . .' (*Poems*, ed. J. Butt, p. xxvii.)
7. Much of Jonson's greatness lies in the tension between observation and ideal: one way of seeing how creatively tense Jonson's finest work is, is to compare it with the complacent conservatism of Massinger's comedy, *A New Way to Pay Old Debts.*
8. The fragmentary *Fall of Mortimer* also shows signs of Jonson's serious interest in Machiavelli and a *Sejanus*-like view of the court as the centre of corruption, but it is interesting that the play's plan suggests that Jonson intended to dramatize a virtuous counter-force. This makes it particularly annoying that we don't know when the fragment was written. Gifford/Cunningham accept Cartwright's statement that it was Jonson's last effort, while Herford/Simpson regard it as clearly early work—neither view is backed by any firm evidence.
9. In, most famously, 'An Execration upon Vulcan' (*The Under-wood*, XLIII), lines 101–4.
10. Camden also apparently hated puritans as men 'greedy of novelties and too eager to root up things that were well established' (quoted by Trevor-Roper, op. cit., p. 21).
11. 'Ethical Thought and Ben Jonson's Poetry.'
12. *Patriarcha and Other Political Writings*, p. 55.
13. Ibid., p. 63.
14. Ibid., p. 96.
15. Ibid., p. 89.
16. Ibid., p. 53.
17. Historians disagree as to how far this was actually happening, but what matters here is that contemporaries felt that there was movement in this direction and that it was socially harmful.
18. *Works*, p. 64.
19. 'Pictura Loquentes' (1631), p. 56.
20. Godfrey Davies, *The Early Stuarts*, p. 21.
21. *The Stuart Constitution*, p. 11.
22. Ibid., p. 12 ff.
23. Ibid., p. 48.
24. Davies, op. cit., p. 4.
25. Ibid., pp. 5–6.
26. Kenyon, op. cit., p. 152; Davies, op. cit., p. 35.
27. *Politics, Religion and Literature in the 17th Century.*
28. *Works*, pp. 256, 266.
29. J. A. W. Gunn, *Politics and the Private Interest in the 17th Century*, p. 68.
30. *Patriarcha*, etc., pp. 63, 105, 55.
31. Hill, *Intellectual Origins of the English Revolution*, pp. 153, 246, 163.
32. Milton, *Prose Writings*, ed. Burton, p. 32.

33. Hill, op. cit., p. 150.
34. Gunn, op. cit., p. 1 ff.
35. Ibid., p. 23.
36. Harrington, *Oceana* (1656), p. 71; Milton, ed. cit., p. 26.
37. Gunn, op. cit., pp. 13–14.
38. Harrington, op. cit., p. 78.
39. Gunn, op. cit., p. 28.
40. 'An Appeal to the House of Commons' (1649), in *The Law of Freedom and Other Writings*, ed. Hill, pp. 119, 114.
41. Overbury, ed. cit., p. 274.
42. Hill, op. cit., p. 285.
43. Hill, *The World Turned Upside Down*, pp. 35, 23, 122.
44. Ibid., p. 24.
45. Ibid., p. 119.
46. *Patriarcha*, etc., pp. 89, 93.
47. Hill, *Intellectual Origins of the English Revolution*, p. 264.
48. Ibid., p. 52.
49. *Jonson's Romish Plot.*
50. Williams, p. 32.
51. Ibid., p. 29.

Select Bibliography

EDITIONS OF JONSON'S WORKS
(Only those texts are listed which are specifically referred to in the course of the book.)

The Works, ed. W. Gifford and F. Cunningham, n.d.

Ben Jonson, ed. C. H. Herford, Percy and Evelyn Simpson, 11 vols, Oxford and New York, 1925–52.

Poems, ed. G. A. E. Parfitt, Harmondsworth, 1975.

BOOKS AND ARTICLES ON JONSON

Bamborough, J. B. *Ben Jonson*, London and New York, 1970.

Barish, J. A. *Jonson and the Language of Prose Comedy*, Cambridge, Mass., 1960.

Barish, J. A. (ed.) *Ben Jonson. A Collection of Critical Essays*, New Jersey, 1963.

Bentley, G. E. *Shakespeare and Jonson*, Chicago and London, 1945.

Berringer, R. W. 'Jonson's *Cynthia's Revels* and the War of the Theatres', *Philological Quarterly*, 1943.

Blissett, W., Patrick, J., Van Fossen, R. (eds) *A Celebration of Ben Jonson*, Toronto, 1973 and London, 1974.

Boughner, D. C. *The Devil's Disciple*, New York, 1968.

Bryant, J. A. *Ben Jonson: The Compassionate Satirist*, Athens, Georgia, 1972.

De Luna, B. *Jonson's Romish Plot*, Oxford, 1967.

Dessen, A. C. *Jonson's Moral Comedy*, Evanston, 1971.

Hibbard, G. (ed.) *The Elizabethan Theatre* IV, Toronto and London, 1974.

Kay, W. D. 'The Shaping of Ben Jonson's Career', *Modern Philology*, 1968–1970.

Knights, L. C. *Drama and Society in the Age of Jonson*, London, 1937.

Noyes, R. G. *Ben Jonson on the English Stage*, New York, 1935.

Parfitt, G. A. E. 'The Poetry of Ben Jonson', *Essays in Criticism*, 1968.

Parfitt, G. A. E. 'Ethical Thought and Ben Jonson's Poetry', *Studies in English Literature*, IX. 1, 1969.

Savage, J. E. *Ben Jonson's Basic Comic Characters*, Mississippi, 1973.

Swinburne, A. C. *A Study of Ben Jonson*, London, 1889.

Symonds, J. A. *Ben Jonson*, London, 1886.

OTHER CRITICAL AND HISTORICAL BOOKS/ARTICLES

Armstrong, W. A. 'The Audience of the Elizabethan Private Theatres', *Review of English Studies*, 1959.

Baldwin, T. W. *Shakespeare's Small Latine and Lesse Greeke*, Illinois, 1944.
Bentley, G. E. *The Profession of Dramatist in Shakespeare's Time*, New Jersey, 1971.
Entry in *Chambers' Cyclopaedia*, 1901.
Davies, G. *The Early Stuarts*, Oxford, 1958 and New York, 1959.
Galloway, D. (ed.) *The Elizabethan Theatre* II, Toronto and London, 1970.
Gunn, J. A. W. *Politics and the Private Interest in the 17th Century*, London, 1969.
Gurr, A. *The Shakespearean Stage*, London and New York, 1970.
Haller, W. *The Rise of Puritanism*, London and New York, 1938.
Hill, C. *Intellectual Origins of the English Revolution*, London and New York, 1965.
Hill, C. *The World Turned Upside Down*, London, 1972 and New York, 1975.
Kenyon, J. P. *The Stuart Constitution*, London and New York, 1966.
Lamont, W. and Oldfield, Sybil (eds) *Politics, Religion and Literature in the 17th Century*, London (Everyman's University Library) and Totowa, N.J., 1975.
Trevor-Roper, H. B. 'Queen Elizabeth's First Historian', *Neale Lectures in English History*, London, 1971.
Williams, R. *The Country and the City*, London and New York, 1973.

OTHER ENGLISH TEXTS

Anonymous. 'The Great Assizes', *Luttrell Society Reprints*, no. 6, n.d.
Aubrey, J. *Brief Lives*, ed. O. L. Dick, Ann Arbor, Mich., 1957 and London (n.e.), 1969.
Coleridge, S. T. *Miscellaneous Criticism*, ed. T. M. Raysor, London, 1936.
Dryden, J. *Selected Criticism*, ed. J. Kinsley and G. A. E. Parfitt, London and New York, 1970.
Filmer, R. *Patriarcha and Other Political Writings*, ed. P. Laslett, Oxford and Totowa, N.J., 1949.
Fuller, J. *The Worthies of England*, ed. J. Freeman, London, 1952.
Harrington, J. *Oceana*, London, 1887 edn.
Henslowe, P. *Diary*, ed. R. A. Foakes and R. T. Rickert, London and New York, 1961.
Herbert of Cherbury, Edward. *Life*, ed. S. Lee, London, 1886.
Milton, J. *Prose Works*, ed. K. M. Burton, London and New York (Everyman's Library), 1958.
Nashe, T. *Works*, ed. R. B. McKerrow, London, 1910.
Overbury, T. *Works*, ed. E. F. Rimbault, London, 1890.
Pope, A. *Poems*, ed. J. Butt, London and New Haven, Conn., 1963.
Saltonstall, W. 'Pictura Loquentes', *Luttrell Society Reprints*, no. 1, n.d.
Stoppard, T. *Jumpers*, London, 1972 and New York, 1974.
Walton, I. *Lives*, ed. S. B. Carter, London, 1951.
Winstanley, G. *The Law of Freedom and Other Writings*, ed. C. Hill, Harmondsworth and New York, 1973.
Woolf, L. *Sowing*, London, 1960 and New York (paper edn), 1975.
Wordsworth, W. *The Prelude*, ed. J. C. Maxwell, Harmondsworth, 1971, and New York, 1975.

CLASSICAL TEXTS

(In all cases the editions referred to are those of the Loeb Classical Library, London.)

Claudian, *On Stilicho's Consulship*, trans. M. Platnauer, 1922.
Horace, *Satires, Epistles and Ars Poetica*, trans. H. R. Fairclough, 1970.
Juvenal, *Satires*, trans. G. G. Ramsay, 1969.
Martial, *Epigrams*, trans. W. C. A. Ker, 1919–20.
Ovid, *Ex Ponto*, trans. A. B. Wheeler, 1924.
Seneca, *Epistulae Morales*, trans. R. M. Gummere, 1917, 1925, 1930.
Seneca, *De Beneficiis*, trans. J. W. Basore, 1935.
Seneca, *Tragedies*, trans. F. J. Miller, 1938.
Statius, *Silvae*, trans. J. H. Mozley, 1928.
Tibullus, *Poems*, trans. J. P. Postgate, 1956.

Index

The index does not include references to every person mentioned in the text, but all references germane to the argument have been included.

179